The Office a facet of urban growth

The Office a facet of urban growth

by

Peter Cowan, *Director*

and

Daniel Fine/John Ireland/Clive Jordan
Dilys Mercer/Angela Sears

of the

Joint Unit for Planning Research
University College London and London School of Economics

sponsored by the Nuffield Foundation

Foreword by Lord Llewelyn-Davies

American Elsevier Publishing Company, Inc
New York 1969

American Edition Published by
AMERICAN ELSEVIER PUBLISHING COMPANY, INC
52 Vanderbilt Avenue, New York, New York 10017

STANDARD BOOK NUMBER 444–19772–9
LIBRARY OF CONGRESS CATALOG CARD NUMBER: 69–18137

Frontispiece

Central London office building: Centrepoint

Printed in Great Britain

Foreword

Professor the Rt. Hon. Lord Llewelyn-Davies, M.A., F.R.I.B.A., M.T.P.I.

Cities throughout the world today present some of the most pressing problems facing society. Violence, race hatred, pollution, overcrowding, and the gap between 'haves' and 'have nots', are just a few of the issues with which city planners must grapple every day. What is more the problems of our cities are getting worse instead of better. Despite the efforts of many dedicated men, we seem unable to deal with the fundamental cause of our problems, and are forced more and more to treatment of symptoms rather than the disease.

Perhaps one reason for our lack of success, is that we lack sufficient knowledge of the urban process. The study of cities has been going on in one way or another for hundreds of years, but it is only recently that the development of new methods of research has enabled significant progress to be made in understanding the urban process. The use of mathematics brings to the study of cities an immensely powerful weapon. For the first time we can begin to see something of the pattern which underlines the city, and which has been more obscured than illuminated by verbal and anecdotal study.

Nevertheless the use of mathematics in understanding the city has still a long way to go, indeed it will never be possible entirely to understand the city by this means. The use of mathematics must be complemented and set in a context by more descriptive studies, case histories, and historical analysis. In this way we build up a composite picture of the city and its work and life, which can be understood and interpreted by students of the city and by policy makers, whose role is so crucial to the future shape of our urban life.

This book is an attempt at such a synthesis. It treats an important phenomenon of our modern cities from a variety of standpoints.

Mathematical models, are combined with statistical surveys, and with studies of the 'actors' in the urban scene, to provide a rounded portrait of the growth of offices in a large metropolis.

Such an attempt, by a team which contained architects, geographers, sociologists, and mathematicians is unusual. Still more unusual is the attempt to combine the work of such different skills in a single narrative. Although different parts of the book have been drafted by different people we have tried in editing it to bring them all together and to make cross-connections between the different approaches. In this way the book tries to present arguments which will be understandable to the general student and layman, as well as to the specialist.

Contents

List of Plates

Preface

This book is about a particular part of urban development, the growth of office accommodation and activities in post-war London. We see this as the first step in a much wider and more extensive enquiry into the relationship between buildings and activities in the modern city.

Our approach is somewhat different from that adopted by previous urban researchers, and it may be worthwhile setting out the background to our work.

The Nuffield Foundation, who provided the funds for our support, asked us to study the problems of growth and change in cities, with special reference to the development of London. We were asked to regard this as a pilot-study, which would test certain themes and methods for urban research in a specific context. This was an exercise in applied research, in which we were expected to speculate a little about patterns of growth and change in cities, develop methods for measuring and describing these speculations, and test our ideas in an actual situation. We were not asked to make any recommendation for the future of the city, nor were we asked to prepare any plans for its development.

Within this general framework, we decided to develop some mathematical models to describe patterns of growth and change. Mathematical models of urban development have come into use in this country only during the past two or three years, although they have been used in the United States for at least a decade.

Interest in model-building in this country was sparked off by the impact of a series of massive transportation studies, carried out in the United States between 1955 and 1964. These studies showed that it might be possible, by means of mathematics, to relate and understand various aspects of urban development, and that the advent of the high-speed computer had opened up new realms in urban research. This was a most exciting prospect, and a number of individuals and groups began to work with great enthusiasm upon the arduous task of model-building. However, perhaps because of their origins, most of the models so far developed in this country have been concerned with transportation problems, and their use for the investigation of other aspects of urban change has been little studied.

Why did we choose to try model-building? It would have been possible in terms of our grant to write an account of growth and change in London, using established historical, geographical and planning techniques. Such an essay would have been relatively easy and straightforward to prepare, and would indeed have been quite interesting. Model-building is difficult and untried, and it carries little guarantee of success. What were the benefits of such an approach? Perhaps such questions are best answered in terms of what we can and cannot expect from a model.

A model is an abstraction of the real world, and we should expect some compensation for the loss of detail entailed in the abstraction. Broadly, these compensations are three-fold.

First, a model should identify the primary factors which influence the phenomena under consideration. In other words, any discarding of detail in constructing the model should help to clarify the situation.

Second, the clarity afforded by a model should enable the consequences of the past upon the present and the future to be understood with greater force than is afforded by more traditional 'anecdotal' work.

Third, a model should confer some degree of generality on the work. This is perhaps the most crucial advantage conferred by a model, but it is also one of the most difficult parts of the model-building process.

The difficulty lies in achieving the correct level of generality. At one end of the scale, it would be possible to make a model describing in great detail a particular phenomenon, but this would simply describe, in a special language, a very particular situation, and a normal historical account might have been as good or better. At the other end, a very high level of generality could be achieved by discarding sufficient detail, but in this case the model might become so general as to be useless when applied to the real world.

In spite of these difficulties we felt that the advantages conferred by a model were significant, and there were thus several very clearly defined guidelines and limits to the kind of study we wanted to do.

Accepting the limits of time, theme, place, culture and resources, there remained an almost infinite number of topics for investigation. We focused our attention on the changes which occur in the city as activities shift from one piece of accommodation to another, and as buildings are 'removed, restored and replaced'.

This project presented a new approach to urban studies and was something of a gamble on the part of the sponsors. We received great help and understanding from the Nuffield Foundation throughout the work, and we hope they will feel their support was justified.

As with any research we have raised more questions than we answered, and some aspects of the work have been more successful than others. We think that some interesting themes have been treated in a fairly novel manner, which may have some use in the future. We leave the reader to judge whether the effort has been worthwhile.

Acknowledgements

Many individuals and organisations have contributed to this study. We wish to thank especially Professor Lord Llewelyn-Davies, of University College, London, and Professor Emrys Jones, of the London School of Economics. Without their help this study could not have been started, let alone finished.

A number of people contributed valuable advice to the project, either as consultants or in a more general way. Among these are Professor David Donnison, of the London School of Economics; Professor Peter Hall, of the University of Reading; Professor Robert Gutman, of Rutgers University; Professor John Parry Lewis, of the University of Manchester; Dr. Christopher Alexander, of the University of California at Berkeley; Professor F. Stuart Chapin, jun., of the University of North Carolina at Chapel Hill; Dr. Norman T. J. Bailey, of the World Health Organisation, Geneva.

We should like to thank the Greater London Council, Messrs. Freeman, Fox and Partners, the London Boroughs, and especially the Location of Offices Bureau, who were most generous with help and information.

Our special thanks go to our sponsors, the Nuffield Foundation, who made the whole thing possible, and to the Ministry of Public Buildings and Works, whose support enabled Chapter III to be prepared.

We are grateful to the following for permission to reproduce the diagrams: Dr. W. T. W. Morgan for Fig. VII 1, L.C.C. Land Use Survey, 1962, for Figs. VII 5 and 6, C. H. Holden & W. G. Holford for Figs. VII 2 and 3.

We are grateful for permission to reproduce photographs as follows: frontispiece, Richard Seifert and Partners (photograph by Charles Wormald); plates 1 and 6, the Hamlyn Group; plate 2, reprinted from *The Geographical Review*, **56**, 1966 (copyright: American Geographical Society of New York); plates 3 and 4, Colin Westwood; plate 5, *The Architectural Review*.

We wish to thank Mrs. Jean Buchanan, Mrs. Marie Hildyard, Miss Sandra Major, Miss Patricia Prescott-Clarke and Miss Lesley Timson, who contributed so much to the work, as research assistants or secretaries. A number of people, too many to mention by name here, helped us on a part-time basis, and we offer our thanks to all of them. Mr. Nicholas Abercrombie gave invaluable assistance in preparing chapters V and VI, and in assembling the large number of references involved in the study.

Chapter I
Introduction

A true history of almost any investigation in the social sciences would relate a series of defeats. The hopes and aspirations with which research workers set out are seldom fulfilled, and often the results of their work are unexpected and upsetting. But such waywardness does have its own rewards. Changes in direction often lead up fascinating byways to new and interesting views. It is one of the tasks of any research worker to seize upon the opportunities presented by unexpected changes in the development of his programme, and to turn them to advantage. Serendipity is an essential ingredient of most research, and this is especially true of the social sciences, with their special interest in the vagaries of human thought and action.

Perhaps the best way to begin is to set our work in a more general historical and cultural context, so that by describing the development and present state of urban studies in this country and abroad we can show how our own efforts fit in.

The General Pattern of Urban Studies

Several clearly defined patterns can be traced in the historical development of urban studies, and there are some quite clear distinctions between the approaches adopted in various parts of the world. Such divisions and distinctions do carry with them some dangers, for it is easy to fall into the trap of believing that a classification which has been made for the purposes of discussion is absolute and exclusive, whereas we know that the real world is full of ambiguities and blurred edges, but it does simplify things if we discuss them in some definite order.

The historical development of urban studies has proceeded in two ways. On the one hand are the action-orientated and Utopian developments which have characterised English planning since the nineteenth century and which are complemented by a tradition of social surveys and discussion of the city as a way of life; while on the other there is the tradition of urban analysis which flowered in Germany during the nineteenth and twentieth centuries and which truly dominates the field in the United States.

Ever since the nineteenth century, British planning thought and theory has been based upon Utopian views. The work of Salt, Owen and others was Utopian in origin, and, through the later contributions of Ebenezer Howard, Geddes and Unwin, these ideas became established as the fundamental core of British planning. And, because of the English capacity for getting things done, Utopian ideals were often translated into real terms. Even during the nineteenth century the model communities of Saltaire, Port Sunlight and Bournville attested to the capacity for action of the Utopians. Later, the Town and Country Planning Act of 1947 enshrined these Utopian principles in the law of the land, and the current existence of some twenty-three new towns points to the strength of the Utopian tradition in Britain.

British planners believe that the city can be controlled, its worst effects relieved, and its benefits magnified by political action and control. They recognise the importance of economic forces in shaping the city, but consider that legislation can override economics, and that direct control is not only possible but a good thing. What is more, much of the British approach to planning has an *architectural* slant. Planners are seen as creators who can manipulate the environment, not as meteorologists who can only observe what is going on.

This direct intervention has taken two forms, one positive and one negative. The positive side has been the construction of new communities, new towns, and, more lately, new cities. These have all been constructed according to certain sets of principles such as the neighbourhood unit, separation of various parts of the community by green areas and the idea of a 'balanced community'. Several of the principles upon which the first new communities were based have since been called into question, but the achievement in constructing so many complete new towns has yet to be matched anywhere else in the world. A great many practical lessons have been learned from the new towns programme. Densities, standards, and many other facts of planning theory and practice have all been affected profoundly by the experience gained in constructing the new towns. The new towns have also provided valuable lessons as social experiments. After many initial difficulties, arising from the transplantation of great numbers of people from a life as city-dwellers to a life in a model community set in the countryside, most new towns are working successfully. But in the course of their development they provided a tremendous stimulus for another strong theme in English planning—the tradition of sociological description and anecdote.

Perhaps it is inevitable that a tradition of Utopian thought must give rise to a parallel stream of sociological comment. Unless Utopias remain in the mind they must affect the way people live. The English genius for putting into practice major political and social experiments has meant that many Utopias have been built. But dreams are difficult to translate into reality, and Utopias as places to live in have often been very different from their makers' intentions.

English planning has therefore given rise to a whole series of social surveys and analyses about the way people live in old and new communities. This work is in turn tied into the main stream of English social science, which has remained firmly rooted in surveys and empirical studies since the nineteenth century. The work of Booth in the first London Survey (itself a successor to the many local statistical and sanitary reform societies which had been at work during the previous fifty years) has continued through to the present day, and we are now seeing the completion of the Third London Survey at the Centre for Urban Studies in London.

This tradition of a social survey in Britain is also linked to the Utopian tradition. Fry, Rowntree and other English reformers and Utopians who were influential in forming the model community movements in the last century were much involved in social surveys and community studies. These surveys were not the result of idle curiosity; they sought remedies for poverty, disease, delinquency and many other social ills. Thus these two strands of English planning thought are interwoven, and as we shall see they are each linked with a third strand—the formulation of controls upon the growth of cities.

In a sense controls upon the growth of cities can be seen as the negative side of the Utopian coin, of which the creation of new communities is the positive. Yet this would be unfair to the thought behind the development of controls. Although many controls have since evolved into restrictive covenants, a great deal of the system had a very positive intention. For example, the idea of a green-belt around large cities was not intended simply to restrict the growth of those areas, but also to provide greenness and open countryside within easy reach of every city-dweller. Nevertheless an effect of the system of controls as they have evolved from the Utopian view of British planning has been to restrict the growth of cities. There is a general view, which has been common among British planners, that large cities are somehow bad and that their growth should be stopped, or at least slowed down drastically. This view has been with us since the industrial revolution, and indeed many of the current attitudes of British planners can be traced back to a retreat from the horrors of the nineteenth-century industrial city. It stems also from certain political traditions. These saw the industrial city as the creation of unbridled capitalism, and considered that the only way to check the onrush of this monster, to prevent it engulfing a majority of the population and forcing them to live in misery, was for the government to step in and set things to rights. Thus the controls which have been erected not only attempt to limit the growth of the city as such, but also try to limit the power of the entrepreneur. This second object has been approached in two ways; firstly by requiring the entrepreneur to obtain permission from the public authority before adding to the growth of the city, and secondly by skimming off some of the profits which the entrepreneur may gain by such addition. In a sense British planning law has been both anti-city and anti-private enterprise. Yet, because of certain unforeseen and unexpected events, the effect of major parts of British planning law has been to make collaboration between public and private enterprise essential. It is becoming common for the central areas of large towns and cities to be rebuilt by joining the efforts of the planning authorities to those of private developers, and although this process is still relatively new it does mark the first steps towards a change of attitude on the part of British planners. It may be clearer than it used to be that ownership and control are two separate things. Public ownership does not solve the problems of the planners. Indeed, if the government owners are aggressive and unco-operative, it may make them harder to solve.

We can now see the traditional and current stance of British planning as Utopian, anecdotal, action-orientated, legalistic, anti-city and anti-capitalistic. Both its strengths and weaknesses stem from this tradition. The tremendous achievements of British planning in the new towns, in the green-belts, in the creation of a climate in which public housing flourishes and is of high quality, and in the gradual development of a continuing partnership between public and private enterprise have placed Britain in the vanguard of world planning practice. But this same background is responsible for many of the weaknesses in British planning today. Perhaps these could be summarised as a basic lack of concern with the scientific bases of planning. It is possible to suggest that the precepts of British planning have remained unchanged for sixty years or more, since they were first hammered out by Geddes, Howard and Unwin. In spite of the radical changes which have occurred in the nature of productive processes, in the character of the labour market, and in the pattern of communications British planners are still working on the assumptions which they inherited from the founders of the movement. Very little research, other than social surveys, has been carried out in Britain, and the little that has been done seems to have left the bulk of British planning practice unaffected. Lack of research has affected British planning education, which remains founded in action, architecture, landscape and law and contains very little research material. The gaps in British planning are thus passed to the next generation, along with the advantages.

Gaps in the theoretical basis of a subject become apparent only very slowly, and, as the achievements of British planning today are considerable, the reasons for changing to a more rigorous pattern are difficult to demonstrate. But unless British planning does achieve a more consistent basis for action, and if it continues to operate upon the *idées reçues* of earlier generations the profession will become redundant and the planning of cities will be taken over by geographers, economists and administrators. The lack of an adequate and growing body of knowledge upon which to base action must lead in the long run to the gradual demise of any profession. It would be a tragedy for planning, not only in Britain but throughout the world, if the profession which has made such a contribution to the subject were to fail because it ignored the need for further thought. The effects of such a failure, upon town and country alike, would be disastrous.

The course of planning thought, theory and action in the United States has been very different. There have been many Utopians in American planning thought, and indeed perhaps the greatest Utopian of all, Lewis Mumford, is an American. But, perhaps because of a fundamental difference in social and political outlook, the effect of Utopian thinking has been far less than in Britain. In the United States the growth of the city is seen as an economic phenomenon which is difficult to adjust and almost impossible to arrest. This view arises partly from the role of the entrepreneur in American society, but perhaps even more from the pioneering tradition and its implications for land owners and their rights. The conviction, so widely held, that free enterprise and the market are sacrosanct has in the past led American planners to accept a fairly passive role in directing and controlling the growth of cities. Another cause may lie in the democratic tradition: there could be no Haussman in this environment. A caricature of the American planner is a man who, although he sees many flaws in the present pattern of cities, finds direct action or intervention is impossible and must always operate through persuasion and negotiation with the real heads of power, the entrepreneurs.

Of course this picture is simplified, and the pattern is changing. Through the allocation of resources and contracts to industry, the United States Government is becoming more and more directly involved in planning by direct intervention. Planners in the United States are acquiring more power both directly through the creation of government agencies at national and local levels, and indirectly through their ability to influence the location of employment by placing industrial contracts. British planning is moving from a centralised and public authority based position, towards a collaboration between public and private enterprise in city development. In the United States, planners are moving from a position where planners have no power but private enterprise has a great deal to one where planners and private enterprise must join together in the development of cities. The two positions are moving closer together.

But there remains one area in which the two countries are still far apart. Because of their traditional inability to act, the planning profession in America has had more time to think, and this has led to a much stronger development of theory. There has accordingly grown up in the United States a view of the city as a phenomenon which can be investigated in a scientific manner, and which can be understood and eventually controlled. This last point is rather crucial, since most investigators of the city in the United States do hope eventually that their efforts will lead to the ability to control the phenomena they reveal, but the first task remains to achieve an understanding. The beginnings of the study of cities from a scientific point of view occurred in Germany in the nineteenth and early twentieth centuries, where Von Thünen and Christaller laid down the basis of a theory of location. But it was in Chicago in the 1930's that Park and Burgess began the work which later flowered as the great Chicago school of urban sociology before and during the Second World War. Here the pre-occupation was not with the size and spacing of cities, but with their internal structure. This remains a solid bed-rock for much later work, and many of the later graduates of the Chicago school occupy influential positions in the hierarchy of urban studies in the United States today.

However a fresh impetus was given to urban studies, as to many other areas, by the impact of the Second World War. The development of operations research and the electronic computer was especially significant, and it was not long before they were used in the study of urban phenomena. Really this was almost inevitable, for cities do seem particularly suitable to such treatment. They contain a great many items which can be counted and whose data can be processed by computer, and they exhibit many of the most obvious characteristics of the subject-matter of operations research being dynamic, self-regulating, competing and collaborating with each other.

The first and most successful application of these new tools and techniques in the field of urban studies was to the general problems of transportation. Here were problems of flow and regulation common to much operations research and massive amounts of data which could be handled by computer. During the last decade a great series of transportation studies has been launched, beginning with the Chicago area Transportation Study in 1955 and leading through to the Penn-Jersey Study of 1964. These showed that it was possible to relate cities and parts of cities by means of mathematics, and that such analysis might be used to predict the outcome of different policies on the future shape and size of the city. The utility of these studies has been in some doubt at a political level, but their effect upon urban studies was profound. Many people saw for the first time that this kind of analysis might bring intellectual rewards of a high order, and that in the long run cities might be brought under better control by such means.

Parallel with the development of transportation studies, which treated the problems of the city itself in a rigorous and analytical manner, the whole field of Regional Science developed. Drawing upon the work of earlier German geographers and economists, the Regional Science movement in the United States also used computers and various kinds of econometric analysis to study the relations between cities, and between cities and regions. This work has gone ahead, and is perhaps the major influence in urban geography in America at this time.

We thus have two main areas of urban research which have developed very strongly in the United States. At city level, recent research has been founded on, and grown out of, the mathematical treatment of transportation problems. At regional and inter-city level, techniques of econometrics have been used to describe the flow of goods and services, from one part to another, and to define the changing hierarchy of settlements in the country as a whole. At both levels emphasis has been on analysis and understanding before action is taken. As is to be expected, the research effort has yet to pay off in terms of practical planning. Indeed, given the general lack of action towards control of market forces, it would be most surprising if the American planning profession were able to use such results in the immediate future. Nevertheless the rapid growth of concern about poverty and racial inequality in cities, which is becoming apparent at every level of America life, is making the role of urban research a critical one. This general concern with urban affairs on the part of the community marks another difference between planning in Britain and the United States. It has to do with the role played by individual citizens in the planning and growth of the city. Perhaps because of the particular mode of democratic procedure in the United States, where many local officials are elected representatives, the degree of interest and influence of local pressure groups, including both businessmen and citizens' committees, is considerably greater than in Britain. In Britain the tradition of an impartial and mandarin-like civil service has lessened the power not only of locally elected representatives either at Borough or County level, but also of the local pressure groups, preservation societies and so on. The points of leverage in American city planning are many and varied, and are distributed at all levels from the neighbourhood to the national government. In Britain such points of leverage are fewer in number and are concentrated more closely around the machinery of central government. Planning by *fiat* is more common in Britain than in the United States. Each system has its advantages, for in the United States a more open and diverse approach to the solution of urban problems is common, while in Britain the capacity to act from a single central position has speeded up the whole process of national strategic planning and implementation. But whatever may be their respective advantages, these contrasting situations are reflected in the pattern of urban studies in Britain and in the United States. In America there has grown up a considerable literature concerning the politics and administration of urban areas and the role of various groups and power-structures in forming the urban environment. In Britain on the other hand there has been an almost total lack of work or interest in these aspects as topics for research. That such problems are indeed urgent is shown by the recent report of the Royal Commission on Local Government, but the Commission itself again illustrates the British habit of planning by edict and by precept rather than from analysis.

We can now summarise the present pattern of urban studies in Britain and in the United States. In Britain we have a situation where planners possess a great deal of power, which they use wisely to implement Utopian principles which were laid down some sixty years ago. The planning law which provides this power has positive attributes in that it aids the creation of new communities, green-belts and other amenities. It also has negative aspects in that a great many controls have been erected. One of their objects has been to limit the growth of cities. British planning has, over the years, learned to collaborate with private enterprise. Planning power in Britain, compared with the United States, is highly centralised, and local community participation in urban affairs is small. Finally, and most important of all, the capacity for action of British planners has until quite recently discouraged research other than social surveys, of which there have been a great number but whose contribution to urban theory has been small.

In the United States on the other hand, planners do not possess very great power, which resides more with the entrepreneur and with the market. The community participates more in urban affairs, and has the opportunity to influence planning decisions at many points from a local to a national level. Partly because of this lack of power, American planning interests have turned to research and analysis, and in particular to the use of mathematics, operations research and the computer to bring order and understanding to urban phenomena.

Having compared and contrasted these two approaches to planning problems, we can see that some kind of mid-Atlantic position would bring many advantages. If it were possible to combine the British capacity for action and construction with the increasing sophistication of American analysis and research, we should stand to gain an immense amount. We might begin to provide the planners and decision-makers with tools which could display the consequences of alternative policies, so that their work could be based upon a firmer foundation than the hunches and guesses which are so common at present. Such a result is indeed the aim of those planners, geographers, economists and mathematicians who are working or are beginning to work on urban research on both sides of the Atlantic. For there is no doubt that one result of the increasing interest in urban affairs in Britain and America has been to bring planning research into academic respectability. Groups and individuals in both countries are now established in university or quasi-university settings, and more and more graduates are turning into the general area of urban research, which is indeed one of the growth points of research today.

But of course the whole field is still very young, and there are many aspects of urban work and life which have so far received very little attention on either side of the Atlantic. In general, transportation and regional analyses have tended to dominate the pattern of urban research, partly because they were the first to get started and partly because their subject matter is particularly suitable and susceptible to analysis. Flows of vehicles, people or goods can be measured with some precision, and their treatment in mathematical form is relatively straightforward. It is also true that transportation and regional economics and location are among the most critical problems in the urban spectrum. But there are other areas which have not so far received very much attention but which are of considerable importance in cities today. Indeed, since cities are one of the most complex products of human endeavour, we should expect them to provide a particularly rich mine of material for social research of all kinds. It is difficult to separate out a single strand from the closely woven and intricate web which makes the city.

A Plan for Research

One such strand is provided by consideration of the buildings from which the city is made. In one sense the city only exists as a collection of buildings, for an uninhabited city, buried deep in the jungle, remains a 'city' even after the inhabitants have disappeared. Indeed, just as the archaeologist reconstructs something of the way of life of the people from the ruins of an old uninhabited city, so we may detect something of the current patterns of city life from a study of the 'stock' of buildings which our cities contain today. For buildings exist only to contain human activities, and it is these which make the city live and breathe, which provide it with a reason for being, and which introduce all the patterns of growth and change which every city experiences.

So that we can begin to isolate a facet of urban studies which has to do do with the pattern of buildings in the city and which seeks to understand their evolution, distribution, growth change and ageing, this theme must be linked immediately to the accommodation needs of all the various activities which make up the life of the city, and upon which the pattern of buildings depends. The aim of such a study might be to understand the interaction of activities and accommodation in the city, to trace the evolution of this interaction, and if possible to predict the future course so that planners and policy-makers may consider the provision of new or adapted accommodation with more confidence.

This is an unfamiliar theme and must rest upon some general view of the evolution of stock and activities. What is more, we shall eventually need to set some limits upon the theme, both in history and in culture, for otherwise an investigation would become diffuse and general to the point of uselessness. However, let us begin by considering buildings and the activities they contain in a very broad manner, gradually narrowing our focus until we achieve sufficient clarity to formulate some hypotheses and means of testing them.

Imagine that all the buildings in the city were arrayed before us, in single line. We should see an immense variety of structures of all kinds, shapes and sizes. Now some of these buildings will be suitable for only a very few activities; for example, concert halls. On the other hand there are some types of buildings which can house many different types of activities. Georgian town houses may be used for housing single families, flats, small offices, factories or many other purposes. Thus we might rearrange our array of accommodation so that at one extreme we have 'highly specialised' accommodation or stock which is suitable for only one or two activities, while at the other end of the array there are buildings or pieces of stock which can house a great variety of activities; that is to say, they are 'non specialised'. Between these two extremes there will occur pieces of stock with varying degrees of specialisation in terms of the number of activities they may accommodate. We thus have a spectrum of stock arrayed according to its 'degree of specialisation'.

Now we could arrange the activities which occur in the city in a similar fashion. That is to say, we could identify those activities which require very special kinds of accommodation, such as symphony concerts, and those which require much less specialised accommodation, such as offices which might be accommodated in new office blocks, old houses or many other kinds of structural stock. The evidence that such adaptability occurs in cities is all around us, for if we look at any large town or city today we can see that many buildings contain a variety of activities, and that many similar activities are accommodated in a variety of buildings.

We have thus erected two arrays, each dealing with a particular aspect of the city. On the one hand we have an array of buildings, on the other we have an array of activities. In one way or another these two arrays match each other, and the degree of fit between them offers us some measure of the working efficiency of the city. But each of the arrays is growing and changing, both as a whole and in the balance between the parts. What is more the arrays do not change at the same rate.

The array of buildings or structural stock changes as new buildings are constructed, existing ones adapted and old ones demolished and replaced. The rate of change in structural stock may accelerate or decelerate over time, according to general economic cycles and trends, local demands for a particular type of building, or political decision. But because of the fairly permanent nature of buildings and the cost of adapting, demolishing or rebuilding them, changes in the 'structural stock' of a city occur fairly slowly.

On the other hand, changes in the activity patterns of a city occur much more quickly. Indeed it is partly the ability of cities to accommodate to rapid changes in activities which gives them their special place in the pattern of social life. Simple observation shows that the quality which can be expected of any city is change. Sometimes changes in the activity pattern will require the adapting of existing accommodation from one type to another. But certainly activity changes are going on all the time in the city and with great rapidity.

Thus the array of structural stock changes more slowly than the array of activities which flows through it. There is a lag between stock and activities, which gives rise to both costs and benefits in the work, shape and life of the city. But the problem and the pattern are more complex than this, for accommodation is fixed while activities are mobile. And the requirements of activities will vary in respect of location and of type of accommodation. To take our earlier examples, for some kinds of activities such as symphony concerts the type of accommodation will be all important, whereas for others location will take precedence over accommodation. And the balance will once again be changing all the time as accessibility to various parts of the city is altered by new communications, and as the spatial distribution of accommodation and activities evolves.

This whole process is acted upon by *public* controls, it is not a simple matter of the balancing out of private choices. In the early days of the growth of cities the original pattern may have represented the outcome of an entirely private dialogue of competition. But very soon public controls in one form or another are imposed upon the privately chosen arrays of stock. As the original 'free market' pattern of stock decays, it is replaced by new accommodation which has been constructed within the framework of public control, and this becomes the basis of choice for the later operations of activities.

The matching between the arrays of accommodation and activities is affected by the behaviour of certain sets of 'actors' in the urban scene. First of all we have the 'providers' of accommodation, those who construct building stock, sometimes for their own occupation but very often for occupation for others. Next there are the 'occupiers' of accommodation, those who take up the space provided and who must choose between the array of stock available in the city, balancing out such factors as the type of accommodation available, its size and location and cost against their own needs and resources. Finally there are the 'controllers', the actors who make planning policy and manipulate the various sets of controls within which the providers and occupiers must operate. This is a simplified account, and approximates more closely to the British than the American situation, where there would be other sets of actors representing politicians and pressure groups involved in the more diffuse situation occurring in the United States.

Thus, even at a very simple level, a view of the city which begins with a consideration of the stock of structures it contains soon unfolds into a most complicated pattern which, like every other aspect of the city, is an extraordinarily rich mine of research themes and materials. The main task is once again to narrow the focus and to evolve a means of attacking the problems which will be both interesting and rewarding in terms of results.

Suppose we begin by limiting our view to the modern industrial city. Thus we should consider the growth of cities in Britain since the early nineteenth century, in the United States since the mid-nineteenth century, and in many other parts of the world since the early twentieth century. Although many attempts have been made to construct a general theory of urbanism which would cover all cities at all times, a number of writers have urged that the modern industrial city can be isolated as a phenomenon in its own right. If we accept this view, our general interest in the pattern of stock and activities immediately springs into clearer focus. We see that the modes of dealing with changes in activities are radically different from those adopted in other settlements and at other times. For example, the accommodation in an African village or encampment may be changed many times as population expands or as new social or family groups come into being. But the main pattern of accommodation remains unchanged, for the buildings are built in the same manner as before. It is also worth noting that the extremely temporary nature of the buildings in African villages does not alter the permanence of the pattern. Buildings in these primitive societies are very simple, and the same form with only minor variations is used for all the different activities which occur. Therefore problems of change can be dealt with fairly easily and without disturbing the form of the settlement. In modern cities on the other hand, as we have seen, the permanence of buildings combined with the increasingly rapid rate of change in the activities produces problems which cannot be dealt with simply by rebuilding in the same manner as before.

A focus upon the modern industrial city, therefore, brings immediate advantages in terms of clarity. But there will also be some difficulties arising from the great complexity of the city as it exists today. Two approaches are possible: to cover the total pattern of change in all its aspects; or to select a single aspect or indicator of change and to study it in some depth.

At first sight the first alternative seems more attractive. Since the pattern of change is very complicated and it is difficult to separate one aspect from the next, it seems sensible to study a total pattern, even if this means restricting the area of coverage to a single part of the city. It might be too ambitious to attempt a description of change across the whole city. But if it were possible to define an area or areas within the city which were meaningful and manageable in terms of a research programme, the idea of attempting to measure and relate all aspects of change affecting activities and accommodation in the city is most attractive. We might try to identify areas of the city in which change was known to have occurred, or in which change was occurring with particular rapidity. We could study the area of the city which lies just outside the central area, known by geographers as the 'transition zone'.

Here we should expect all kinds of change to be occurring, since this is one of the characteristics which defines this part of the city in most geographical analyses. By studying changes in buildings and activities within this zone we might well gain most valuable insights into the processes of change across the whole city. Alternatively, it would be possible to compare the pattern of change in different parts of the city, in which case we should need to select for study areas which were either spatially or functionally separate and discrete. We should then devise comparative measures of change, and develop indices which could be used or applied to other parts of the city to predict the future patterns of change. Yet another alternative might be to define a segment or sector leading from the centre to the periphery of the city, and to trace the patterns of change in this sector as an indication of changes of the city as a whole. All these variations are possible while studying the total pattern of change within a city or part of a city.

But there are some problems. It is extremely difficult to define or isolate an area of the city which has sufficient coherence to support exact hypotheses and which can be related to other parts of the city in a useful way. The task of formulating testable hypotheses about the general pattern of change in the city becomes very complicated. How should we know what to measure? And if adequate measurements were possible, how could we judge whether the answer were right or wrong? The more we think about the proposal to consider all aspects of change in a particular part or parts of the city, the more we see that it is not susceptible to rigorous analysis. It would be possible to describe such a pattern of change in great detail, and this has indeed been done in many socio-geographical case histories, but the results of such an investigation would be difficult to generalise, and if our work is to benefit urban studies in general we should need to be particularly interested in the wider relevance of our studies.

There are thus good reasons for moving on to consider the second approach. Here we might consider the changing pattern of a single aspect of the city, so far as it affects activities and accommodation. By isolating a single facet for study across the whole face of the city we gain a number of advantages. First, and most important, our studies gain in precision and clarity. Because a single topic is brought into focus it is possible to handle the problems with more rigour. Second, data problems become more manageable as it is easier to describe the kind of measurements which are necessary. Third, it is possible to formulate *testable* hypotheses about the behaviour of a single aspect of the city, and to decide with some degree of accuracy upon the correctness of the answers we obtain. Finally, if the facet is chosen carefully, the work will act as a useful pilot study, in which methods and techniques can be tested for use in connection with other facets of urban activity. In this case the study might be seen as extendable; that is to say that the methods used for studying one aspect of urban change should be capable of dealing with other and different themes. New facets could be incorporated one by one into the research, until an overall picture is built up. The end result of the process is the same as if we set out to consider the total pattern all at once, but the road towards this goal is taken in a series of modest steps instead of a single leap.

If we decide to adopt this approach, then the selection of a topic or facet for study becomes of immense importance. What kind of criteria should be used to isolate such a topic? First, the facet chosen must be easily distinguishable from other elements in the patterns of urban growth. Second, it must be an important element in forming the general pattern of growth and change in the city. It would not be of great profit, except as a purely methodical exercise, to consider a topic which played an insignificant role in the activity of the city as a whole. Third, there should be a well-documented history of policies and controls concerning the topic chosen, so that the effect of these constraints can be judged, making the investigation of some use to planners and policy-makers concerned with the controls in the future. Fourth, there must exist coherent and well organised data relevant to the subject, so that measurements of patterns of growth and change can be made easily and with accuracy. Finally, the facet chosen must be some kind of index of urban growth in general, and must be extendable to other topics; that is to say, it must be possible to see the connection between one facet and others, even if they are each treated separately as research tasks.

There are of course a number of subjects which fulfil these criteria, but one particular topic stands out in the modern city—the growth of offices. There is a great deal of evidence to show that office growth is a major index of urban growth today. Efforts to control the growth of modern cities have often failed because they concentrated upon the control of industrial locations and employment to the exclusion of control of other aspects, especially offices. But it is now recognised that one of the primary reasons for the continued existence of the modern city is because of the focus it gives to communications. The vehicles for such communication are many, but much of it is carried in pieces of paper which emanate from offices—the paper metropolis is indeed a major phenomenon of urban life today.

Thus it is appropriate and useful to deal with the patterns of growth and change in office activities and accommodation in the city. But in order to assemble data with which to test research ideas and hypotheses, it is necessary to consider these problems in a real-life situation. Comparative studies might be made of a number of cities at similar times, national or international comparisons might be made; or a single major city might be studied in some depth.

As a beginning it may be best to consider a single city, for the problem and the approach to it have not yet received much attention. There are no tried and tested methods available for such a study.

The choice of a city is fairly clear. London has acted as the prime focus of communications and transactions in Britain, and its development has been closely connected with every phase of national growth. What is more, the phenomenon of office growth in London fulfils all the criteria necessary to the kind of research programme we need. Office growth has been important to London for many years, and the post-war era has been especially critical. Major policy decisions and regulations have been developed concerning the office growth in London, and these are well documented. A great deal of data is available from various sources concerning the pattern of office development in London. Finally, office growth can be fairly clearly distinguished from other facets of urban growth in London, and lends itself to treatment in model form.

Having decided upon a topic for study and a venue for investigation, it remains to set some limits on the span of time to be considered. Should the whole history of the office pattern of the city be looked at, or the 'modern industrial' phase only? How should we set the limits? In fact the period available for study is largely dictated by data problems and resources. It is only since the Town and Country Planning Act in 1947 that office growth and development have been subject to controls, and, as with many other controls, these have given rise to a considerable amount of most useful information, largely as a side-effect of the need to obtain permission for every new piece of office space provided. There is thus a strong practical reason for concentrating upon the post-war years in a study of office growth, but there are also some theoretical arguments for such a choice. The post-war years have seen a general increase in communications activities of all kinds. Television is perhaps the most striking invention, but the rapid rise in air-travel, the use of telephones and teleprinters, to say nothing of the increase in car ownership and use, all point to an increasing emphasis upon the relay of messages of one kind or another during the post-war years. Letters, telephones, telegrams and all the other accoutrements of communication on the city require people to send and receive information. The growth of communications in the post-war years suggests that this period must be especially significant to the growth and change in activities and accommodation in the city. This narrowing of the view brings with it once again a considerable sharpening of focus and we can begin to see the way forward in the research.

But having got this far some problems still remain. These concern the kind of questions which we might ask about the pattern of offices in London. Before we can begin to ask the right questions we must set up some hypothesis—however crude—about the process we are looking at. Such hypotheses may be modified during the progress of the work, but they are an essential starting point for any study of this kind. What kind of hypotheses can we erect for our study of offices?

As a start, let us imagine the development of office activities as a birth-growth-death process. Each activity seeks different accommodation at different stages of its life cycle, balancing space, rent and location against age and condition of structural stock, tenancy conditions and so on. Activities are 'born' at a rather small size, and the circumstances of birth often affect their location, as when a small off-shoot breaks away from a parent company, upon whom it continues to depend for support. Most activities begin life in adapted premises, for it is here that they find cheap rents which they can afford while they are still struggling to survive and succeed. Some enterprises do not progress beyond this point, but gradually wither away and die, leaving their premises free for occupation by another generation of activities. Others manage to succeed and grow. In the process of growth they need more space, and begin to move around among the stock of structures in the city, acquiring more space each time and balancing out location and rent against the kind of premises or accommodation they need. Because each move is made to acquire more space, more investment is required each time. Therefore the length of stay in each successive piece of accommodation becomes longer, as the activity sinks more and more funds into its accommodation. At the same time the activity, because of its growing resources, is able to devote more effort to acquiring information about available accommodation over a wider and wider area. Therefore moves, in addition to taking place at longer intervals, may be made over increasing distances. Finally, the most successful activities grow sufficiently large to build their own accommodation, where they settle down for a very long time indeed. A new phase begins as these successful activities continue to grow and experience problems in arranging their dependent activities in a satisfactory manner. Such very large activities may also begin to generate other small new ones, and thus the whole cycle begins again. Such an outline is very crude, and does not deal with many special cases of the growth of activities. For example, the pattern of size and growth in professional offices may be entirely different and the patterns of size and moving may be conditioned by other factors altogether. Neither does this outline deal adequately with important issues such as the role of prestige, or of the growth of special 'office regions' in the city. But for the majority of commercial offices which are not tied to industrial plants, the general pattern may have some meaning.

If the general hypothesis is correct, it follows that old and converted accommodation should contain a predominance of small, young activities. These would have a history of moves confined to their local area, although their latest move would be over the longest distance; they would also be planning to spend longer in their present accommodation than in any place previously. On the other hand new accommodation should contain a wider mixture of larger scale activities, all of them successful and growing, many of them having moved some distance from their previous location.

We can thus begin to frame the kind of questions we should ask about the process. Not all of them will be answered, but they will serve as a starting point for our work. Who builds offices? Who occupies them? Why has office space grown at particular speeds? Why is it located in particular areas of the city? How has the social control and intervention affected the development of offices? How do office firms make decisions about their accommodation? These and other questions form the basis for our study. The next step is to evolve a pattern of work which will help us answer them.

We have previously seen that a possible aim of urban research today might be to combine the rigorous analysis and development typical of American work with the interest in policy and controls which is so strong in Britain. Thus we should seek to construct models of office growth and development which would analyse and provide an understanding of what has happened in London since the war, and we should seek to surround these models with complementary studies of different facets of the city which have affected the process. For it seems unlikely that models alone, at the present time of writing, can provide a full understanding of urban patterns. The time will surely come when mathematics can handle the problems of urban growth in all their complexity, but just now certain aspects remain outside their scope. These concern the behaviour of city-dwellers and workers, and the effects of policies and controls.

These aspects of urban life are beginning to receive attention, but their development has been slower than the more mechanical treatment afforded by models of transportation and so on. Thus a study of those who occupy office space, their behaviour, decisions and the preferences and choices which influence their reasons for occupying a particular building will be necessary. Similarly the providers of offices must be investigated, for it is their decision which must govern the final pattern of office growth in the city. And these must be joined by an analysis of the patterns of policy and control within which each set of 'actors' operates.

If this pattern of work is successful it should enable us to combine the advantages of each approach. What we might achieve is a new kind of insight into the urban growth process. Thus the analysis afforded by treatment in mathematical model form could be used to evaluate the effects of controls and policies upon the behaviour of the various groups in the urban scene, and then the effects traced through to their eventual results upon the shape and size of the city.

It is at this goal that we are aiming, for the ability to evaluate in advance the effect of different policies would be of immense value to planners. It is not the task of research to recommend policies or programmes; that is the job of planners and politicians. But it is the task of any research to display to those who make decisions the consequences of their actions. The advent of mathematical analysis of cities and the availability of the electronic computer have brought nearer the day when such things may be possible.

In the concluding chapter of the book we suggest some possible lines for future work. Some of these are already being done either in our own activities or elsewhere. But whatever the immediate results of this particular piece of work in connection with offices in London, there is clearly a considerable need for more research of all kinds and on many different aspects of urban development. The resurgence of interest in the problems of cities must be encouraged in every possible way. The study of offices is only one small aspect of the total complex of urban studies, which must be seized and understood by research if the future is to be better than the past.

Chapter II
The Evolution of the Office Function

Until quite recently the 'office function' was considered relatively unimportant by students of the city.

Although the subject has not been neglected entirely, the majority of urban research has been concerned with other issues. Service industries and especially office activities and accommodation are late comers in the urban scene, and are only now beginning to receive the attention of research workers and planners.

As Goodwin (1965) points out,

> In the literature on the classification of cities little or no attention has been given to management *per se*, or to management centres. A recent bibliography of central place studies by Berry & Pred (1961), which lists the significant studies of tertiary activities, does not contain, among its more than five hundred entries, a single reference explicit to management centres; and neither this work nor any of the extensive bibliographies in Isard's *Methods of Regional Analysis* (Isard, 1960) makes any mention of management functions.

A major obstacle to the systematic treatment of office functions within a theoretical framework lies in the problem of classification. As Vernon (1959) says, 'Whereas manufacturing, transportation, retail trade and wholesale trade are economic activities whose existence is easily recognised and catalogued, many aspects of office activity are more difficult to classify.' The intangibility of office activity is a prime block to proper analysis.

An exception to this story is the huge New York Metropolitan Region Study, carried out between 1956 and 1959 under the direction of Raymond Vernon. The nine volumes of this study contain perhaps the most complete account of office activities in a regional setting, and the ideas and speculations of this group have influenced a good deal of the thinking in this chapter. The volumes by Hoover and Vernon, *Anatomy of a Metropolis* (1959); Robbins and Terlecky, *Money Metropolis* (1960); Lichtenberg, *One Tenth of a Nation* (1960); and Vernon, *Metropolis 1985* (1960), contain particularly useful information and insights. However, the New York study is an isolated example, and only shows how far we have to go in order to bring our knowledge of the office to the level of understanding we have about other aspects of urbanisation.

This is a serious gap, for the office function is becoming more and more important in our cities. Gottman (1966) has put the situation very well:

> But . . . those sectors of employment which were, and still are, regarded by the classical economists as *external* because they did not seem to be important elements in the economic process (production through processing and distribution to consumption)—those external activities are now becoming major sources of employment. They were, of course, peripheral to the economic process of old. It was useful to have people to do the research, take care of management, look after speculation and investment, gather and spread information, but though qualitatively important, quantitatively the group was negligible. Now their number is increasing fast: non-production workers employed by manufacturing establishments numbered 2·7 million in 1950 and 4·5 million in 1964, by which time they constituted more than one quarter of all manufacturing employment.

The neglect of a function which is increasing in importance at such a rate must have serious consequences. On a theoretical level, models of the urbanisation process and urban research in general lack a whole dimension. Although the office function by itself will not account for the whole of urban growth, it is a necessary counterpart of those other aspects, transportation, housing, manufacturing and so on, which have received intensive treatment by urban research workers.

The practical consequences of ignoring or neglecting the office function are equally serious, and we can see them all around us. An outstanding example is London, where policies and controls directed towards limiting the growth of the city failed because they omitted to control office employment. The Barlow Report (1950) set out to limit London's growth, using the control of industrial employment as its main mechanism. But the Barlow Commissioners failed to take account of the growth in service employment, which was to account for such a major share of total growth in post-war years. As Hall (1963) says,

> The Barlow Commission (then) were right in thinking that employment in London and the Home Counties had been growing much faster than elsewhere. They were right in stressing the importance of certain 'growth industries' in this rapid development. But they failed to put sufficient stress on the growth of service industries, because the statistics before them underestimated employment in these industries.

Foley (1963) also remarked upon this deficiency in the policies directed towards controlling London's growth. He says, '...a serious shortcoming of the emphasis on controlling the location of manufacturing plants is that so significant a proportion of new jobs are not in manufacturing at all, but are in service-type and particularly in office type activities.' The Town and Country Planning Association in a recent policy statement explained: 'In the entire conurbation, factory employment now represents only a third of the $4\frac{1}{2}$ million jobs.' The consequences of this omission have been well put by L'Institut d'Aménagement et d'Urbanise de la Region Parisienne (1967). In Volume 8 of their report they state, 'Certain measures taken in order to favour industrial decentralisation have been minimised by the counteraction of offices. Until recently the tendency towards concentration in large towns and especially in London does not seem to have slackened; on the contrary.' Thus the post-war growth of London, especially of the central area, went almost unchecked through neglect of the office function. It was not until 1964 that this facet of urban growth became so pressing that action was taken to control it. But by this time the face of London had been changed by the addition of millions of square feet of office space, and the pattern of London's transportation and economy had been altered by a corresponding addition to the office employment in the region.

If we are to understand the place of the office function in our cities today we must look back into urban history, for the rise of the office function as we know it is closely bound up with changing patterns of urban life, with major economic and social developments—especially the industrial revolution—and with a series of inventions and innovations in the field of communications. These changes have altered the role and place of the city in society, and are continuing to affect the whole future of urban development. Without some appreciation of the general urban process, our study of the office function will lack depth and may loose much of its meaning. We must sketch in the story of the modern city, and show how the evolution of the office function fits into the urban picture.

For a great many years, from the middle ages until the beginning of the industrial revolution, the primary role of most cities was for defence, for trade or in some cases for political or religious administration. As Dickinson (1964) says: 'Market place, through route, ecclesiastical stronghold and the castle of the feudal lord became the generating forces in both the functions and the form of the medieval town . . .'. And although great changes occurred in Europe under the impact of the Renaissance their effects on urban life were not by any means uniform. Mumford (1938) puts the situation very clearly:

> Between the fifteenth and the eighteenth century a new complex of cultural traits took shape in Europe. Both the form and the contents of urban life were in consequence transformed. The new pattern of existence sprang out of a new economy, that of mercantilist capitalism, a new political framework, that of a centralised despotism or oligarchy, usually focussed in a rational state, and a new ideological form, that of mechanism, whose lines were first laid down in the monastery and the army. But until the seventeenth century all these changes were sporadic and tentative; they were restricted to a minority: they were effective only in patches: they were in an embryonic state, receiving nourishment from an older society, from which they were soon to emerge with a lusty squawk.

Mumford's identification of the baroque city with 'Court, Parade, and Capital', points to the underlying continuity of the main springs of urban life during this period. There were many exceptions to the rule; cities which were centres of leisure or healing, or cities which combined many roles at once. Nevertheless, the main symbols of the city, for several hundreds of years prior to the mid-eighteenth century, were the castle, the cathedral, the palace and the market place.

In such a context the place of the office was very small indeed. Affairs of state and of the military required some administration, but no very elaborate machinery was needed and the size of the civil service in England remained very small. Morgan (1960) tells us that even as late as 1793 the Treasury employed only thirty-seven people! The affairs of the Church could be administered from the cathedral chapter house, while the market place itself and the surrounding coffee houses, counting houses and the homes of merchants could contain all the office functions necessary for trade. The East India Company, founded in 1600, operated from a private house for 126 years until, in 1726, a special headquarters building was put up in the City. The same applied to many banks, which occupied private houses for much of the period. The Bank of England was built in 1732.

In some large cities there might grow up certain professional office districts, especially in connection with the law, and these would centre upon some focus, such as the courts of justice. But the commercial office function as we know it today was accommodated generally within other structural elements of the city.

It is really not surprising that the office function was obscured in this way. With the comparatively simple organisational and financial patterns of the time, there was no call for much elaboration or increase in office activity. The main focus of the city lay elsewhere, though the expansion of trade through explorations and discoveries was preparing the ground for fundamental alterations in society and the city.

The industrial revolution broke the form of the baroque city. The era which opened in the middle of the eighteenth century with new machines for spinning and weaving cotton had its roots in the great expansion of trade opened up in the previous century by exploration and colonisation. The latter part of the eighteenth century saw the beginning of the industrial revolution, and the expansion of the city to cope with it. For some time it was the capital cities which grew the most; the rise of the industrial centres did not come until later. Mumford (1938) shows this very clearly:

> . . . the capitals continued to monopolise population. In the eighteenth century the cities with over 200,000 including Moscow, Wien, St. Petersburg and Palermo, while already in the 100,000 class were Warsaw, Berlin and Copenhagen. Toward the end of the eighteenth century Naples had 433,930 inhabitants, Paris around 670,000 and London over 800,000; while the trading cities like Bristol and Norwich, or the industrial cities like Leeds, Manchester, Iserlohn and Paderborn for the most part remained small in size: that is with less than fifty thousand inhabitants.

It was the nineteenth century which carried the industrial revolution to its climax, when the role of the city changed utterly. As H. G. Wells says in *The Shape of Things to Come*, 'In the nineteenth and twentieth centuries the story of mankind upon this planet undergoes a change of phase.' The role of the city in the West, and especially in Britain, changed out of all recognition. The city became a centre for manufacture, cottage industry declined, and workers flocked from the country to the towns, partly in search of richer rewards and partly because they had been displaced from agricultural labour by the enclosure movement.

And the industrial revolution changed the form of the city. New machinery required labour in large amounts, and as the expansion of production and trade proceeded so more and more labour was required. The workers had to be housed near to the factories, and their dwellings huddled against mill or foundry. The nineteenth century industrial city was born.

Blake saw the beginning of this, and foresaw its conclusion. In *Jerusalem*, written at the very beginning of the nineteenth century, he describes London:

> I behold London, a Human awful wonder of God!
> He says: 'Return Albion, return! I give myself for thee.
> My streets are my Ideas of Imagination
> Awake, Albion, awake! And let us awake up together.
> My Houses are Thoughts: my Inhabitants, Affections,
> The children of my thoughts walking within my blood-vessels.
> Shut from my nervous form which sleeps upon the verge of Beulah
> In dreams of darkness, while my vegetating blood in veiny pipes
> Rolls dreadful thro' the Furnaces of Los and the Mills of Satori.

The symbol of the city was no longer the cathedral, the palace or the market place, but the factory chimney.

All this wrought tremendous changes in the pattern of office activities and accommodation. The need to control and to finance the industrial revolution is closely linked to the growth of offices as we know them today, and illustrates two aspects of the office function—communication and the control of complexity.

It is obvious that the office function has a great deal to do with communication. The jobs that people do in offices have always been concerned with writing or transcribing messages of one kind or another, and with relaying information. Therefore, we should expect that, when there is an increase in the number of financial or other transactions, there will be a corresponding growth of the office function. The explorations, discoveries and empire building of the previous three centuries had already opened up whole new realms for exploitation, and had increased trade enormously. Clearly this would in turn lead to a growth in the number of messages, bills, agreements and so on which poured into the banks, counting houses, exchanges and coffee houses of the city. Mumford (1938) says,

> Food-chains and production-chains of an extremely complicated nature were being formed throughout the planet: ice travelled from Boston to Calcutta and tea journeyed from China to Iceland, whilst machinery from Birmingham and Manchester found its way to the remotest corner of the earth. A universal postal service, fast locomotion and almost instantaneous

> communication by telegraph and cable synchronised the activities of vast masses of men who had hitherto lacked the most rudimentary facilities for co-ordinating their tasks.

The office function was clearly due to grow, and to grow quickly. And in addition it would need to separate off from other facets of urban activity, because of the growing complexity and intricacy of organisation needed to finance, administer and support the industrial revolution.

We have seen that, until the industrial revolution, the office function was generally an integral part of other facets of urban life. But it is a commonplace that, as an organisation or an organism grows in complexity, certain parts or functions become separate from others. The office function of communication and control is just such a case. When an organisation is fairly simple, as in a cottage industry or a small workshop, the office function is integral with the production process itself. But as the enterprise grows and increases in complexity, and especially as more and more links are added to the networks of internal and external communications, so the office function begins to separate off. Haire (1959) has shown this process at work in all kinds of enterprises, and has suggested certain models. He shows that the office function has to do with communication and control, and that the clerical aspect in particular has a special place in growth; 'They are part of the general function of control, co-ordination and communication, which increases rapidly as the size increases . . . The clerks' job is largely concerned with information-recording, duplication, disseminating, keeping and finding information—to support the integrative function.' Haire also shows that the growth of the office function is not constant in relation to total growth of an enterprise; it rises rapidly as a proportion of total employment during the first ten or fifteen years of the life of the enterprise, after which it slows down, and runs parallel to other sections.

The separation of the office function at the level of the industrial firm is repeated on a city-wide scale during the nineteenth century. The need to support and sustain the process of industrialisation called new institutions into being, and changed old ones into new forms. The financial and administrative arrangements necessary for rapid industrialisation are formidable, and all the apparatus of distribution and marketing requires a great deal of co-ordination and control. As Mumford (1938) says,

> Plainly, no great corporate enterprise with a world-wide network of agents, correspondents, market outlets, factories and investors could exist without

> relying upon the services of an army of patient clerkly routineers in the metropolis: stenographers, filing clerks and book-keepers, office managers, sales managers and their varied assistants right up to the fifth vice-president whose name or O.K. sets the final seal of responsibility on an action.

Lichtenberg (1960) shows that the separation of the office function was inevitable, given the changes in other sectors which were occurring in the nineteenth century U.S.A. He says,

> Indeed, the same developments that were essential to the rapid growth of the industrial complex in the mid-west in the late years of the nineteenth century—the rise in speed and the fall in costs of transportation and communication—were fundamental to the establishment of the detached office. Before a manufacturer could hire specialists in administration, planning, sales promotion and finance, who were to make up some of the key personnel in central offices, he needed a large volume of business. And this volume was generated by the rise in scale of plant production that accompanied the falling costs of transportation and communication. The separation of the office from the plant also rested in part on the development of the long distance telephone in the 1880's. With the telephone, it became possible for management to choose one location for production and another for part of the office work.

As the separation and specialisation of the office functions continued, there grew up a new kind of building to house them. Once again Mumford (1938) has identified the pattern.

> Not merely did the bureaucracy itself require office space and living space: but the by-products of its routine came to occupy an increasing share of the new quarters. . . . This age found its form in a new type of office buildings: a sort of human filing case, whose occupants spent their days in the circumspect care of paper . . .

So that we begin to see the growth of 'office quarters', where the new office buildings cluster together. In New York a cluster of central offices—especially larger enterprises—began to accumulate in the late 1880's or early 1890's, although the evidence is incomplete. In London, the effects of the industrial revolution were felt earlier on, and the building of offices got under way during the first part of the century. We have already seen that the Bank of England, the Admiralty, the East India Company offices and Somerset House had been built in the eighteenth century. They were now joined by a whole series of new office accommodation. A number of insurance companies erected buildings in the area of the Strand and Fleet Street during the 1830's, and this cluster survives today. A little later, a whole series of exchanges were built to accommodate expanding office functions which had previously been housed in the Royal Exchange or in the city coffee houses. The Coal Exchange was built in 1849, the Stock Exchange in 1854 and the Wool Exchange in 1874. The Manchester Exchange had been opened in 1809, and was extended in 1838 to become the largest Exchange room in Europe. Again in London the latter part of the century saw the construction of great 'office streets', such as Victoria Street (1871), Queen Victoria Street (1867–1871) and Shaftesbury Avenue (1877–1886). The growth of government and municipal offices also accelerated, and more and more office jobs were created by the social and economic circumstances of the time.

Morgan (1960) has shown the extent of the growth of office employment:

> The development of the West End as a specialised commercial area during the latter half of the nineteenth century was influenced by factors which were making for an overall expansion of the entire central office district. These factors included an increase in the number of office workers. Problems of definition make difficult the comparison of the total number of office workers in different censuses, but an illustration may be made of the number in London enumerated as 'commercial clerks'. In 1851 these totalled 16,420 or 0·7% of the population, whereas by 1891 they had increased to 78,180 or 1·85%. Part of this increase was due to the growth of London itself, which had increased in population by 78% . . . The number of commercial clerks, however, increased by 476%. During this period the proportion of clerical employment was increasing throughout the country following the increasing complexity of larger firms, particularly after the Joint Stock Companies Act of 1856 had made limited liability easily obtainable. London gained disproportionately, however, because of its attraction both as the commercial centre of Britain and the world, and as a location of the headquarters offices of large amalgamations. This increased employment refers only to men, and it was not until after 1891 that a new element entered with the widespread use of women as commercial or business clerks.

Clearly, the socio-economic forces at work were powerful; and the growth of the office function was not to be a short-lived episode.

These social changes were complemented by a series of inventions and technical innovations, which gradually shaped the development of the office building as we know it today. Three inventions shaped the office activity, and each has to do with communication. They are the telegraph, the telephone and the typewriter together with its complementary skill—shorthand writing.

The telegraph had been invented by Watson in 1746, and the first telegraph line had been erected by Gray and Wheeler in 1753, but it was not until 1851 that the Dover–Calais cable was successful. In 1856 the Atlantic cable at last connected the two continents, and by 1862, according to Derry and Williams (1960), the world's telegraph system covered about 150,000 miles in Britain, 80,000 miles in the rest of Europe and about 48,000 miles in the United States, where telegraph lines had spanned the country from coast to coast in 1861. A method of printing the message was invented in 1854, and was developed in the United States as 'Hoase's printing telegraph'. In 1867 the New York Stock Exchange installed the electric stock ticker. Throughout the latter part of the nineteenth century telegraph lines multiplied in Europe and in the United States, connecting central offices and exchanges with distant branches.

McLuhan (1964) had discussed the impact of the telegraph, pointing out that, because it enables information to be passed instantaneously and directly to any branch of an organisation, the telegraph tends to destroy rigid and hierarchical systems which characterise most businesses. This is true, and certainly the structure of office organisations had to adjust to deal with a new kind of instruction system. But the major effects of the telegraph were, first, to make the detachment of administration and production even more possible, and, second, to increase the volume of work done by the office. As messages came in over the telegraph they would have to be recorded and processed. And the very rapidity and ease of this new form of communication would increase the volume of messages. In order to keep up with competitors, or with the news of world events which now flowed in with increasing rapidity, an administrator must issue orders and directives more quickly. He would respond ever faster, and this would in turn throw an increasing demand on other more routine office activities. The telegraph created an accelerating pattern of office work in which electric instantaneous external communication was slowed down within the office where it was processed by manual labour.

But perhaps the two inventions which had the greatest effect upon the nature of the office function were the telephone, invented by Bell in 1876, and the typewriter.

The telephone changed office activities in a similar fashion to the telegraph a few decades earlier. Not only did the ability to speak directly with people at a distance affect the dispersal of office functions, but within the office itself the telephone changed things and increased the work load. Confirmation of orders, instructions, appointments and so on became one of the major parts of office activity. But the telephone and the typewriter together effected even more far reaching changes in office activities and in the arrangement of the office space. McLuhan (1964) has described in some detail the impact of these inventions.

> At first, however, the typewriter was not seen as indispensible to business. The personal touch of the hand-penned letter was considered so important that the typewriter was ruled out of commercial use by the pundits. . . . Once any part of the economy feels a step up in pace, the rest of the economy has to follow suit. Soon no business man could be indifferent to the greatly increased pace set by the typewriter. It was the telephone paradoxically, that sped the commercial adoption of the typewriter. The phrase, 'Send me a memo on that', repeated into millions of phones daily, helped to create the huge expansion of the typist function. Northcote Parkinson's law that work expands to fill the time available for its completion is precisely the zany dynamic provided by the telephone. In no time at all the telephone expanded thework to be done on the typewriter to huge dimensions. Pyramids of paperwork rise on the basis of a small telephone network inside a single business. . . . Northcote Parkinson had discovered that 'any business of bureaucratic structure functions by itself, independently of the work to be done'. The number of personnel and the quality of work are not related to each other at all.
> In any given structure, the rate of staff accumulation is not related to what work done but to the intercommunication among the staff itself . . . Parkinson's law says that the rate of accumulation of office staff per annum will be between 5·17 per cent and 6·56 per cent irrespective of any variations in the amount of work (if any) to be done. . . . What Parkinson carefully hides from himself and his readers is simply the fact that in the area of information movement, the main work to be done is actually the movement of information.

Morgan (1960) has dealt in some detail with the impact of all these inventions upon the offices of London, and reaches the same general conclusions:

> The importance of rapid communication to the rise of modern business has been frequently stated. The introduction of the penny post in 1840 had little significance within London, which had an efficient internal postal service for some time, although the ability of a London head office to maintain control of factories and warehouses in other parts of the country was undoubtedly enhanced. More important was the introduction of the telegraph and telephone. The former was first used for railway signalling, but

> after 1846 a number of companies began to offer telegraphic facilities for commercial firms. Edison and Bell introduced their telephone systems in 1879 and 1880 respectively, and it is interesting to note that their first ten exchanges were in the city or the West End, except for two which were The Leather Exchange, Bermondsey, and the Hop Exchange, Southwark. The telephone has geographical significance in providing more or less instantaneous contact with branch offices and warehouses or the docks, and with stock and commodity exchanges, all of which therefore were no longer as strongly restricted to adjacent situation as they were previously.

Mumford (1938) summed up all these patterns of invention and their impact upon the office.

> With the manufacture of the typewriter in the seventies, and the coincident spread of high speed stenography, more and more business could be conducted on paper. Mechanical means of communication and mechanical means of making and manifolding the permanent record, mechanical systems of audit and control—all these devices aided the rise of a vast commercial bureaucracy, capable of selling in ever remoter territories . . . The housing of the bureaucracy in office buildings and tenements and residential suburbs constituted one of the major tasks of metropolitan expansion: their transportation back and forth to work within a limited time span raised one of the difficult technical problems that confronted the city planner and the engineer.

And, of course, the typewriter drew into the office a whole new class of worker-women, whose labour had been previously confined to the factory or to domestic service. We noted earlier that it was not until 1891 that women were employed in offices in England. But after that date the number of female office workers rose quickly, so that they very soon began to outnumber men in the more routine sections of the office. Derry and Williams (1960) note that in 1881 there were only 7,000 women clerks in England and Wales, yet by 1911 there were some 146,000. The office job was cleaner and more respectable than factory work, and it offered opportunities for social life which were not available to domestic servants. Quite soon 'office girl' became the rule rather than the exception, and the secretary became the symbol of the office girl. Mills (1956) says:

> The secretary has been the model of aspiration for most office girls. The typewriter too, of course, has been the woman's machine, and in itself has not led to factory-like effects. In and out of the office world, it has been a highly respectable machine. Its operator, equipped with stenographer's pad, has managed to borrow prestige from her close and private contact with the executive.

Since the nineteenth century the office has become more factory-like. Business machines have been introduced to speed up the internal functioning of the office, in response to extra demands placed upon them by a higher volume of external transactions. The function of the office girl, has in turn, become more centralised and routine. The typing pool grows, and as Mills (1956) puts it:

> The skill of shorthand becomes obsolete; the white collar girl becomes almost immediately replaceable; work in offices becomes almost immediately a blind alley. . . . The work is regulated so that it can be speeded up and effectively supervised by non-executive personnel. In short, the prized white collar spot for women is becoming more the job of a factory-like operative.

But if we look back to the end of the nineteenth century we can see that the office function had become well established as a separate entity in the city: new buildings were being constructed to house it; more and more of the labour force were working in offices, and women especially were beginning to go into office work in large numbers. The outlines of the office as we know it were laid down.

With the twentieth century, the office function and the office building began to assume an ever-increasing importance to the western city. In London the Kingsway-Aldwych development (1905) joined the nineteenth-century 'office streets'. Fletcher (1946) gives the following list of 'large office buildings' completed in London prior to 1939: The Port of London Authority Building; Metropolitan Water Board Building in Clerkenwell; Underground Railway offices, Westminister; I.C.I. Buildings; Lloyds Headquarters, City; Royal Mail House, City; Bush House, Aldwych; Britannic House, Finsbury Circus; Courtaulds Offices, City; 37 Lime Street, City; Adelaide House, London Bridge; Unilever House, Blackfriars. Others could be added, such as the Shell Building, Strand; B.B.C. Headquarters, Portland Place; and County Hall on the South Bank of the Thames, but the list indicates the great amount of office building going on in London during the first part of this century. In New York the story is the same. New skyscrapers joined those which had begun to cluster at the southern tip of Manhattan around Wall Street, and others began to form a new group at mid-town on 5th and Park Avenues, The Woolworth Building (1913); the Chrysler Building; the New York Telephone Building; Panhellenic House (1928); and the skyscraper par excellence—the Empire State Building (1931)—were all springing up during the first three decades of the century. And they were joined in the 30's by the greatest single collection of office space yet assembled—Rockefeller Centre. Chicago, too, was expanding the office function, and the space needed to accommodate it. The birthplace of the skyscraper in the nineteenth century saw the form continued through into the twentieth, although in a rather adulterated architectural style—neo-gothic or neo-classic trappings being applied to the steel frame. The Palmolive Building (1929); '333' North Michigan Avenue (1928); the Wrigley Building (1924); the Tribune Tower (1922) were joined by many other office buildings during the succeeding decades.

The symbol of the city was changing once again. The office and the skyscraper were displacing the industrial plant and the factory chimney. Why was this happening, and how did it occur? For, after all, this is the kind of city which we have today, and with which we are trying to grapple.

The cause is once again rooted in fundamental changes in society, which had a profound effect upon the role and shape of the city as a whole. What we see in our cities today is a reflection of a new kind of urban life arising from what Gottman (1966) has called the 'transactional society'.

We have seen that the office function is closely linked to the patterns of communication in society, and that we should expect any changes in such patterns to have a profound effect upon the office. Now a number of writers have put forward the idea that the fundamental role of the city has been changing over the past few decades. The old functions of the city, for defence or for religious headquarters, were swept away long ago, and replaced by the city as a manufacturing unit. Now, the need to assemble large numbers of factory workers around industrial plants is fast disappearing. Automation is making inroads in the number of workers needed in a factory, and the day of the completely automated and remote controlled factory is not far off. In these circumstances what remains as the main focus? It is, of course, the need for co-ordination and control, and the need for swift executive decisions—just the kind of role which the office fulfills. Dyckman (1962) puts this process very well.

> In the early stages of the evolution of the city, industrialisation, though only one of many social changes, was the decisive one. Without it the metropolis would have been impossible; without it the metropolis would have been unnecessary. The city, in turn, was an important artifact in

> the creation of an industrial civilisation. Now, however, the marriage faces possible dissolution. For one thing, industry is freer than it has ever been to set up outside the city. For another, both the 'city' and 'industry' are less clearly defined. The former has been submerged in a tide of urbanisation which does not respect clear-cut boundaries. The latter has evolved from recognisable processes of shaping materials to a range of activities shading in some cases from pure science to manipulation of human motives.

So that, as the traditional props of the city are removed, its role as a mechanism for facilitating communication moves to the centre of the stage.

Deutsch (1962) says,

> Any metropolis can be thought of as a huge engine of communication, a device to enlarge the range and reduce the cost of individual and social choices. . . . The facilities of the metropolis for transport and communication are the equivalent of the switchboard. The units of commitment are not necessarily telephone calls but more often face to face meetings and transactions.

And, indeed, people nowadays, in the west at least, no longer migrate to the city only for jobs but also in order to make friends and contacts and, possibly, to meet a marriage partner. In this context the city as a point of confrontation is supreme. Mead (1966) has compared such a city to an inn; a place where strangers can meet and converse. 'A great city like London or Paris or New York is a place which attracts young and excited people and one to which people from other countries go to meet one another, make new plans, invent new things, talk about new kinds of politics and paint new pictures.' Dyckman (1962) sketches in another aspect of this same phenomenon. 'Clearly we have entered upon an information-organisation drive for the whole world that dwarfs the old task of taking the message to the small towns. Cities play a convenient role in all this process, as the metropolis continues to provide a favourable habitat for a large volume of transactions . . .'

We now begin to see how the growth of offices and the office function reflects some underlying changes in the role of the city. But we need to probe more deeply and to expose the connections more clearly before we can fully understand what is going on. For the 'office function' is itself difficult to define, and has changed considerably over the years, becoming in some parts more factory like, while in others the need for individual action and decision has remained paramount. Such internal changes must affect the place of different parts of the office function in the city.

The story of the changes inside the office function during the past decades is fairly clear, and reflects the earlier separation between office functions and production activities. A great deal of office activity has become mechanised and 'routinised', leaving a certain elite function of decision making and action as the nucleus. Mills (1951) has sketched in the stages of the development in the United States. In 1919 the National Association of Office Managers was formed to promote the ideas of scientific management. The same period saw a rapid growth in office machinery. In the second decade of the century some hundred new office machines were placed on the market every year. By 1930 some 30% of women in offices were, in the course of their work, using machines other than typewriters. But it was the Second World War which accelerated the mechanisation of large sections of the office routine: the pre-war rate of office machinery sales in the United States was $270,000,000; by 1948 it was $1,000,000,000. All this mechanisation has enabled the office to cope with the volume of work produced by automation and scientific management in the factory, and to deal with the increasing complexity of the office itself, as the business unit grows bigger through mergers and so on. Business machines have also led to centralisation. Machines and centralisation go together to increase output and lower costs. They open the way to factory-type procedures in the office function, and a great many firms have by now introduced time and motion studies, leading to splitting of complicated tasks and to specification of many activities. The planning and layout of the office have also undergone change of machinery and centralisation. The private office gives way to the large open spaces needed for a straight line flow of work. Mills quotes an office where 200 former private offices were reduced to 17, with consequent gains in quality production and supervision.

The Town and Country Planning Association (1962) have put the position in Britain:

> Modern equipment has brought a new conception of office routine, and in large concerns integration has become a key word. Great improvements have been effected in the spread of recording and processing information, in output capacity and organisational flexibility, and in storage facilities. Where the volume of work justifies it, there is a strong trend towards the establishment of a centralised data-processing unit serving many departments, divisions, and even companies. In many cases mechanisation brings no reduction in staff but enables a far longer volume of work to be handled.

In others separate sections can be reduced and combined with routine staff, being replaced by a smaller number of higher grade employees able to interpret or edit the processed information. But the high cost of buying and installing the new machines, often in rooms with air conditioning, sound proofing, and special ducts for power supply and servicing, and of the pneumatic tubes, punched card stations and even closed-circuit television to distribute information is a strong incentive to seek greater centralisation so that machines and equipment can be used nearer to capacity.

In harness with this is the trend through take-overs and mergers to concentration of industrial and commercial concerns in larger units. New headquarters offices are demanded which proclaim by site, size and appearance the new organisation's enhanced importance, its 'prestige'. And with London the dominant centre of almost every aspect of national life, what city, asks the board of directors, could possibly confer greater prestige—if the question is ever asked.

We can now begin to see the effects of these internal changes in office activity upon the location and role of the office function in a city which is itself changing into an engine for communication.

Some work has been done in Britain during the past few years on the locational patterns of office accommodation. Wabe (1965) has studied the moves of a number of office firms, and has shown that the size of firm is related to both the distance moved and to the kind of move (total, partial and so on). Very broadly, large moves are the most difficult to make, while small firms seem to be able to move only a short distance. It is the medium-sized moves (20–79 people) which are easiest, for these firms are growing rapidly and can consider complete decentralisation as a whole unit. Wabe also puts forward some hypotheses about the relation between firm size, moving characteristics and profits. Williams (1965) has also considered the problem of office growth and movement in London. She concludes that there is no "office problem" as such, and that the growth of offices is inextricably bound up with general regional development. She demonstrates conclusively that the large amount of office activity in south-east England is caused by the type of industry clustered there and by the growing forces of metropolitan concentration. She does not hold much hope for policies of restraint or voluntary dispersal of office growth, in the face of the major forces underlying the whole process of development in the south-east.

Another report by the Department of Economic Affairs (1965) explores patterns of office development outside the south-east. This lays stress upon the importance of communications in determining office location, and considers in detail various modes of communication and their availability in different regions. The general conclusion is that London holds a dominant position for most kinds of office work, although certain routine activity might be moved out. A policy to achieve such decentralisation must include financial assistance to communication functions and a tax on floor space in central areas. Thus these British studies confirm the importance of communications as an element in deciding office locations, and point to the forces which are affecting two distinct sections of the office functions—centralised decision making and dispersing routine data processing. The same two things seem to be occurring in the United States. First, the decisions makers, the leaders of industry, finance, communications and so on—what has been called the 'elite group'—are finding it more and more necessary to locate in the centre of the city. These people are those whose business, and indeed survival, depend upon rapid communication—they flourish upon the newest ideas, and must react instantly in order to maintain their place in the system. These people, the elite, also need to be near, or have immediate access to, their own information which is contained in the more routine parts of the office organisation. The second trend is for those more routine parts of the office function to become more footloose; able to locate in the suburbs, near to the female labour force and away from the high rents and access difficulties of the centre.

Lichtenberg (1960) points to this process at work in the New York region, and suggests that there are very practical economic reasons behind the desire of the elite to remain in the city centre. He says,

> Questionnaires designed to elicit the views of executives on the attractions of New York. . . . often emphasize the 'mystical spark' of Gotham, the stimulating and challenging atmosphere, the 'prestige of plush New York facilities', of New York's central location for transportation, business, and finance. These facts undoubtedly play some role in the attraction of New York City. But we are strongly inclined to the view that the fundamental explanation is the more prosaic one, which also accounts for the high concentration in New York of the external economy manufacturing industries or the money market specialists.
>
> Like producers of unstandardised products, the central office executives 'produce' answers to 'unstandardised' problems, problems that change frequently, radically, and unpredictably. . . . These problems are solved quickly only by consultation with a succession of experts. But, like stock-brokers or high style dress manufacturers, most central offices would find

> it inefficient, if not impossible, to staff themselves internally with all of the specialised personnel and services that they must call upon from time to time to solve their problems. Nor it is convenient to transport the experts to their plants or maintain effective contact by telephone or letter. The importance of speed blunts the effectiveness of the fastest means of transportation, and the complex and subtle nature of the problem often precludes the use of the telephone. All of these considerations dictate a concentration of offices in a tight cluster near each other and near their 'suppliers'.

So the reasons for the elite remaining in the central city are practical and economic as well as intangible and preferential. But what of those other, routine, sections of the office? How are they evolving and what locational choices have they made? Once again Lichtenberg (1960) tells us what has happened in New York. 'Routine office work is growing in size. With the steady growth of data processing machines, such work is also growing in complexity of production technique. In consequence, routine office work is no longer effectively supervised by the elite corps of executives in Manhattan's central offices. In addition, the labour requirements for the processing of routine data are changing. Instead of employing a huge staff of book-keepers and clerks, concerns are hiring business machine programmers and operators. As the years pass, this kind of skill becomes available in more and more areas of the country. The special attraction of the New York area, generated out of its external economies and communication advantage, therefore decline.

On these grounds we should expect most routine office functions to move out of the central area. That this is not occurring with greater speed is in part due to the attraction which a great metropolis holds for certain kinds of people—especially the young women upon whom much of the work depends. Hoover and Vernon (1959) have told us something of this problem in relation to the New York area.

> The young women's preference for a job in the central business district today, therefore, is not based quite so solidly as before upon the compulsions of the transport net; it is based instead on the increased opportunities for after-hours recreation, lunch-hour shopping (or window shopping) and the greater opportunities for husband hunting. This means, as we observed in connection with life insurance companies, that office establishments with a large complement of workers—our field work suggest that the critical level may be 500 or so—would have a considerably easier time recruiting and maintaining a staff of clerical workers in the

> central business district. For smaller office establishments, however, the advantage is not nearly so great.

It may be worth noting in passing that this point concerning the size of establishment may conflict with the economic ties to the central areas. For it is just these smaller establishments, the ones who would recruit routine labour outside the central area, who need to stay there in order to 'service' or 'supply' the elites of major national company headquarters. They are particularly vulnerable to changes in the communication pattern, and a move outside the central area might well be fatal to many.

The office function has thus become split, and the two elements have different location and space needs. There is a conflict here, but it may be resolved by modern communications. Lichtenberg (1960) has once again summarised the situation very clearly:

> Modern jet planes are providing, and closed circuit television will soon provide, a solution to a major locational dilemma of these executives. On the one hand they need to be located in a tight cluster to obtain information in a hurry from a large number of possible sources. On the other hand they need to be near their plants to keep a close check on the implementation of their programmes. But today they can more easily carry out both functions from one or other of these locations. And since uncertainties and variability of requirements are much greater in decision making than in carrying out the decision, we suspect that most of the elite corps will choose to locate in the tight cluster.

We can now see that both the internal organisation of the office and its location in the city depend to a very large extent upon patterns of communication. Elite groups locate in the centre where they can have immediate face to face contact with a wide variety of people. Routine functions may be suburbanised at the end of an airline, a telephone wire, or a television circuit—the finer nuances of communication are not necessary for the kind of messages which flows between executive and routine office plant. But how have these patterns affected the building of offices? We know that there has been a great boom in office building in London since the war, and that New York has also experienced a skyscraper boom. What part have the forces and factors we have just discussed played in the process? Perhaps the main point is that the kind and amount of space needed by each office worker is changing. Office work is now recognised to need proper conditions, light, heat, space and air, which are not always provided in old structures. New office buildings provide proper conditions and an efficient use of space in which machinery can be installed properly. And the amount of space required per worker is rising. The recent 'Office Workers' Charter' (1964) in Britain laid down minimum space standards, and could create a demand for more office space, even if there were no increase in office jobs in the cities. A recent survey of New York offices carried out by Kroos for the New York Metropolitan Region Study estimated that, for all types of employees the average space per employee increased about 20% between 1947 and 1958. Hoover and Vernon make the following comment:

> Whether the skyscraper community continues to grow does not depend alone upon the number of office workers in Manhattan. It depends also on who those office workers are, and what they do. Manhattan's position as an official location, we have suggested, is weakest for repetitive, standardised office work, strongest for the elite activities of the office. Therefore, if standardised office activities peel off from Manhattan locations in the next decade or two, the space demands of the average office worker in Manhattan will almost certainly increase and this will happen whether or not the office elite continue to expand the amount of space per person that they occupy. In the decade ahead no requiem will be sung for the skyscraper.

We have concentrated upon New York in this last section because it is better documented than most other cities, largely through the work of the New York Metropolitan Regional Study. But the general pattern can be seen in other cities of the world, most especially in London, where the post-war boom in office space has been a feature of the city scene, and has indeed made over parts of the city in a new image.

What of the future? Such speculations are more appropriate to a concluding chapter, when the themes raised in this chapter will be taken up and woven with those developed in other sections. But we can, even at this early stage, see some broad trends in the role of the city and of the office within it. Hall (1966) has sketched part of the picture.

> Yet the general principle is evident enough. At the very centre of the structure of the central business district of each world city there is found a relatively small nucleus of highly skilled professionals. All these people in one way or another, live by creating, processing or exchanging ideas . . . all these people live only on their ideas, on transmitting those ideas readily and economically to others, and in receiving their ideas in exchange.
>
> The central business district therefore can be seen as a highly specialised machine for producing processing and trading specialised *intelligence*. . . .

> The process is a continuing one, for the ideas industries are growing many times faster than industry as a whole. As late as 1850, they included only a very small number of traditional professions like banking, medicine or law. But as increasing mechanisation and then automation have reduced the physical agony of growing wheat and turning it into bread, of picking cotton and processing it into shirts, so new types of economic activity come into existence. . . . The overall likelihood therefore is that the ideas industries will continue to grow in the metropolitan centres. They will displace other activities long associated with the centres; many types of manufacturing, wholesaling and warehousing, the more generalised and popular types of retail shopping, and those types of office activity which involve the assemblage, processing and storage of data, and even the taking of routine decisions on that data. Such routine activities will increasingly be performed by electronic machinery with the help of a small staff of skilled programmers and computer operators. Though electronic storage should lead to dramatic savings in space, it is likely that wherever the routine activities can be economically split off from the decision-taking processes they can be displaced from the high rent central sites into the suburbs near to their labour force.

For the next few decades this pattern is by far the most probable, but are there any longer term prophecies we might make or are there details of this general picture which we might refine?

The answers to such questions will depend upon how far we think electronic communications can become an effective substitute for face to face meetings in the future metropolis. There is a considerable divergence of views on this issue. At one end of the scale are those who believe that a total substitution is possible, and that in the future we shall all live entirely physically separate lives, although bound together by electronic links of all kinds. Such views are common in science fiction—E. M. Forster's *The Machine Stops* is an early example of the genre. At the other end there are those who think that very little advance can be made upon our present systems of communication, and that the investment in existing cities is so great that they cannot be changed much, even over a very long period. Most observers fall somewhere between these two positions. Their views are summed up by Fliesher (1962) when he says that, although television may replace many kinds of face to face meetings 'it may not be adequate for transactions which would terminate in a handshake or a fist fight'. What this means is that developments in communication technology are selective in their effects; that although some more routine types of transaction—

for instance, the instructions necessary to pass orders from an executive to his staff, or from an office to the factory floor—may be carried out by remote control, others, especially those requiring a sensitive awareness of a multitude of surrounding circumstances, will still require direct contact between individuals. Project MAC, now developed at M.I.T., illustrates this. There will be one central computer with peripheral and display installations in many locations—for example, in the homes of the scientists—so that anyone who needs to use a computer can have as much time as he needs in any location that is convenient to him. Thus the routine part of a scientist's job can be handled at a distance and by remote control. But a large part of the scientist's work will still occur in meetings with colleagues on the campus, where the free interchange of ideas goes on in face to face situations. This seems a probable pattern for the office function in the city for some time to come. But it may well be that the *number* of the *elite* decision-makers decreases, as improvements in communications enable each individual to deal with a greater number of problems in the course of a day. Therefore, the actual concentration in the centre of the city may grow smaller, there may no longer be a need for large office buildings, and businesses may be run from social gathering places such as restaurants or private houses or apartments in the city centre—a return to the coffee houses of the baroque city!

Our brief survey of the place of the office function and its accommodation in the city has suggested some clearly defined phases.

First of all office functions were diffused throughout the city, in the houses of merchants or in coffee houses; with certain concentrations around the court and government or in professional enclaves. In the second phase, which was ushered in by the industrial revolution, the office function became detached and concentrated in specially designed accommodation, where economies of scale, and the rapid transmission of information were facilitated. During this phase the office function grew, both because of social and economic changes connected with the need to finance and administer the industrial revolution, and because of several inventions in the field of communications.

We are now entering upon a third phase in which the impact of technical advance is altering the balance once again. Automation is reducing the importance of manufacture as part of the role of the city, while at the same time the interchange of ideas and the information handling activities, of which the office function is one, are increasing in importance. Soon the further impact of improved communication may lead to another dispersal of the office function to the homes and gathering places of those with ideas to exchange. The wheel will have come full circle.

Chapter III
The Growth of the Office Function—Some Case Studies[1]

The previous chapter sketched in some of the major outlines of office evolution in the changing city. It took a very broad view of social, technical and economic changes which affected office functions in the western city. But within these major secular changes are contained smaller patterns of development. Each office organisation has an individual history. How do these histories fit into the overall pattern of change in the city, and what factors affect the individual office activity as it grows and changes?

As part of our work at the Joint Unit for Planning Research we have undertaken a series of case studies of different kinds of organisations and the problems posed to them of growth, change adaptability and location in the city. This work was planned to link on to this present study of the office function, and for this reason four large office organisations were chosen as part of the sample.

A more detailed report of the whole study is contained in Cowan and Sears (1966), but for the present purposes it will be sufficient to concentrate upon the four office case histories.

First of all we must point out that the organisations are examples of 'commercial' offices. Other types of offices, such as those of professional firms or of government, do experience problems of growth and change, but it is likely that their patterns of development will be very different, and will perhaps be conditioned by rather special circumstances. Morgan (1960) has pointed to the evolution of 'office regions' in London, and has shown how certain quarters of the city attract government and

[1] This chapter draws upon material acquired in the course of a study of the problems of change and adaptability, financed by a generous grant from the Ministry of Public Buildings and Works, to whom we are very grateful.

professional offices. Our enquiry has dealt with a more 'general' kind of office, one which is perhaps more affected by the overall patterns of change in the city and by economic circumstances.

The natural history of institutions has been little studied. Some consideration has been given to the growth of firms by Steindl (1965) and Archer and McGuire (1965), but this has usually been couched in terms of economic models, related to the current size of firms and so on. The growth rate of buildings has received even less attention, and very little is known of the way individual buildings behave over time. On the other hand, a great deal of work has been done on the growth of cities and large aggregates of buildings. Various models of city growth have been developed in the United States over recent years, and a most fruitful line of enquiry has been opened up. But these efforts have not yet been related to individual buildings and, while investigations of the behaviour of large aggregates may offer some methodological clues to the study of change in buildings, they have not so far provided any very clear insights into the process of such change. We are therefore entering an unknown territory in this chapter.

We have considered each organisation from the point of view of changes in the overall size of the institution and internal changes which have occurred in staff numbers engaged in different activities. These are related to building growth and change, in terms of floor space occupied by various parts of the institution at different times. Four organisations were chosen because they were available for study, they were large enough and had been in existence long enough to make a study of changes worthwhile, and they were able to supply statistics and other information about their life history as organisations. These were the four organisations:

1. The headquarters premises of a computer firm. This firm was the result of a merger which occurred in 1959 between two previously existing companies. The period since this merger was studied. The headquarters offices currently employ some 2,000 people.

2. The London and head office of a mechanical engineering firm. The period studied for this organisation was the decade 1955–1965. At the end of this period, these offices housed some 800 people.

3. The offices of a London advertising agency. This firm has been in existence for some forty-two years. However, a number of moves have been made during this period, and the study has concentrated in depth

upon the five years 1960–1965, when very great changes were occurring which occasioned a number of complex and significant changes in building needs. By 1965, the firm employed some 170 people.

4. The offices of an insurance company. This company has been in existence for over 100 years, and the period chosen for study is the thirty years between 1935 and 1965. By this time the company was well established, and problems of expansion, changing methods of work and technical innovation were becoming urgent. In 1965, these offices housed about 5,900 people.

In some cases, it was necessary to select parts of organisations for study. In such cases, we tried to deal with parts of the organisation which are reasonably complete in themselves. For example, in the case of the insurance company, we decided not to concern ourselves with local branch offices, but only with the central headquarters. This was possible because the headquarters organisation performs a distinct and separate role in the total organisation of the company. For the same reason, we have not considered the manufacturing side of the computer firm, but have concentrated upon the headquarters offices. Such decisions may seem somewhat arbitrary, and indeed we would have preferred to deal with the total pattern of each organisation, but in the perspective of the resources available we had no alternative.

The data required from each organisation concerned the numbers of employees in various categories at each stage of development, and the amount and kind of floor space which was occupied.

One variable factor was the length of time over which each institution's growth could be traced. In some cases, only a short period has been treated whereas in others, periods of thirty years or more have been considered. Once again, the reason was dictated partly by the availability of information and partly by the intrinsic interest of certain periods of growth in the organisation's history. In each case the history of the organistion has been brought up to date and the final description is of the institution as it exists today.

Case History Number 1

The headquarters premises of a computer firm

In 1959 a merger took place between two large computer companies (referred to throughout as *A* and *B*) and their subsidiaries, to form one new company (*Company C*).

The original firms had each been founded in 1907 to produce, market and develop punch-card systems. Their history was marked by frequent bursts of expansion in turnover, staff employed and premises. Such expansion usually occurred because of major technical advances in the industry or because of new applications for punch-card systems.

Since the early 1950's expansion in the entire industry has been at an unprecedented rate.

In order to meet expansion, both companies started acquiring premises close to their original head offices. But by 1959 the need for space had resulted in the use of many buildings spread over a wide area.

A great amount of organisational change took place after 1958, when the merger was planned, but this cannot be followed in detail, as certain records are not available. Annual staff totals, and breakdowns of staff and buildings by function are available for only a few buildings for a few years, and it would have been foolish to use such incomplete information.

Thus the study deals only with buildings used as headquarters premises within the Greater London area between December 1952 and December 1965. We have concentrated especially on the process of consolidating and rationalising premises after the merger in June 1959.

Fig. III 1 shows the overall pattern of change in floor spacc during the period. The bars above the lines of dates show total London headquarters floor space in use at the end of each year, while those below the line show the area given up during the same year.

By 1958 floor space belonging to *Company A* was half as much again as the 1952 total. *Company B* meanwhile did not increase its headquarter area. Between the merger, at June 1959 and the end of 1964, the area for headquarter purposes more than doubled. Almost none of the buildings which were used as headquarter premises in 1959 remained in this use by 1964. The 170,000 sq. ft. shown in Fig. 1 on the extreme right comprised premises acquired by *Company C* after the merger (with the exception of one very small area in a block acquired long before by *Company B*, where part of the headquarters had moved back in).

The process of replacing individual buildings is of particular importance. An examination of Figs. III 1 and 2 will show exactly what occurred.

Fig. III 1 Computer firm. Total HQ floor space on lease or given up each year.

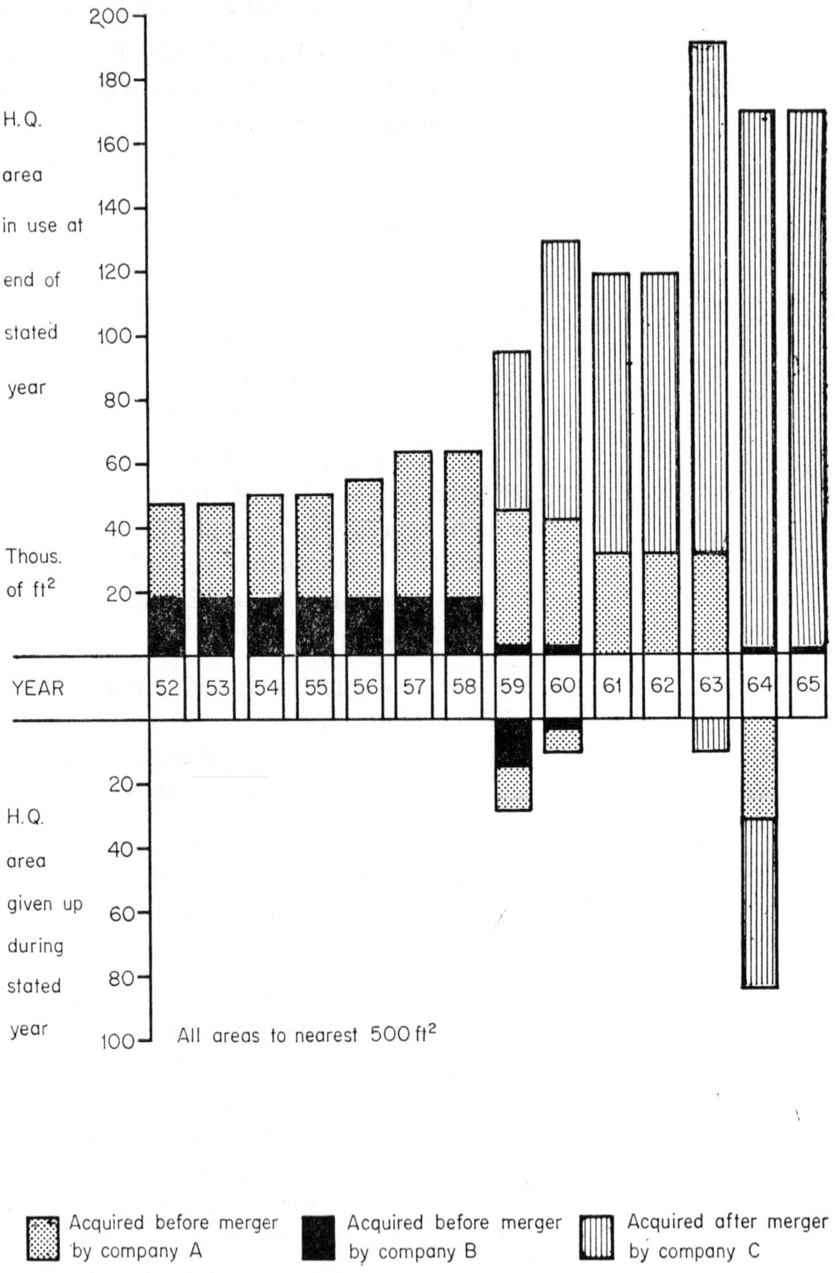

Fig. III 2 shows the nineteen London headquarter buildings used during the period 1952–1959, their length of time in use, size, and the company that acquired them.

Until the merger, Building 1 was the head office of *Company A* with Buildings 2 and 3 opposite. However, of the extra headquarter space taken up by *Company B* before 1959, only Building 8 adjoined these original three, and Building 5 was some considerable distance away. All the new buildings were comparatively small.

This scatter was lessened after the merger, as the three buildings given up (5, 7 and 9) were away from the Hyde Park Corner Group. Buildings 10, 11 and 12, which replaced them, were all at Hyde Park Corner. After the merger the head office for the newly formed *Company C* was Building 11, which was the largest single unit of headquarter area used till then.

After the merger various headquarter computer sections were spread throughout many buildings, and in April 1960 one building of 23,910 sq. ft. was acquired to house them all. (Building 15.) This was the first building to be taken at Putney. The choice of this location was largely fortuitous. It happened to offer the only suitable building in size, availability and accessibility at a time when new premises were being sought for a fast-expanding division. Office deployment had long been divided into three categories: (1) Central London; (2) the periphery; (3) the Provinces. Already Research Division had suburban premises inherited from a mutual agreement with another company, but the move to the suburbs was new in that it united certain sections, previously scattered in London, with others from outside London, and rehoused them in a decentralised building.

By the end of 1961 the management was seriously worried about general deployment of premises.

It was decided that a Central London headquarters must be built by the Company to their own requirements. This would house certain staff for whom a central location was essential while further expansion would be taken up on the 'periphery'. Within the Park Lane complex there was no room for expansion, and no available long-lease building was large enough. It had been proposed to take temporary accommodation in a new building under construction at Putney, and this would have taken some of the pressure off the Park Lane area, but by the end of 1961 this new building was a year behind schedule. The accom-

Fig. III 2 The nineteen Central London headquarters buildings used—by years, by size.

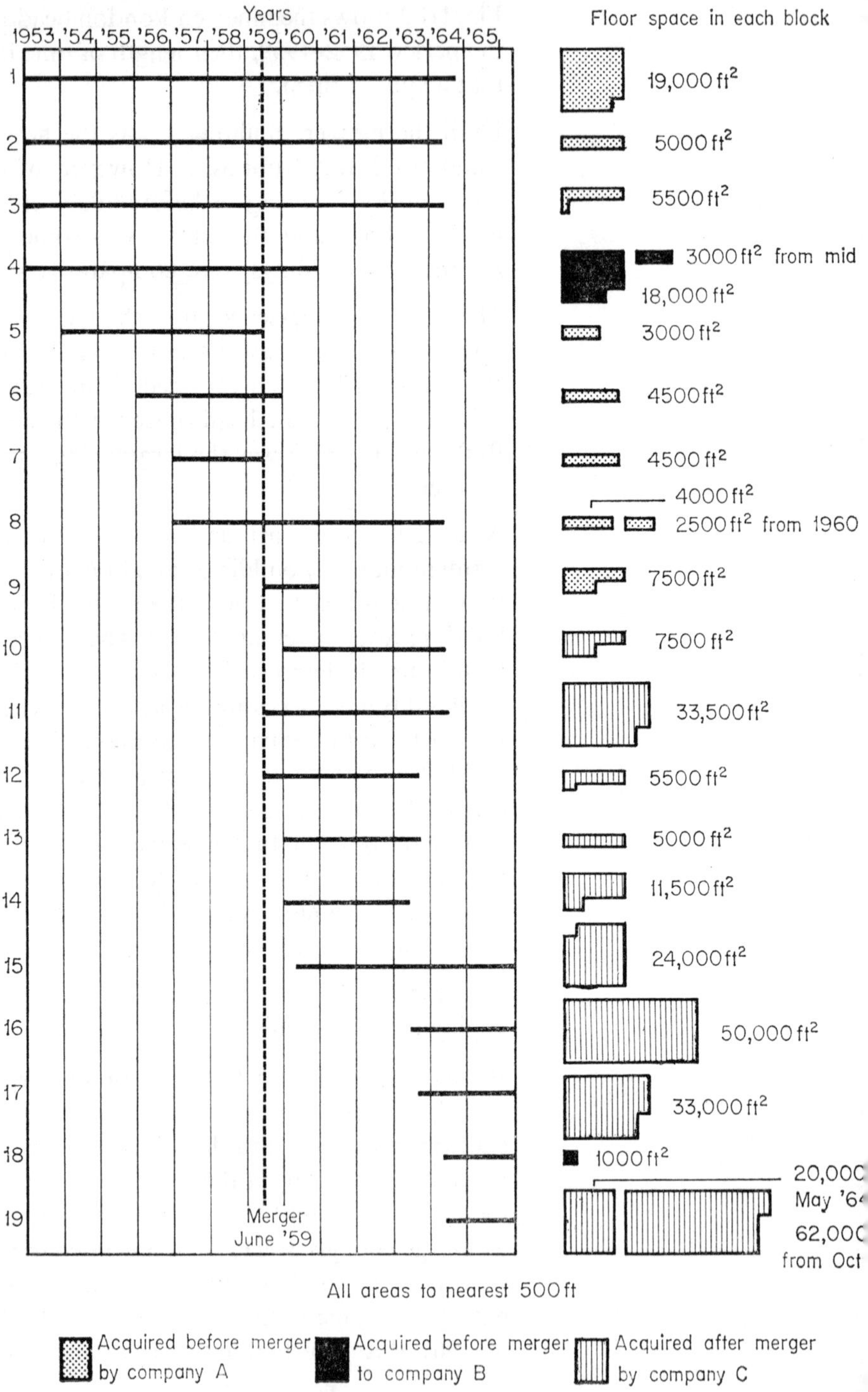

modation problem at Park Lane was now becoming acute. Space allocation had been tightened up and it was felt that there might be difficulty in satisfying the new working premises legislation.

There were two problems. First, which staff must stay at a central location and which must or could be at the 'periphery'? Second, could planning permission and building space in Central London be obtained, plus suitable premises to rent at the periphery?

It was estimated that a building containing between 90,000 and 120,000 sq. ft. was needed for the Central London head office. It was also felt that, if occupation was to be possible by 1965–1966, a site would have to be found by mid 1962. The building should be planned with sufficient adaptability to allow segregation between the company itself and any sub-tenants who might take up surplus space. Preference was expressed for Mayfair and Knightsbridge. Marble Arch and Victoria were also favoured. Failing these, any other West End site would be considered. Three ways were put forward for using a new central block to cope with expansion requirements.

First, the development could be built and occupied in two stages.

Second, it was suggested that the building should be larger than required for the 'kernel' of headquarters staff, and that the remainder should be occupied by headquarters staff destined for the periphery.

The third suggestion was that immediate excess space should be sub-let on short leases. This solution was felt to be the best, as it would enable unused space to earn for the Company at London rentals, until London staff expanded.

By Spring 1962 inability to find a suitable site was causing concern. It had been assumed that the Company would be able to build on a site of their own to their own requirements, but nothing suitable had been found. The alternative was to stake a claim to new office development. This would mean that plans for disposing of the Hyde Park Corner complex might depend on a completion date, supplied by a developer. The management was worried that if completion was delayed, Park Lane buildings might be disposed of before the new building was completed, and temporary premises would have to be acquired; or that Park Lane might be retained longer than necessary, and rents would overlap. While the latter would be a financial burden, the prospect of taking stop-gap premises was even more unsatisfactory.

By September 1962 an analysis had been made to show which staff required a Central London base, and which could be at the periphery. Predictions were made of expansion up to 1976. It was anticipated that, by 1976, 83% of staff would be deployed in the periphery and 17% in Central London. The aim of getting permission for the Company's own development scheme had not been quite abandoned, and it was felt that planning authorities might regard an application for a Central London 'prestige' building more favourably, if the Company's long-term expansion policy was based on greater expansion at the periphery.

An estimate of future peripheral space requirements was calculated. At mid-1962 it was estimated that the Company already needed an additional 50,000 sq. ft. By late 1963 it was hoped that this would fall to 24,000 sq. ft. when the second Putney building of 50,000 sq. ft. was taken. Buildings 12 and 13 in Piccadilly could then be given up. But meanwhile an anticipated staff increase of 130 would maintain the gap between the area acquired and that required.

Building 16 was occupied in July 1963 and the two Piccadilly buildings were given up in October 1963. However, the next stage did not go according to plan. It was assumed that by 1966 a Central London headquarter building would be in occupation, all the original Park Lane premises would be disposed of, and 231,300 sq. ft. at the periphery would house all non-Central London staff. But no Central London site building could be found, and by the end of 1965 virtually the entire headquarters staff was housed at Putney in four buildings totalling 169,000 sq. ft.

Thus, because of a misfire, the suburban site was chosen to house all London headquarter staff and to deal with all future expansion. Since late 1964 the Company have had no property foothold or redevelopment potential in the central area.

There is no surplus space to lease out to tenants at Putney and more premises will undoubtedly be acquired. On the other hand, the feeling that visitors should not be taken 'right out' has caused certain changes. As a result of the move to Putney, a *pied à terre* (in Carlton Gardens) was acquired by the Company for entertaining overseas visitors, for press conferences, and for visiting directors. In spite of this the story shows that the Company was virtually forced to leave Park Lane through the inadequacy of premises available at the centre to meet expansion requirements, and there is no indication that the process is in any way reversible.

Case History Number 2

The London and head office of a mechanical engineering firm

The Company had its origins in Wiltshire in 1816. Since this time it has established branches in London and fifteen provincial cities and at the end of 1965 employed nearly five thousand staff.

The London premises house both the main London offices and the national administrative headquarters. By the end of 1965, head office and London office were split between two buildings, but, as the two sections are closely linked, both are covered in this study.

It is necessary to describe what had happened immediately before 1955, the first year of the decade studied. In mid-1954 premises of 18,500 sq. ft. were occupied (Building 1) by about 250 London and head office staff. Stores buildings, a mile away from Building 1, were replaced by premises much closer to it (Building 2). Part of these stores were let to a sub-tenant. At mid-1955, when the sub-tenancy expired, some space in the stores building was turned into makeshift offices and used for staff overflow from the main building.

Between mid-1955 and mid-1956, the staff in London and head office doubled. Within five years newly acquired premises became overcrowded. It was decided to acquire another large building, not only to contain current overflow but also to provide a main reserve.

After a wide search, an office development in a new town was selected for particular consideration. A detailed study was undertaken of the implications of such decentralisation.

Fig. III 3 shows the total floor space leased at June of each year between 1955 and 1965, and the amount given up during each year. The firm's physical expansion is planned around the gradual absorption of extra space as sub-tenants' leases expire. For this reason, Fig. III 3 goes on to show the expiration date of all sub-tenants' leases taken up during the ten-year period.

Fig. III 4 shows all the buildings used between 1955 and 1965 as London and/or head office premises.

Fig. III 5 shows the relationship between total space actually in use, (i.e. not in reserve or sub-let) and the number of staff employed. It should be noted that staff totals were not available for such regular intervals as floor space totals, and we sometimes had to make an assessment when only a sub-total was given. For instance, it was known that apprentices were sometimes omitted from a grand total, and in such

Fig. III 3 Engineering Firm. Total London and head office floor space on lease or given up during each year.

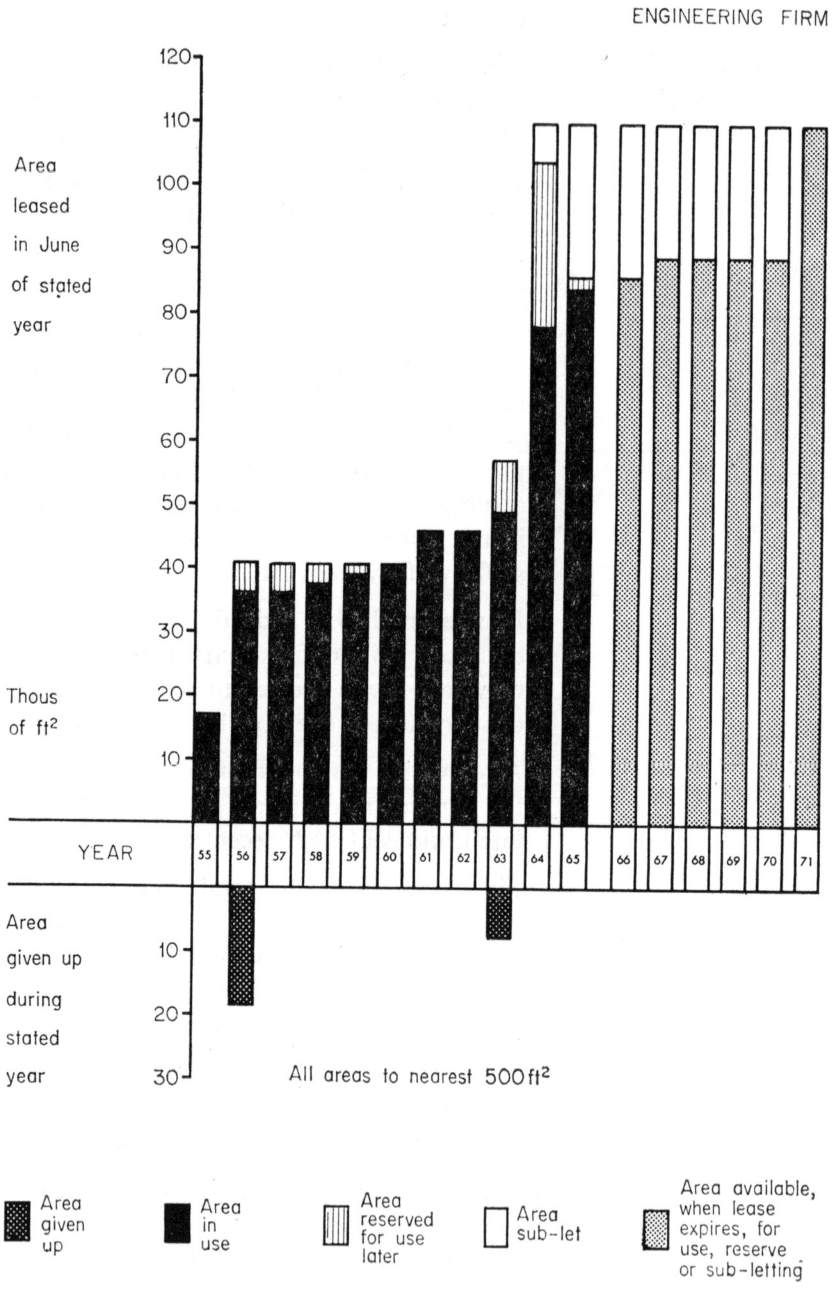

Fig. III 4 The six London and head office buildings used—by year and by size.

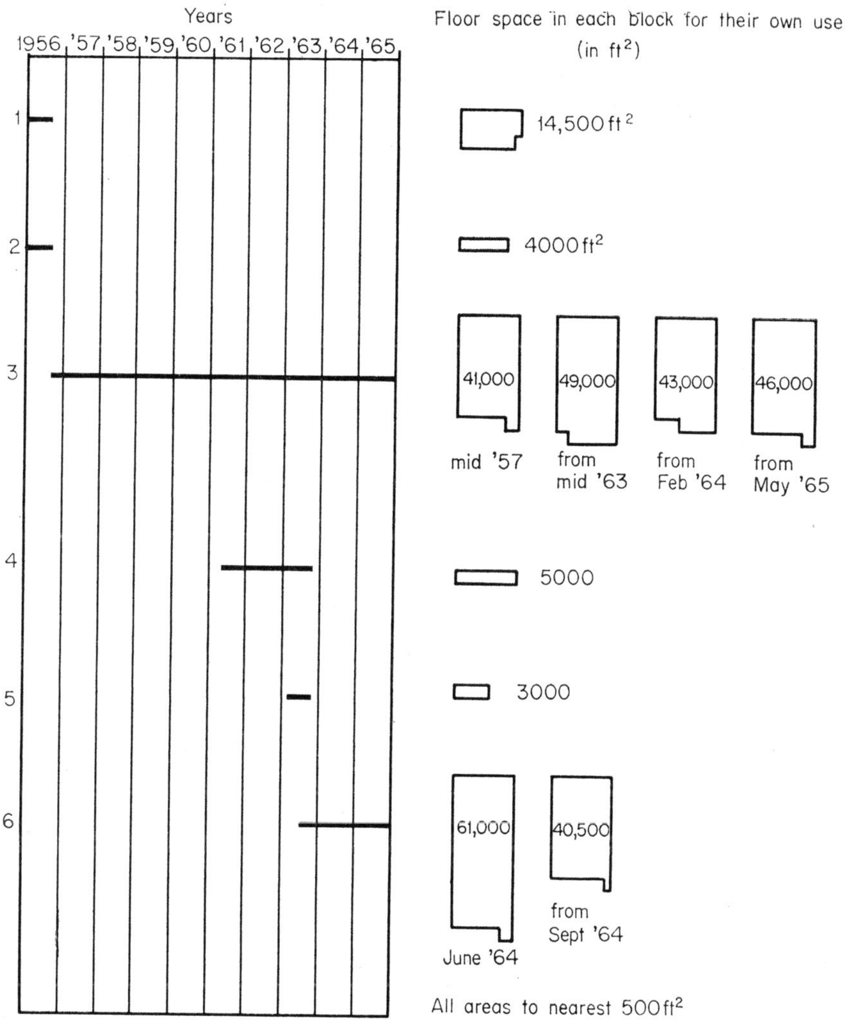

cases 100 has been added to the sub-total. Fig. III 6 shows the location of various buildings mentioned in the text.

Approximately 285 staff occupied 18,500 sq. ft. at mid-1955 and no expansion was possible within either main building.

It was felt desirable that one building should be found to provide some 28,500 sq. ft. plus expansion room, and that Building 1, with a lease running till 1981, should be sub-let. A large development company offered all eight storeys (80,000 sq. ft.) of a new office block nearing completion. The firm took four floors of this building (Building 3),

Fig. III 5 Floor space actually in use and staff totals or estimates (1955–1965).

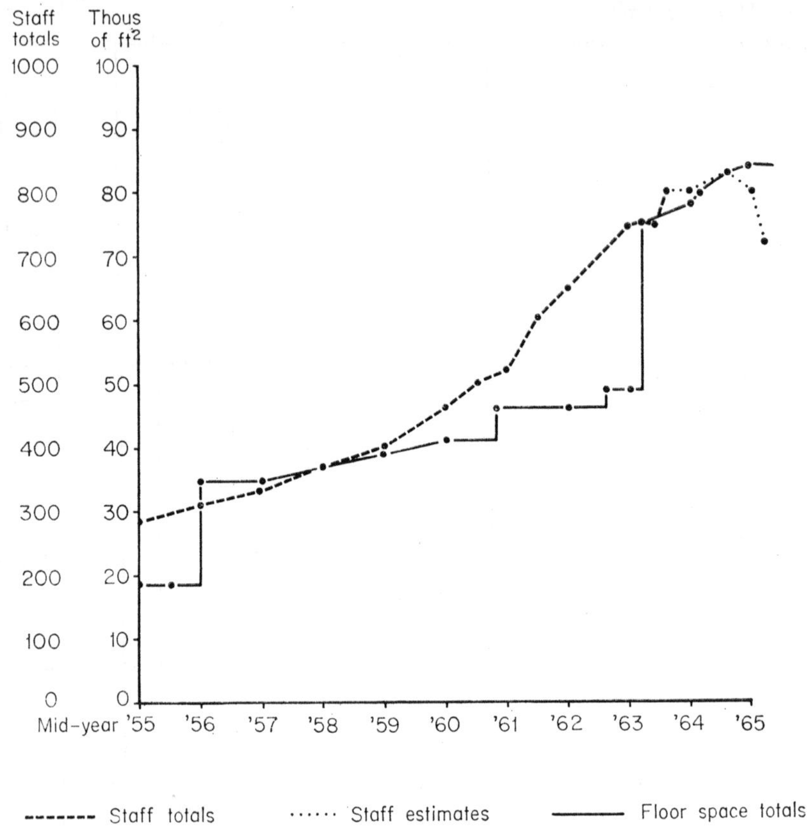

feeling that they were taking a great risk with so 'large' an area (41,000 sq. ft.).

The company was cautious in its estimates of future space needs. Continuing at the expansion rate then proceeding (see Fig. III 5, lowest prediction curve made at 1960), within eleven years the overcrowding would be as bad as 1955.

i.e. At 1955—285 staff in 18,500 sq. ft. = 65 sq. ft. per person
At 1967—630 staff in 41,000 sq. ft. = 65 sq. ft. per person

As the lease for these floors was taken until 1991 it can only be assumed that the caution reflected uncertainty as to whether demand for services the company supplied would increase as steadily in the future as it had in the past.

Three and a half of the four floors were occupied at mid-1956. A reserve was left unoccupied which was gradually taken up over the next three

Fig. III 6 Location of main buildings mentioned in text.

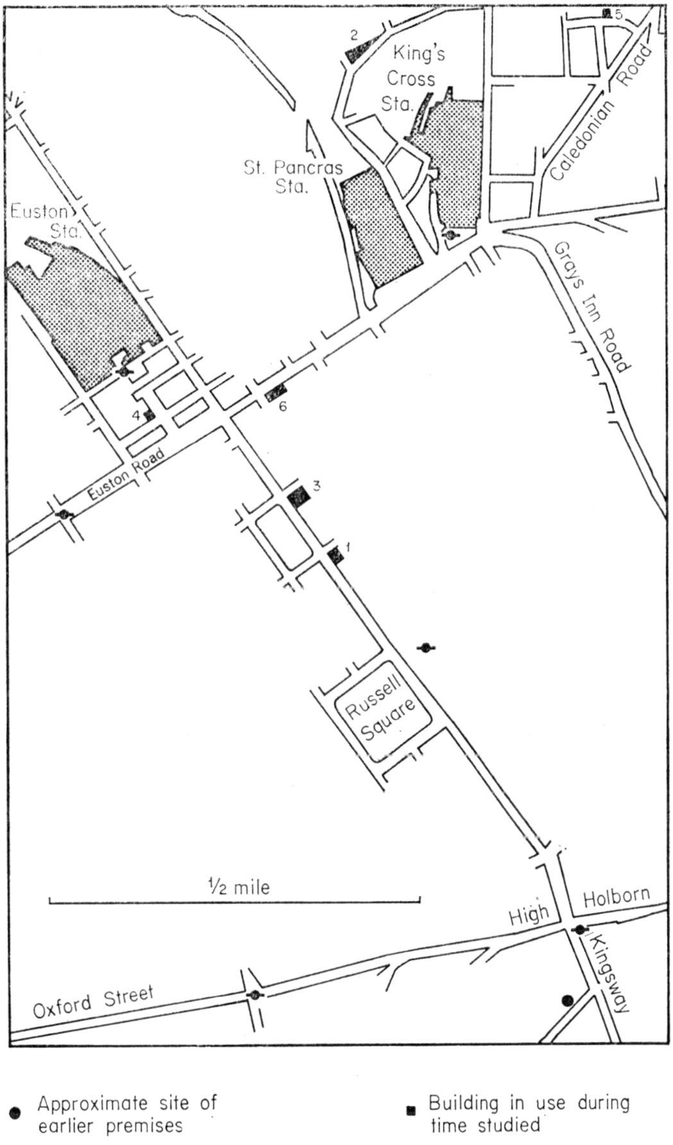

years. Thus, by the end of 1959, the whole building was in use, and the area per person was falling below 100 sq. ft. By the time new premises were occupied in September 1963, Buildings 4 and 5 had been taken to hold staff overflow, as Building 2 had done in 1955. Even so, by 1962 the area per staff was lower than at 1955.

Before the situation could be resolved, four main issues had to be clarified. 1. What was a realistic estimate of the company's probable expansion? 2. Should the entire London and head office staff move to new premises, should only one move, or could divisions within one or both be split off? 3. Were all departments inter-dependent, or dependent on a particular location or communication system? 4. What type of premises were to be looked for and where?

New projections were prepared in mid-1960, based on a minimum of twenty and a maximum of forty extra staff per year. (See Fig. III 7.) The upper curve is compromise between the twenty to thirty increase per year between 1951 and 1959 and the unusually sharp increase between mid-1959 and 1960. A maximum increase of forty staff per year, evenly spread over all departments, was the basis of ensuing discussion on size of building required.

Building 3 could be retained if the number of departments housed there could be reduced. It was necessary to analyse the administrative inter-dependence and locational and communication needs of all London and head office departments.

However, this analysis did not reveal any satisfactory means of dividing up the office. The most favoured pattern of division would have provided space for expansion of the departments kept in Building 3 until 1962, but by 1967 there would have been forty-five staff more than desired. Thus, while this analysis of the characteristics and degrees of autonomy in departments was a most valuable fact-finding exercise, it was not crucial in deciding what building to look for and where.

There were at least two schools of thought within the management regarding the most desirable deployment.

One 'faction' felt that top management could exist on its own—probably in Building 3—and all other departments could be housed in one new building. Liaison between the two establishments would be more formalised if appointments had to be made for meetings, and more travelling might be necessary, but it was felt that the need for planning such contact may impose a useful discipline. Those not favouring such a split felt that it might be motivated by 'empire-building', and felt that poor departmental management would not be sufficiently visible in one enormous unit.

The opposing argument was for some dispersal into at least two large units. Advantage should be taken of the fact that some departments

Fig. III 7 Staff growth predictions compared with actual staff growth.

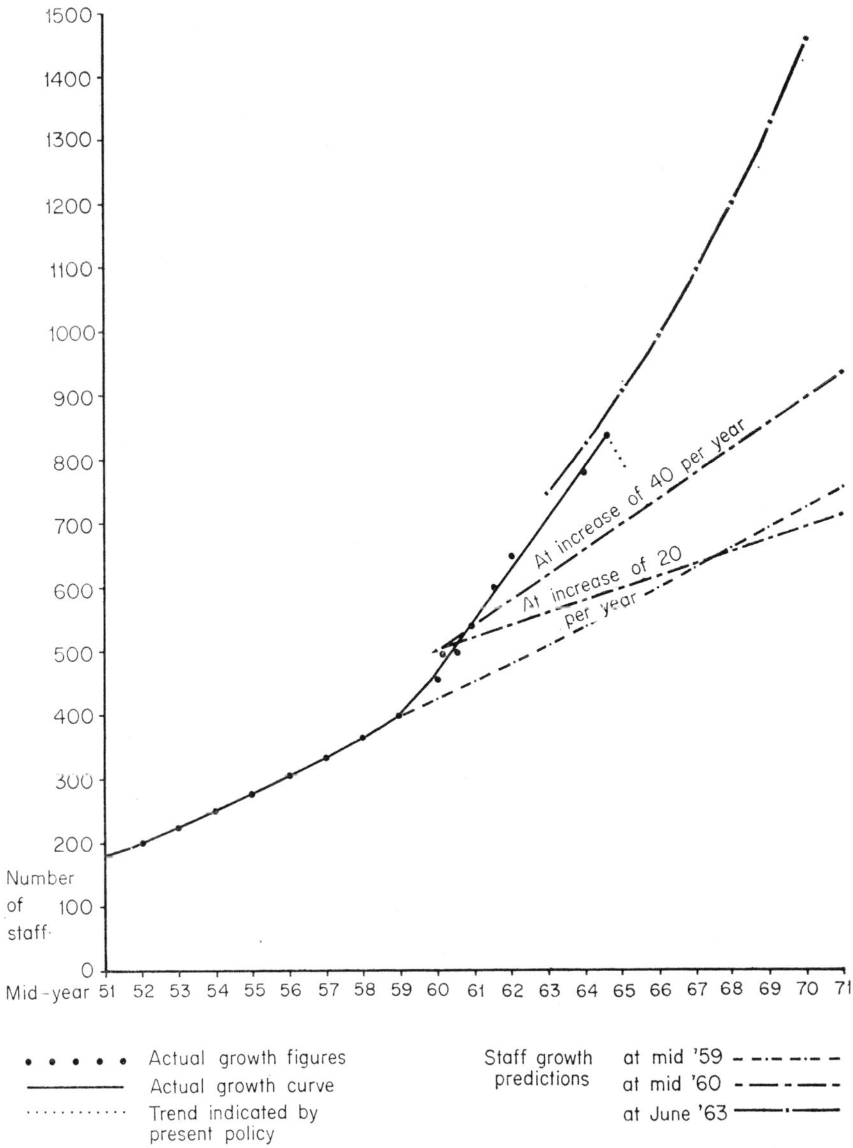

were virtually autonomous and could be more cheaply housed away from head office. Also smaller units, would be easier to control, and incentive to good management might be sharpened.

No final decision was taken on these alternatives before a search began for suitable buildings, although it was decided to look at all developments providing up to 150,000 sq. ft.

As early as 1959, when it was apparent that any reserve was soon to be swallowed up, planning permission had been sought for the company to build on an empty corner of the site of Building 3. However, it was soon realised that the small floor space obtained would be of little use. When the hunt for space began in earnest, the firm investigated the possibility of constructing their own accommodation, but it soon became clear that professional property developers were able to find and acquire all the sites in any way suitable—whether in central London, outer London, or the perimeter area. The firm also realised that, even if a site could be found, the time involved in acquisition, planning and building would be far longer than they could possibly wait. The search for premises was quickly confined to those to rent. The search included only those planned, under construction or very recently completed. It was necessary that any building taken should contain up-to-date heating and air-conditioning, more easily installed when the building is incomplete and when modification is comparatively easy. By July 1960, an intensive search had been made for developments offering up to 150,000 sq. ft.

Certain buildings were considered in central London but all were rejected.

The development company from which Building 3 was leased offered the firm a building being put up five to ten minutes' walk from Building 3. The rent of twenty-five shillings per square foot, though twice the rental of the floors taken in 1956 in Building 3, was considerably cheaper than others considered. Double-glazing could be installed for air-conditioning and noise reduction. A decision on the type of organisational split to be made would be virtually forced upon the firm, as the area of the whole building was 61,000 sq. ft., and therefore the desired 150,000 sq. ft. could be achieved only by retaining the current area within Building 3. On the other hand, the new building was very close to the existing main building and stores depot, and was near to tube and main line stations. The firm was generally predisposed to this location through being already familiar with it.

By autumn 1960 four broad solutions seemed possible. (1) A total move to Hemel Hempstead; (2) A partial move to Hemel Hempstead; (3) A new London building (such as the one of 61,000 sq. ft. offered) and Building 3; (4) One new London building to house everyone. Costs were estimated for each alternative as follows.

(1) *Total move to Hemel Hempstead offices of 150,000 sq. ft.*

Rent (at 14s. per sq. ft.)	= £105,000	
Rates (at about 9s. 4d. per sq. ft.)	= £69,000	
Outside repairs (a condition of the lease)	= £7,500	
Services (heating, lighting, cleaning, lifts, porters, insurance, etc.)	= £44,000	
		£225,500
Minus potential profit rental from most of *Building 3 which would be sub-let		£17,000
		£208,500

(* It was felt that if most of London and head office moved to Hemel Hempstead the minimum facilities that would have to be retained in Building 3 were a conference room, an office for each London director and for a secretary, receptionist and typist, three standard offices for the use of senior engineers visiting London clients, and a telephone switchboard. The total area was estimated at 4,000 sq. ft., which would reduce the potential rental profit for sub-letting Building 3 from £23,000 to £17,000 per annum.)

(2) *Partial move to Hemel Hempstead offices of 60,000 sq. ft.*

Rent (as 1 above)	= £42,000	
Rates (as 1 above)	= £28,000	
Outside repairs (as 1 above)	= £3,000	
Services (as 1 above)	= £17,500	
		£90,500
Plus cost of retaining all of present Building 3 area (40,800 sq. ft.)		
Rent		= £22,500
Rates } An over-estimate as this includes 2 small non-H.Q.		= £13,000
Services } stores buildings		= £13,500
	Approx.	£49,000
		£90,500
		£49,000
	Approx.	£139,500

(3) *Partial move to new London offices of 60,000 sq. ft. plus Building 3*

Rent (at 24s. per sq. ft.)	= £72,000	
Rates (at 16s. per sq. ft.)	= £48,000	
Services	= £17,500	
		£137,500
Plus Building 3 retained		
	Approx.	£49,000
	Approx.	£186,500

(4) *Total move to new London offices of 150,000 sq. ft.*

Rent	= £180,000	
Rates	= £120,000	
Services	= £44,000	
		£344,000
Minus profits rental from sub-letting Building 3		£23,000
		£321,000

Sub-letting would be a problem at Hemel Hempstead. In London sub-letting was expected to be easy.

On the basis of these costs, alternatives 2 and 3 appeared most suitable. But there were factors involved in a move to Hemel Hempstead. A detailed analysis was carried out of the implications—mainly in terms of cost—of a move to Hemel Hempstead. The main findings were as follows:

(a) Travel to Work

Trains from Euston to Hemel Hempstead took about forty minutes, no longer than many staff would take to travel to a London office. But there was only one train morning and evening leaving Euston at a suitable time. In addition there was no transport from the station at Hemel Hempstead, and a fifteen-minute walk would be necessary.

Rail and road transport combined, could provide a better service. It was suggested that if there were sufficient demands a commuter bus could be provided to Watford or Stanmore. For business calls, private or pool cars could be left there. Such a car pool would involve costs to the firm estimated at about £2,000 extra per annum.

Car travel to London would take just over an hour. To South London or Southern England it would take considerably longer, as there was no alternative to going right through congested Central London. On the other hand, travel to the Midlands would be very fast via the M1, and access to the West would be fast.

If a Euston building were taken, the problem for staff getting to work or to South London would be less, as three tube and three main line stations were within easy walking distance. On the other hand, the advantage of speedy access to the North would disappear.

(b) Staff facilities

It was presumed that many staff would wish to move to Hemel Hempstead if a building was taken there. The Development Corporation could provide some houses but could not guarantee all that might be required at an exact date. Certain private housing developments might provide some owner-occupier accommodation, and towns and villages around Hemel Hempstead would also be possibilities, but the general impression was that housing might not be easy to find. Grants for removal expenses were investigated. On the basis of maximum grants recommended by the Heating and Ventilation Research Council, 150 employees' pre-removal, removal, legal and agents' expenses would cost the firm a maximum of £62,350, assuming that only 150 out of about 500 employees would move.

Apprentices and young staff already with the firm provided one of the most difficult problems. Forty-two out of sixty-seven apprentices lived south or west of London and would have to move, as would twenty-nine out of fifty-three staff under thirty. Living accommodation and social facilities for these young people presented problems. The Corporation considered leasing the firm hostel accommodation, but did not make a definite offer. Whatever solution was found it would certainly involve a cost to the firm not incurred in London. This cost was estimated at a subsidy of £3 per week for the first few years for about eighty men, i.e., approximately £12,500 per annum.

The recruitment of student apprentices could have been a problem in a comparatively young town. In fact there was only one local grammar school with a sizeable sixth form, although there were many others in nearby towns. If a move was decided on it was suggested that recruitment should start immediately in Hemel Hempstead and commuting into London be subsidised until the move was made.

(c) Staff liaison

By 1960 Building 2 had reverted wholly to its intended use as a stores and service depot. It was never considered that this should be moved, even if all London and head office went to Hemel Hempstead. Certain local car servicing would have to be established near the new office but this was not regarded as a problem. However, if all but this service department and top control did move out of London, liaison problems would arise for certain supervisory staff with duties split between the Service Depot and Building 3.

(d) Client liaison

A census of staff travel was made over a fortnight in early 1960 to check the destinations and amount of travelling done by technical staff to clients and sites. It was estimated from this census that the 175 people making such trips would waste one-third of a day every three days in additional travelling time if they had to travel from Hemel Hempstead. In order to make up for this loss most economically, it was estimated that another twenty engineers would have to be employed at a total cost of £25,000. Additional fares could add £6,000 to this total. In fact these extra costs were a pessimistic maximum, as they assumed that all trips would pass through central London. But it was felt that the additional cost for travel and supplements to staff would fall somewhere between £23,000 and £31,000.

(e) Telephone communication

An additional expense concerned telephone communication with clients. The retention of a direct line switchboard in Building 3 was regarded as very important. Any hindrance to contact with clients presented serious problems. Various clients were sounded on their reactions to possible decentralisation, and several of them felt there would be no disincentive to their using the firm if direct contact were no harder than before, and if a London telephone number was retained. It was therefore decided that, if a total move was made, five direct G.P.O. landlines would be provided between Building 3 and Hemel Hempstead, at a cost of £600 per annum each. A longer time travelling for meetings with clients would not be a problem as contractors usually visited clients. In the rare cases when clients visited the firm, Building 3 could be used. In addition the clients agreed that, even in an extreme emergency, it was unlikely that they could not be given two to three hours notice of a meeting, and this would allow time for travel from Hemel Hempstead.

The average length and designation of business telephone calls out from London and head office was estimated and calculated at Hemel Hempstead rates. It was found that an additional cost of £14,000 per annum might be involved, although STD installations in the future would reduce this.

Analysis showed that many extra costs were involved in a move to Hemel Hempstead, costs which would have to be added to the basic rent/rates/services total. At the beginning of the search, when the best division of departments was being investigated, a warning had been given that '. . . on balance, the decision to split or not will probably depend on (other) factors . . . viz. financial, the risks involved in provision for uncertain growth, ability to choose whether the split is made to a local building or to one out of London or others'. The financial and locational aspects of the decision mentioned here became crucial deciding factors. This can be seen when the possible total costs of moving entirely to Hemel Hempstead is compared with staying entirely in London.

Possible total annual expenditure if move made into 150,000 sq. ft. at Hemel Hempstead:

Rent/rates/repairs/services with profit deducted for profit rental from most of Building 3		– £208,500
Out of London car service/maintenance		– £2,000
Apprentice subsidy for first few years		– £12,500
Extra staff travel to clients/extra staff	Approx.	– £27,000
5 G.P.O. landlines from London		– £30,000
Extra telephone bill anticipated		– £14,000
Maximum removal expenses		– £62,350
		£356,350

The cost estimated for one London building of 150,000 sq. ft. was £321,000 (see previous estimates) but it must be remembered that sub-letting of any surplus space was expected to be no problem, whereas at Hemel Hempstead sub-letting was felt to be extremely unlikely.

It had also been suggested that a split could be made and only 60,000 sq. ft. taken to Hemel Hempstead. This had been the cheapest estimate for basic rent costs. However, the departments assessed earlier as most easy to hive off from an administrative point of view were contracting departments which were the very ones involving these extra locational costs. If the firm had decided to take 60,000 sq. ft. in Hemel Hempstead, the proportion of these costs still incurred would have made a partial move more expensive.

On the basis of these analyses the firm decided to take Building 6, totalling 61,000 sq. ft. and developed by the same large company from whom they leased Building 3.

Building 6 was not completed and occupied until June 1964, by which time Building 5 and 6 had been taken as emergency space. Overcrowding was as high as it ever had been.

'The risks involved in provision for uncertain growth' in the past had caused extreme caution. One important reason for frequent mis-calculation of future needs was the unreliability of growth predictions.

The maximum staff total predicted in 1960 for mid-1964 (middle curve for Fig. III 7) was 660. The 1963 prediction for mid-1964 was 820. In fact, the actual total was 750. It is obviously better for a prediction to err on the side of over-estimating a staff total than under-estimating it, but it is also clear that given an uncertain growth rate a flexible reserve space is of great importance.

Sub-letting is now an important factor affecting the firm's supply of reserve space. Building 3 has one sub-tenant on a three-year lease till 1968. Building 6 has two sub-tenants on a seven-year lease till late 1970.

At mid-1964, part of Building 3 was already sub-let and a small reserve space left there. Building 6 had three empty floors, part scheduled for reserve and the rest for sub-letting. By the end of 1964 two and a half floors were let for seven years and the half floor of reserve was thinly occupied. By granting these leases, expansion space was being cut rather fine for the next three years, but seven years was the shortest time and two and a half floors the smallest area acceptable to two valuable sub-tenants.

In splitting the firm insufficient contact was taking place between management of the two buildings. While close proximity means that contact should be possible without making formal appointments, inertia is caused by the effort to put on a coat, leave the building and walk along the road. It has been found that even a slight actual distance between the buildings causes a disproportionate feeling of distance between them.

Case History Number 3

The offices of a London advertising agency

This firm was founded in 1924, in premises off Fleet Street. This area was the traditional home of advertising agencies, as blocks of advertisements were originally delivered straight to the press. Necessary intermediaries in the transactions were space buyers and sellers, who also worked around Fleet Street. Local pubs and restaurants were useful meeting places for contacts and business between press, space sellers and advertising men.

When the firm moved to Piccadilly it became one of the first advertising agencies to leave the Fleet Street area. Their Piccadilly premises were bombed during the war and the firm moved again, this time to Mayfair. They remained in two buildings in Mayfair for almost twenty years, before taking their present premises in Marylebone Road.

The firm was among the top twenty-five London agencies in terms of the total value of accounts handled in 1964. (There are approximately four hundred agencies in London.)

Within the five and a half years examined, several major decisions had to be taken about office space. Overcrowding occurred, the original buildings were judged to be unsatisfactory, a thorough search for new premises was made, a building was selected and considerable thought went into planning a system of flexible dividing walls.

Fig. III 8 shows the total floor space leased at the end of each year from 1960–1965, and the amount given up during each year. It is also extended past 1965, to show the expiry dates of leases granted to subtenants during the five years studied.

Fig. III 8 Advertising agency. Total floor space on lease or given up during each year.

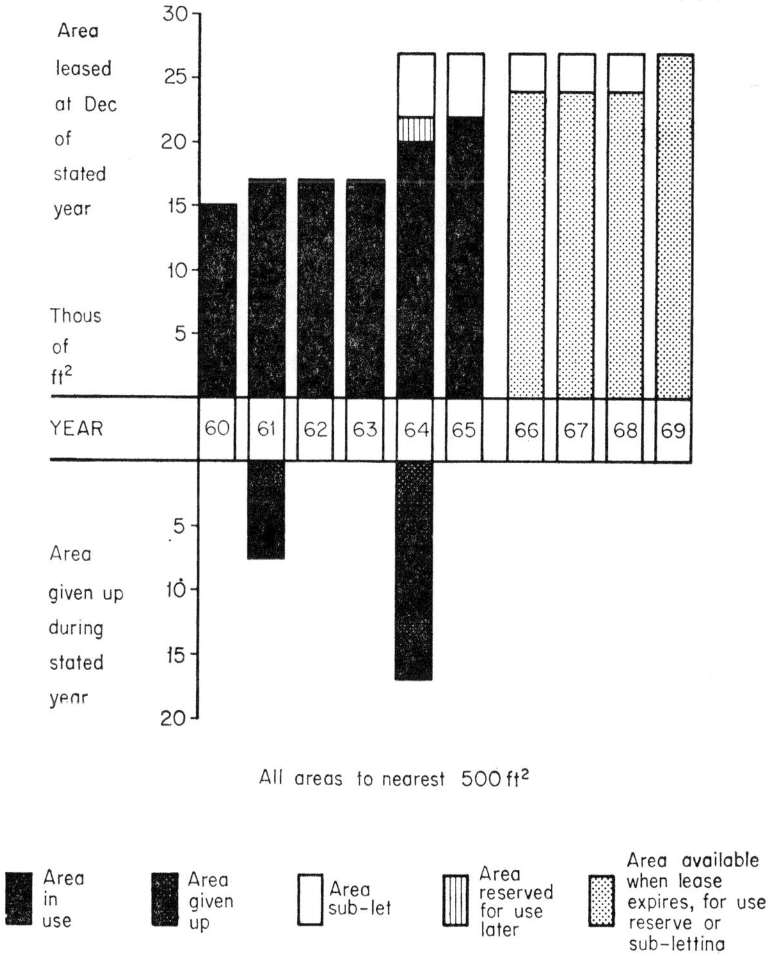

Fig. III 9 shows the four buildings used between 1960–1965, the number of years they were in use and their area.

Fig. III 10 shows the relationship between total space *actually* in use (i.e. not in reserve or sub-let) and the number of staff employed.

Some trouble arose over the lease of Building 1, and by April 1961 it had been replaced by two floors of Building 3.

Fig. III 9 The four buildings used—by year and size.

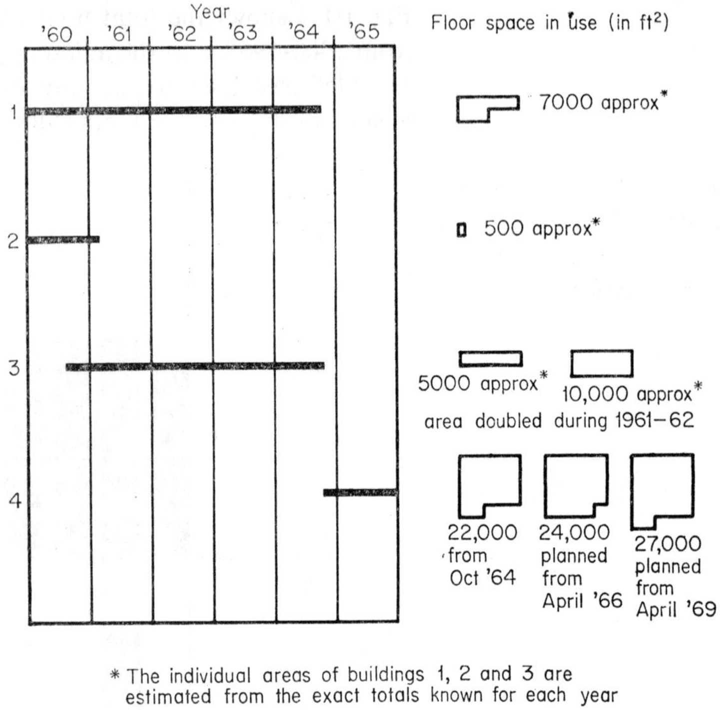

Fig. III 10 Floor space actually in use and staff totals.

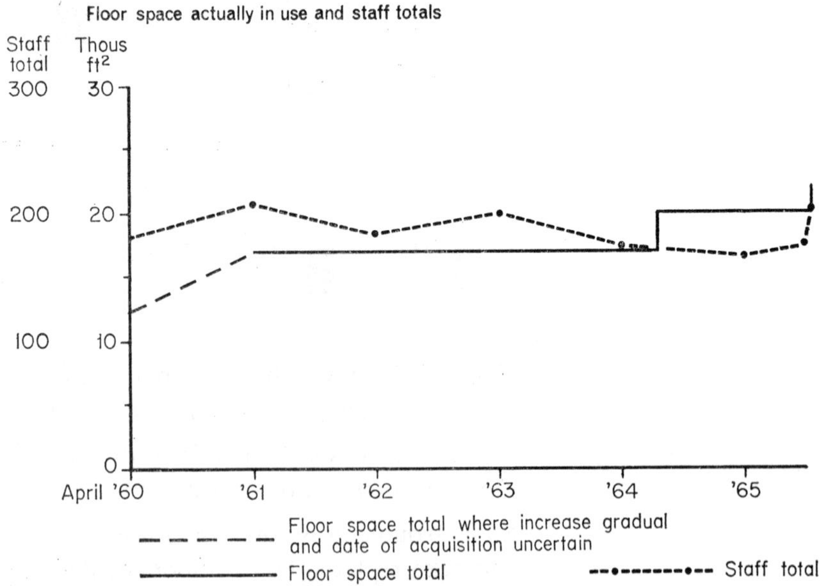

This case differs from the others studied in that staff expansion with consequent overcrowding was only one of the reasons for new premises. Although the area per staff member was regarded as too small, by the time the search for a new building began in mid-1963 staff totals were falling slightly. The feeling of urgency about new premises was caused by a combination of factors.

A new company Chairman appointed in 1961 decided that the firm's 'image' needed modernising. The Chairman felt that, while the buildings in Mayfair had positive merits by being Georgian, gracious and possessing a 'snob' address, they were also inconvenient and had connotations of a 'conservative' tradition which he was anxious to change. They were also likely to become very expensive when new leases were negotiated. In addition, the division into new buildings caused actual administrative inefficiency, as certain services, such as reception, kitchen and despatch staff, had to be duplicated. Although the distance between the two buildings could be covered in only four to five minutes, the split was disproportionately disruptive, and acted as a barrier to contact.

It was felt that a harmful 'us and them' attitude was growing up between the staff in the two buildings.

The main complaints against Buildings 1 and 3 can be summarised as follows. First, two buildings caused liaison problems. Second, rooms were small and of uneven size. Third, it was not possible to change the internal layout. Building 1 had load-bearing walls and was split up into units too small to be further sub-divided. Building 3 had been divided by a former tenant with permanent partitioning.

Other factors which weighed in favour of moving were the impending expiration of leases for Buildings 1 and 3 in 1966, and the uncertainty about official council policy on the continuing use of such buildings for offices in Mayfair. After a long and unsettling delay, a favourable renewal decision was confirmed by the L.C.C., and new leases were negotiated with the owners of Buildings 1 and 3.

When the original lease was taken towards the end of the Second World War, the owners had intended to redevelop the entire Park Lane block in the late 1960's. For this reason the lease had been granted only until 1966. The original lease for Building 1 cost £21,000 and the rent was 4s. per sq. ft. By the early 1960's, when Building 3 was taken, rents had risen considerably, to 20s. per sq. ft. In 1962 the estate owning both

Fig. III 11 Advertising agency—1936 and 1963.

properties were prepared to give a lease for £64,000 until 1990, when they again hoped to start redevelopment. In order to have security the agency accepted this offer, and took a new lease until 1990, although by this time they were beginning to think seriously about moving.

In autumn 1963 the agency started to hunt for premises, but an initial search in the West End produced nothing suitable. Another agency, previously near them in Mayfair, had moved to Paddington at a rental of 19s. 6d. per sq. ft. Inspired by the apparent success of the move, and tempted by what seemed a reasonable rental, the agency contemplated extending its search away from the centre. They were offered 20,000 sq. ft. in a new block at Chiswick, and learned that other suitable property was available at Croydon.

The possibility of these two locations provoked much discussion about the nature of the firm. They regarded themselves as a 'London' agency, and felt that as such they should remain as close as possible to the main concentration of other agencies in 'central' London. A map was drawn up of the location of all London agencies, in order to clarify their own impressions of where their chief competitors were, and in order to locate the 'centre' in these terms. The agency's own map is no longer available but Fig. III 11 gives the same information for 1963. It can be seen that in 1963 the greatest concentration of agencies was in the West End and City, with a scattering around the fringes of this central area. Fifty more agencies, usually very small, were scattered even more sparsely outside the area of Fig. III 12. Although there had been a lot of talk in advertising circles about London firms decentralising, it appeared that none but some of the smallest agencies had gone any further out than Chiswick. This seemed so much like frontier pioneering that the Chiswick building offered was turned down. It was felt that to retain their identity as a 'London' agency, competing with certain London firms, they could not consider a move to Croydon.

If the agencies in London had been less centrally concentrated, and the area between the centre and Croydon more consistently scattered with larger agencies, then Croydon might have been considered. Such a distribution might occur in the future, but until then the risk of becoming a 'provincial' agency by such a move was considered too high.

Two other maps were drawn up to show; (1) the place of residence of all staff and (2) all stations and airports used by staff and clients. It was important that as few staff as possible be inconvenienced by any move.

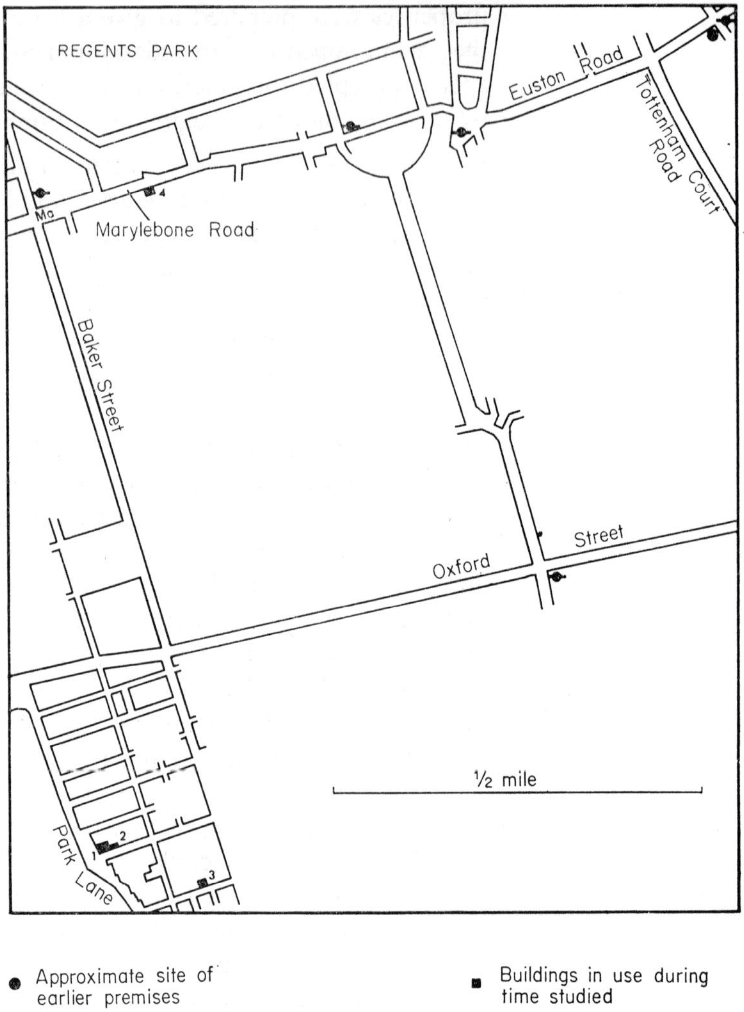

Fig. III 12 Location of main buildings mentioned in text.

While there is considerable turnover in lower grades among all advertising firms, the Chairman estimated that there were only about 18,000 people in advertising in the whole country. Fierce competition existed for higher grade staff, and it was of major importance that no senior staff be lost as a result of a move. Contact with clients was invariably a matter of agency staff visiting clients. For the infrequent visits of clients to the agency, transport from airport or station could be provided.

As a result of the three maps, of the firm's experiences in Buildings 1 and 3, and of the desire for a 'modern' image, specifications were made for the type of building required.

1. It had to be as close as possible to the central concentration of agencies.

2. It had to be easily accessible by public transport.

3. It had to provide parking facilities for at least fifteen cars—five visitors and ten staff cars, some of which would be for visits to clients.

4. The building had to be architecturally modern.

5. Internal sub-dividing had to be sufficiently flexible to contain work-units of any size at any time.

6. There had to be reserve space for future expansion. Although there were problems in predicting expansion, the overcrowding experienced in Buildings 1, 2 and 3 must not occur.

Thirty-four buildings were considered. Their location is not recorded, but it is safe to assume they were all outside the area of heaviest concentration in Fig. III 12, yet well within the boundary of the map (with the exception of the early considerations of Croydon and Chiswick). Costs weighed when considering each building included rent, rates, heating, lighting, servicing and transport. Difficult access due to inadequate transport services meant that several otherwise desirable buildings were rejected.

A year after the search began it was decided to take space in a new block on Euston Road, which seemed to fulfil all requirements. However, the day the lease was signed it was discovered that the promised space for fifteen cars was not available. On the same day a new block (Building 4) was spotted by chance in Marylebone Road. After immediate inspection, this was judged more satisfactory than Euston Road, and it was taken instead! (See Fig. III 12.)

The cost of moving to Building 4 was covered by a profit of £24,000 made from selling the leases of Buildings 1 and 3. They were also sold at precisely the right time to avoid paying any double rents.

In order to prevent future reserve from becoming a financial burden, it was necessary to capitalise on space which was surplus to the firm's immediate requirements.

Fig. III 8 shows that, by the end of 1964, 2,000 sq. ft. were in reserve for the firm's own use, and 5,000 sq. ft. was sub-let. The agency were hoping to increase their staff in 1966, and 2,000 of the sub-let area was leased until April 1966—an exceptionally short term letting to part of a firm desperate for any space they could get. The other 3,000 was let for five years.

By the end of 1965 all the reserve for their own use had been taken up, partly because of an unsatisfactory merger. The thirty-odd staff who arrived with this merger in 1965 caused some congestion. It meant that certain rooms normally reserved for conference use had to be taken over for offices. When the first lease expired in April 1966, a big space reorganisation was planned to absorb new staff.

Case History Number 4

The head offices of an insurance company

The insurance company studied in this section was founded in 1848.[1] The Company's first offices were at Blackfriars, in a street of 'handsome brick houses principally occupied by life and assurance companies'.

In 1851 larger premises near Ludgate Circus were acquired. In 1852 the Company was approached by a group of 'operatives' with a request that the Company start a scheme of industrial assurance payable in weekly instalments.

Payments of this frequency and small size were a feature of friendly societies, which enabled workers to provide against ill-health and loss of work. At a time of rapid industrialisation, accompanied by insecurity and unrest, demand was growing for greater security than workers could achieve through the self-help means of friendly societies. Industrial policies were started after this, and the industrial department soon became the largest department in the Company.

By 1876 the Ludgate offices had become inadequate although rebuilt and extended several times. The Company was loath to leave the immediate area but could find nothing there at a 'reasonable price'. The basis of their resistance to moving appears to have been mainly sentimental attachment to the area which had seen their growth. Eventually a site was found half a mile away from Holborn. In 1879 the Company moved into their new Holborn building, designed by the architect Waterhouse, which still forms the nucleus of their head offices premises, although in 1931/1932 the whole building was demolished and rebuilt with a replica of the original façade.

The National Health Insurance Act of 1911 brought at the beginning of this century additional work for the Company, and two new buildings were erected. By the time of the 1946 National Health Act, this aspect of the Company's activities had four and a half million members and employed over 1,300 staff at head office. The two buildings, providing

[1] Passages quoted are from the Company's Centennial Publication 'A Century of Service'.

56,700 sq. ft. of floor space, were taken over by the Government at the time of the Act, and most of the staff were also transferred. For this reason these activities are omitted from the next section, except in Fig. III 16, where their location is shown, and in Fig. III 15, where these staff cannot be accurately identified in the total.

In 1915 all forms of general assurance were taken up, such as fire, accident and motor insurance, but no business was done until 1919. Until this time the company had concentrated on industrial and ordinary policies. Fairly early the new general branch was permanently decentralised to branch offices which had wide powers under general direction from the chief office. Decentralisation of all or part of a department now plays an important part in the Company's development, and the entire industrial department was moved recently from Central London.

The period chosen for detailed study is from 1935–1965. By 1935 the Company was very thoroughly established in terms of the business they transacted and the population they served. Between 1931 and 1935 the main office was modernised. This change marked more than the final move from a Victorian office image. It was a result of rapidly increasing mechanisation affecting many features of the Company, from methods of work to the type and location of buildings.

Fig. III 13 shows the cumulative floor space total in headquarters buildings for each year from 1935–1965 and the area, if any, given up during each year. This total is also divided to show the area of separate buildings.

Fig. III 14 shows the seventeen headquarters buildings used at any time between 1935 and 1965.

Both Figs. III 13 and III 14 are slightly simplified, and do not record temporary arrangements during the Second World War, or other temporary space occupied during later alterations.

Fig. III 15 shows total floor space and staff, year by year. During the war period only two complete totals were available, but the sub-totals omit only a fairly constant number of female staff. The section of Fig. III 15 below the date line shows the growth of the Company's Reading staff and buildings. Although no floor space is indicated before 1961 in Fig. III 15, the Reading staff were not without accommodation until this time; they had been temporarily housed in rooms of branch offices and buildings owned by the Company. The rebuilding and

Fig. III 13 Insurance company headquarters total floor space and amount given up each year.

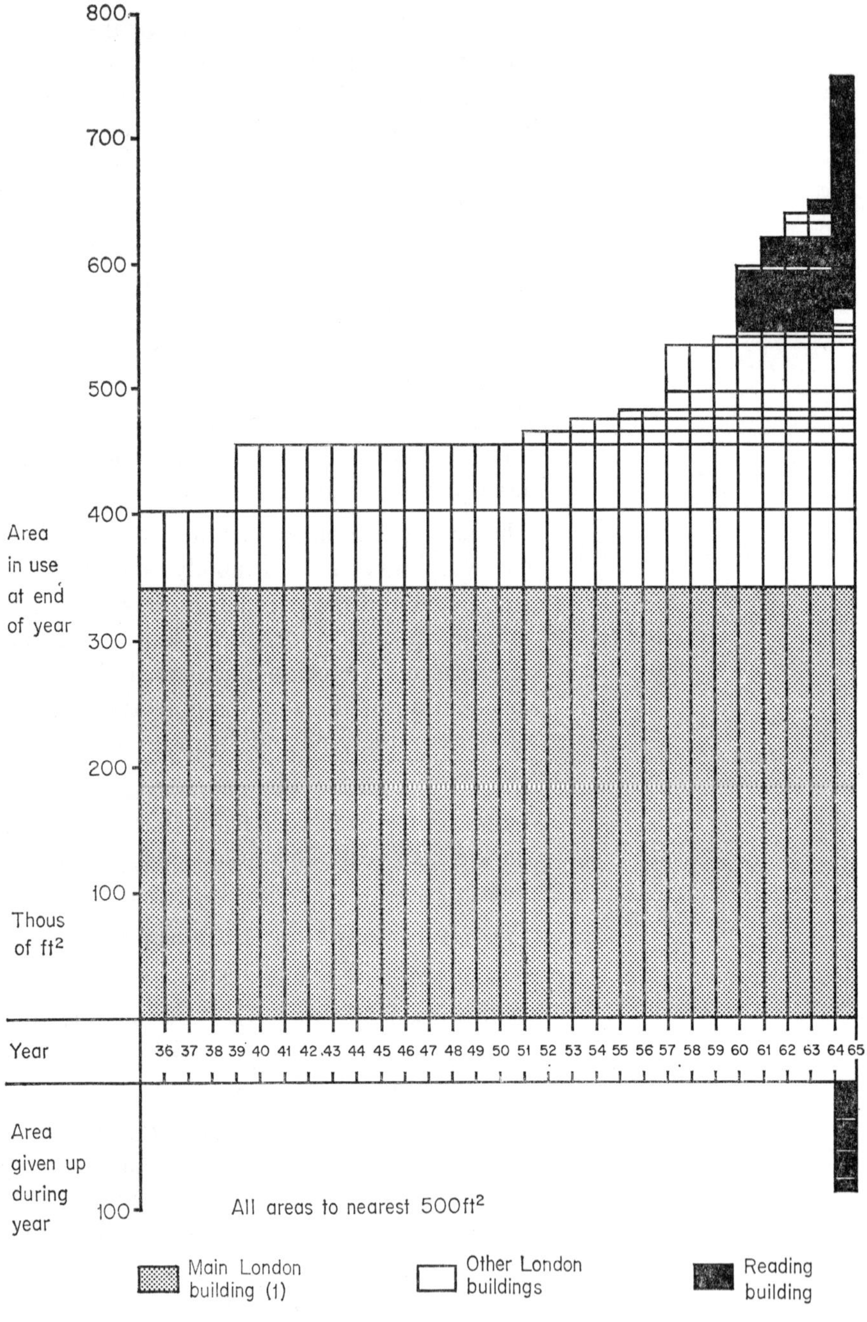

Fig. III 14 The seventeen headquarters buildings used—by year and size.

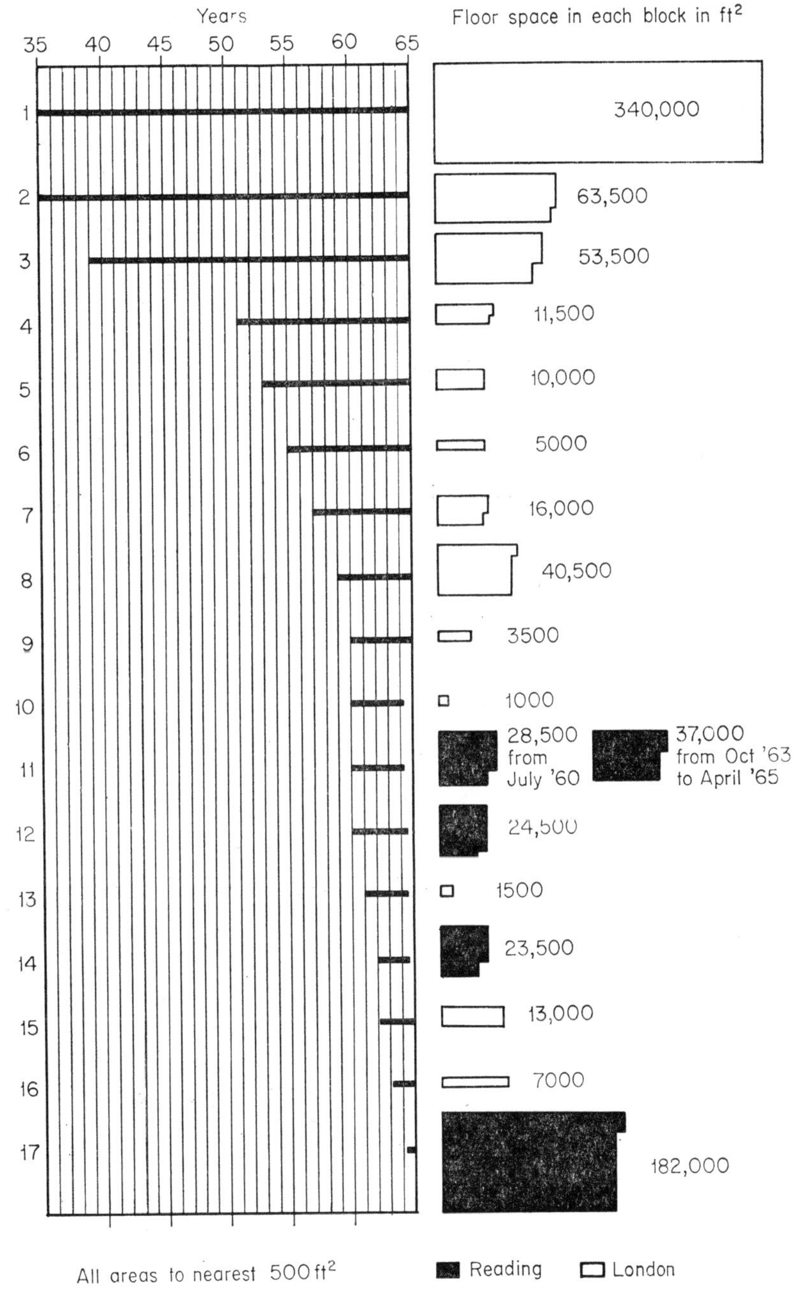

Fig. III 15 Floor space in use and staff total.

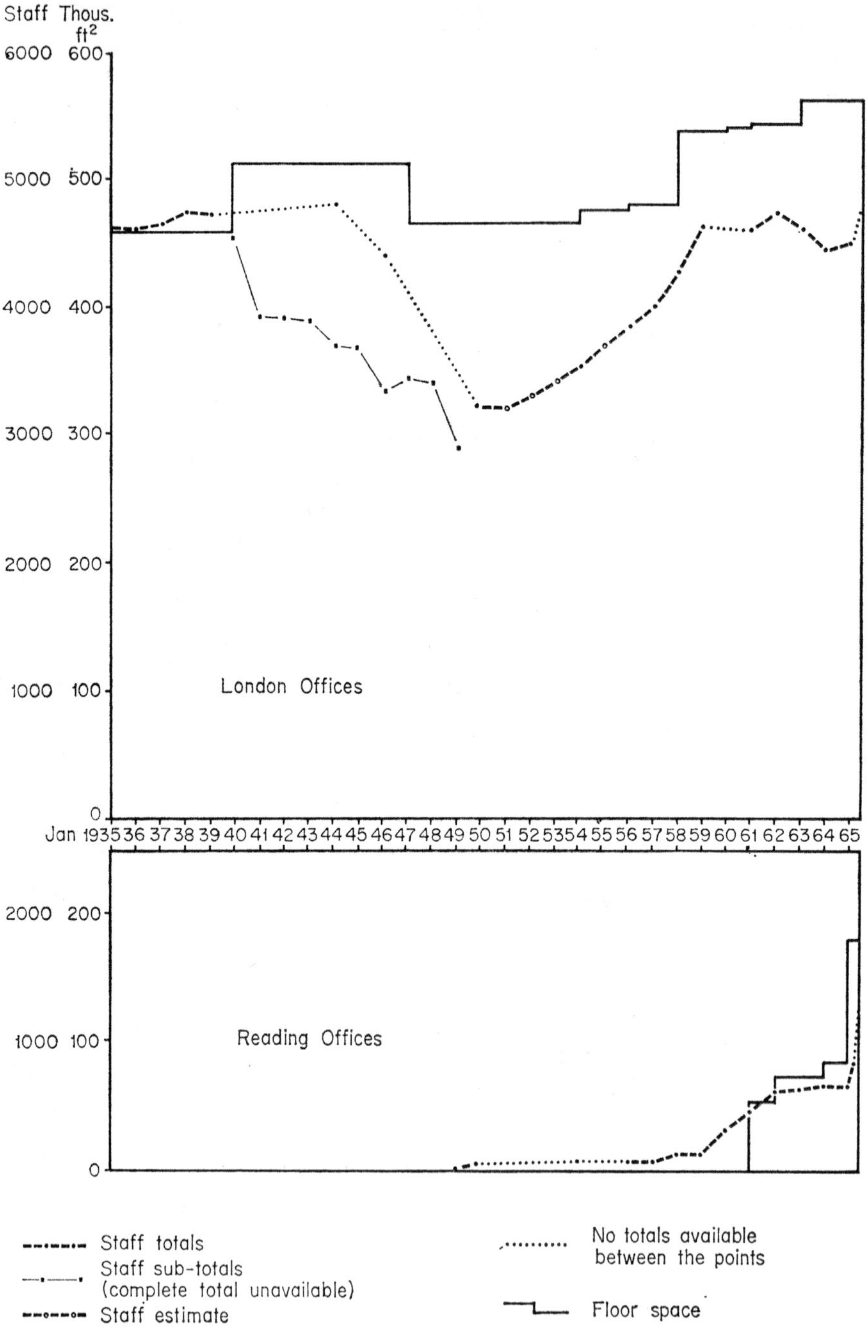

occupation of the first headquarters building at Reading in 1961 marked the beginning of a stage of planned decentralisation of a large department.

Fig. III 16 shows the approximate square footage per staff member at November 1964 in each building, omitting non-work areas such as storage and recreation space. There is no significance in the choice of 1964 as an example. 1964 was simply the year for which staff numbers are known for the greatest number of buildings.[1]

In 1935 two headquarters buildings were in use. Building 2 was for document storage only. All other departments were housed in Building 1. It can be seen in Fig. III 13 that Building 1 has provided more space than any other single building during the thirty years studied. Also it has been the locational nucleus of London expansion. Building 1 is very large. The architect commissioned was a well known man, whose style by modern standards was monumental. Staircases, corridors and halls are wide and sweeping. Ceilings are very high and encrusted with bright, elaborate decoration.

There is an element of grandiose opulence in its structure, which suggests that the building was intended to enhance the prestige of the Company, as well as to provide a base for its work.

Working areas are commonly in the form of large halls providing open working areas, made possible by the use of rows of supporting pillars. Many of these halls open straight into each other without connecting corridors, but dividing walls are solid and soundproof, an important factor if machinery is to be installed. Within these large rooms it is possible to erect a great variety of sub-divisions, providing that an adequate source of light can be obtained.

The clerical nature of much of the work means that there are many large groups of staff performing the same tasks, and these are best kept together in large units. On the other hand the sheer size of the Company and the departments, sections and sub-sections within it involve a complicated hierarchy of authority, within which status is indicated by the amount of space, size of desk, type of partitioning or room allocated. The most senior staff occupy single-person offices, oak panelled rooms lining the impressively wide corridors in the main administrative section

[1] Three buildings are not included: 9 and 10 because they did not contain working space or permanent staff, and 17 because it was not then completed and staff and floor space breakdowns were not available by the end of the study.

Fig. III 16 Average working area per staff member at November 1964.

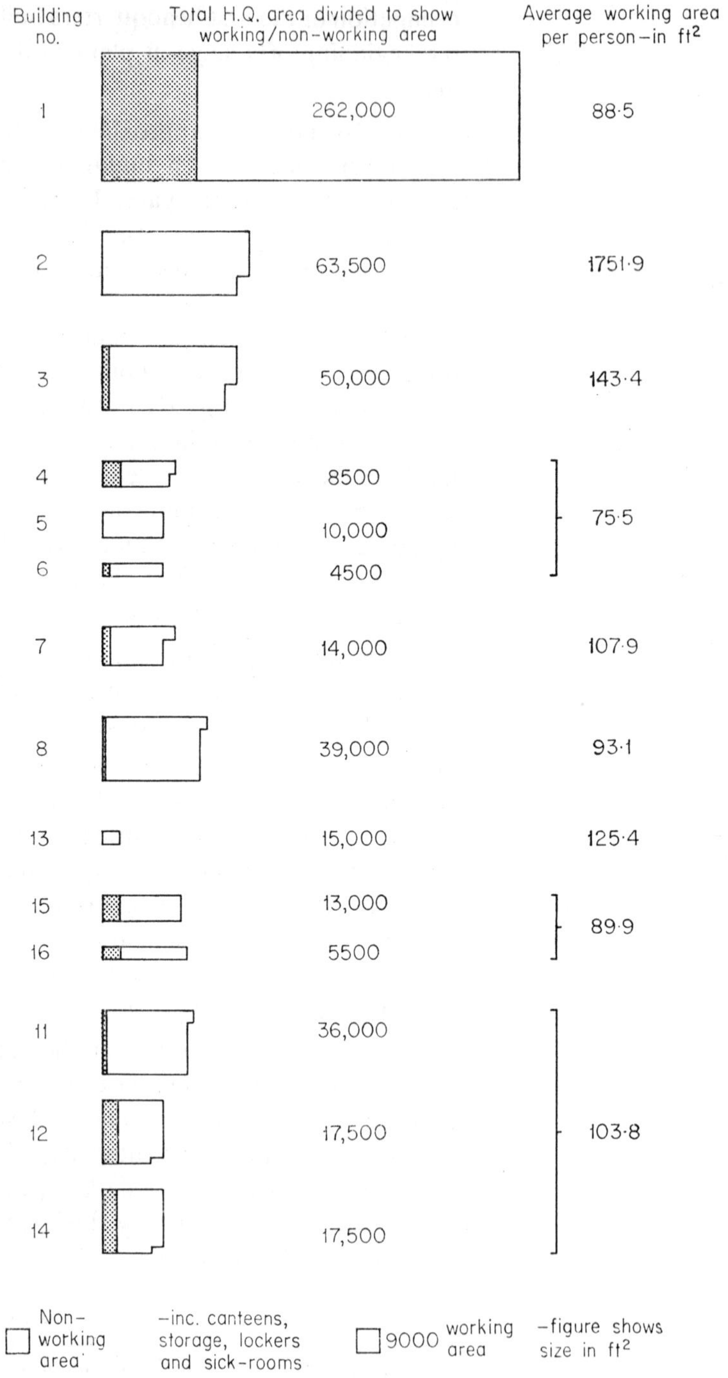

of the building. Administrative heads of a section or department have substantial floor to ceiling oak partitions forming offices within the main room, usually with the upper walls of glass to maintain a light source. Senior supervisors of departments have a greater space allocated than the workers they supervise, and their desks have a 6 ft.-high glass partition around three sides to give a higher degree of privacy without impeding the light or a view of the office. Below this level status is indicated within sections by desk size or space per person, although this varies between departments according to the task being performed. Space for a draughtsman and his drawing-board will of necessity be greater than for a copy-typist and her small typewriter table.

Use is made of light demountable partitioning for sub-dividing large areas. This may be because some reduction of sound is needed, or because smaller functional units are required, or sometimes because doors at each end of a long room are used by through traffic which causes distraction to those working.

Although the degree of internal flexibility is very high it has not been easy to achieve certain other standards which are common in more modern buildings. Building 1 is scheduled as a Historic Building, which means that the exterior must be preserved in its present form. It is difficult to assess the positive advantages that a firm gains from being housed in a Historic Building of such grandiose eccentricity, though the prestige could be considerable. On the other hand there are some clear disadvantages. It is difficult to clean a building with highly ornamental pillars and ceilings and windows 30 ft. high. It is hard to heat rooms of such height, and harder still when they are covered with ceramic tile. In order to make heating and maintenance easier, false ceilings have been put in many rooms, and many pillars and sections of ornament have been covered. However, nothing short of rebuilding could give Building 1 all the advantages of a modern purpose-built building, and this is neither being considered nor likely to be allowed if it were considered.

Building 2 was in use for document storage from its acquisition in 1927 until 1965, when the section moved out and its place was taken by a computer. Building 2 was staffed during these twenty-eight years by a small number of messengers. Building 2 shows an average working area per staff member of 1,752 sq. ft., which had formerly been even higher, as the number of messenger staff rose from 28 to 36 over the thirty years studied. It was essentially a service to other departments.

Few firms, even in their administrative head offices, would be likely to require such a large proportion of their total floor space for storage, but the nature of the insurance business means that vast quantities of records are accumulated which must be retained and must be immediately accessible. Space-saving storage, such as microfilming or computerising records, is a comparatively recent development. (In fact the transfer of records in Building 2 to computer tape accompanied the move of this section to Reading in 1965, and future storage space needs will now be greatly reduced.)

From the characteristics and history of Buildings 1 and 2 it is possible to see some pattern in the organisation and resources of the company as a whole.

First, the Company own its own buildings and possesses security of tenure. Second, it can redevelop sites, or add to buildings or undertake major internal alteration to its own requirements. Third, investment forms a major part of the Company's business, and they own a considerable amount of office property, including much within the immediate vicinity of the headquarters. Much of this property is let, but a certain amount is kept as a pool for temporary use or semi-permanent overflow. Such space is a valuable resource, of even greater significance than internal flexibility. This Company is unlike other firms, in that unavailability of premises in London is unlikely to cause any problems. Building 1 remains the nucleus and the company possesses more than resources of space for it to continue indefinitely in this role.

If the Company had decided to keep all its departments in London, it would undoubtedly have had sufficient space in buildings around Building 1. In fact decentralisation of sections and departments has occurred, which means that the growth of staff in these departments and the buildings they acquired away from London do not appear in Fig. III 13 and III 15.

Throughout the history of the Company new working methods have been introduced, which have resulted in the more economic use of staff. The company takes pride in the fact that staff do not lose their jobs as a result of mechanisation, but this policy is assisted by a naturally high turnover-rate of staff in clerical departments most likely to be affected. It also claims to keep a stable total of headquarters staff, by introducing further mechanisation at the same rate as business expansion.

The Approved Societies Section expanded during the 1930's and Building 3 was acquired in 1939 to house their staff overflow. This building was retained for the Company's use after the post-National Health Act requisition of the two original 'Approved Society' buildings. This requisition caused the only net loss of floor space between 1935 and 1965. Staff decreases around the same time are explained partly by transfers which accompanied the government takeover, and partly by staff unavailability during the war. Mass evacuation started in August 1939, so that only a few specialised sections, directors and top management stayed in London. After the war the build-up to pre-war staff totals in London was slow. Between 1950 and 1965 three main trends are discernible. First of all the expansion of engineering and workshop sections and increased mechanisation, particularly the introduction of computers, required highly specialised use of space, and buildings were especially acquired for this purpose. Buildings 4, 5 and 6, which were put into headquarters use between July 1951 and the end of 1955, were all premises for engineering and maintenance staff. These departments were moved out from Building 1, after it was decided that the Company would profit by building up its own engineering departments.

The second significant post-war trend was simply one of staff expansion. Buildings 7 and 8 are examples of space taken up for headquarters use because certain departments in Building 1 expanded and pressure on space had to be relieved. Each building houses a complete departmental section. In addition, a higher standard of comfort for staff has had a marked effect upon space needs.

Building 9 has housed one small headquarters section, and has also contained workshops, but in 1964 it contained only storage space and offices connected with staff recreation. Building 10 is used as a temporary overflow to hold staff during alterations or other short-term disruptions. For this reason many sections have passed through the building, and the area used is fluctuating continually. It was also used for new mechanisation sections, which began to be formed in the early 1960's. Research into the feasibility of installing computers had started in 1956. By 1965 two computers were in use and a third projected. At this time three new buildings were in use (Buildings 13, 15 and 16), and these contained seven mechanisation sections employing nearly 200 staff. While clerical space within these buildings occupies a greater area than the computers themselves, the physical specifications required for computer installation mean that the building housing them have been extensively adapted and are likely to remain serving this specific function.

The third main change visible after the war was the systematic transfer of a department to Reading and the redevelopment of the Company's sites there. Various sections had been evacuated to Reading during the war and, as some tabulating machinery had been installed, a small number of industrial branch staff had remained to run it when the bulk of the staff returned to London.

The Company had an investment foothold in Reading dating from 1939, when they had acquired the leasehold of several sites suitable for future development. During the war some evacuated sections used the buildings, and by 1950 they were occupied by those evacuees who remained to work with the machines, by staff of the Company's branch offices and by some sub-tenants. In the early 1950's it was decided to go ahead with redevelopment, and freeholds were acquired for the three sites. The phasing of staff transfer and local recruitment was related to the completion of three ensuing office developments in 1960, 1961 and 1963. (See Fig. III 15.) In 1962 another site was bought, and the fourth Reading building (Building 17) of 182,000 sq. ft. was completed in February 1965.

All these sites are in the centre of Reading, and all contain commercial offices to let on the ground floor. When Building 17 was completed the entire industrial branch moved in, collecting in to one building staff and sections transferred from 1939 onwards, local recruits from Reading, and the last sections of the department still left in London—over 900 staff. When Buildings 11, 12 and 14 were vacated by headquarters staff, the surplus, after district offices were housed, was let. Similarly, in Building 17, the space surplus to that of the industrial branch has been let. The post-war decision to try decentralising the industrial branch was regarded as an experiment. It proved very successful and the company could repeat the process with any department. The tremendous advantage that this company has over most firms is that it has so many buildings with which to experiment in so many locations that it can always find somewhere suitable to fit needs or wishes as they arise. Its problems arise from splitting work into suitable sections, as so many departments are closely attached to others.

Conclusions

The most surprising fact to emerge from this part of our work is the extent to which organisations moved entirely or in part because of dissatisfaction with a building, and the variety of reasons which caused the building to become, or seem to become, unsatisfactory. The search for new premises, the expense and reorganisation required by a move, the effect on travel to the building for staff and clients, the possible disruptive effect on business—all make it desirable that as few moves as possible are made.

Clearly, the time will come when any organisation experiencing growth and change is likely to have to move. The rare case which may escape this necessity would be something like a government organisation owning buildings, possessing compulsory purchase powers and the ability to recruit the type of staff they need.

The need to move is brought about not only by lack of space to house increased staff, or lack of flexibility to house changing functions. All too often, it is because of an organisation's lack of resources or foresight, or by inability to rearrange idealistic priorities to fit less pleasant realities.

In order to remain stable in satisfactory buildings, with room to expand and adapt to meet the needs of the foreseeable future, it is essential that an organisation analyses its own characteristics, and on this basis determines the assets and liabilities that these present. It must be able to avoid being forced to move against its will because of a present crisis which foresight could have averted, and it must also avoid clinging to a building after it becomes unrealistic to do so.

Can we draw any general conclusions?

First of all each organisation was reviewing constantly its accommodation pattern. It seems that the provision of space is a major factor in the decision structure of any growing organisation, and that it is a continuing problem. That is to say, none of the organisations was able to make a 'once for all' decision about its accommodation. The patterns of growth of each one forced them to change plans, to improvise, and to accept expedients which they would, in many instances, have preferred to reject.

Second, none of the organisations looked very far ahead when planning its accommodation. The 'next move' or the 'next move but one' is often the limit of a firm's planning horizon. Chess strategies do not enter into the hunt for accommodation. This is surprising, for most other aspects of business do command considerable planning ahead, or at least crystal gazing. But the provision of accommodation for office functions, although it may require considerable investment, does not seem susceptible to this kind of pre-planning which goes into other aspects of capital equipment.

Third, decisions about accommodation are often referred to Board level. It might have been expected that, once the Board had laid down a broad strategy for accommodation, the actual implementation of such decisions could be left to executives. But it seems that the nature of the decisions is such, each one being a unique and new event, that the whole position is reviewed afresh each time a new piece of accommodation is required.

Fourth, the centre of the city maintains its hold. Although one organisation had decentralised and another has moved to the periphery of the central area, there is no doubt that all would have wished to stay right in the middle of London. The reasons are difficult to disentangle, but not hard to find. A combination of prestige, links to clients and to other organisations, and a feeling of being 'where everything happens' makes the centre desirable, in spite of the costs of space, staff and travelling. These links and sentiments are very real, and emphasise the importance of communications in an office setting, and in the role of the city. The pattern of these case histories is a struggle to remain in the centre. Some failed, more often by unfortunate combinations of circumstances, and are making the best of things in the suburbs, but the pull of the centre remains an overriding concern in their hunt for accommodation.

Chapter IV
The Occupiers of London's Office Space

This chapter describes two separate but related studies concerning the way in which London's office space is occupied.

Fitzroy Square

The first of these studies concerned changes in the occupation of a London square, between 1880 and 1967. Although the main project had to be confined to the provision of new office accommodation, the function of converted office premises could not be ignored. Fitzroy Square was chosen for a pilot study of changes in occupation of accommodation, as it was on the fringe of the central area proper, originally residential but subsequently invaded and taken over by commercial activities. Using street directories, it was possible to uncover this process.

Not a great deal is known about London offices, and even less about office occupiers in general. Furthermore, the work that has been done has either tended to concentrate on special aspects (e.g., decentralisation) rather than on their general behaviour and characteristics, or been confined to the individual case study approach.

The most extensive of the larger studies was a survey carried out by the Economist Intelligence Unit in 1964 for the Location of Offices Bureau on the factors governing the location of London offices. Much of the material relates to the firms' attitudes to or experiences of decentralisation. Similar surveys have been done for other areas, e.g., Croydon, and in 1961 the Town and Country Planning Association compared the experiences of sixty firms which had moved out of central London.

Factors affecting the location of London offices have also been investigated from the records of the Location of Offices Bureau. This study, of course, is confined to firms with an interest in decentralising who have approached the L.O.B. for advice.

More general studies on central area location factors include Morgan's work (1961) on West End offices, and several studies by J. Goddard (1966), dealing with the grouping of similar kinds of activity in the City and also with the movements of certain types of firms in London.

Among case-studies of office firms, those of relevance to this particular project are of firms which have decentralised from London. One of the first publications of the Location of Offices Bureau (1963) contained several brief case-studies, and more detailed accounts have been produced by several of the Greater London planning authorities, e.g., Surrey, Kent and Middlesex. In 1964, the Institute of Directors' publication *Better Offices* contained ten valuable studies by W. C. Norris (1964) which describe the whole moving process from the time when the decision was first made.

As far as possible we have attempted to relate the findings of the work mentioned here to the results of the studies carried out for our own project.

Although this was intended as a pilot study to test the usefulness of street directories as a source of data on central area activities, this particular area—Fitzroy Square, W.1.—was chosen so that various hypotheses could be tested. It was thought, for example, that the process of central area invasion of fringe residential districts probably involved distinct stages. The first pressure on residential uses would possibly come from activities which could not compete for central area space, either because they were not strictly commercial activities or because they were newly established with limited resources. Such a district might also, in the early stages of take-over, attract activities which do not require a central area location but which must be reasonably accessible to the centre.

It was also thought that such an area would accommodate generally less stable firms than those in the central area itself, possibly even in the later stages when it was completely taken over by non-residential functions. It is obvious that certain parts of Central London, where residential properties have been converted to office use, have become prestige locations because of the *kudos* conferred by the age and architectural merit of the buildings. These properties, though converted, command rents just as high as those providing modern, purpose-built offices, but in general, most adapted accommodation would be regarded as less desirable. Unless Fitzroy Square had developed into a prestige location, therefore, it would be more likely that its occupants would use accommodation there as a temporary measure, until the higher rents of modern offices could be afforded.

Although instability was expected to emerge as a strong characteristic of the area, the average length of stay of the Square's post-war occupants was in fact shorter than had been anticipated. Of those activities which had both entered and left the Square in the post-war period, over half stayed less than two years.

Two separate exercises were carried out. In the first, the change from residential to commercial use was examined, using directories for selected dates from 1886 to 1965.

Over this period, the number of non-residential activities in the Square increased from 21 (1886) to 84 (1965). The increase was mainly due to the take-over of residential properties by other users, but also to some extent it was the result of the greater subdivision of many of the houses in later years. (See Fig. IV 1.)

In 1886, half the houses in the Square remained wholly in residential use, and several more were predominantly residential. The non-residential properties, however, were mostly converted to semi-residential uses of one sort or another—hotels, boarding houses, hostels, schools, hospitals and clubs.

By 1912 only six houses were wholly residential, with another two partly residential. But the most significant change appears to have occurred in the early 1920's. In this period, the total number of non-residential activities nearly doubled, and by 1925 there were only two houses in wholly residential use. The increase in activities in this period was largely due to the influx of manufacturing firms.

Between 1936 and 1950 there were also considerable changes; the number of societies and associations accommodated in the Square nearly doubled, as did professional and industrial services.

By now only one house is in residential use.

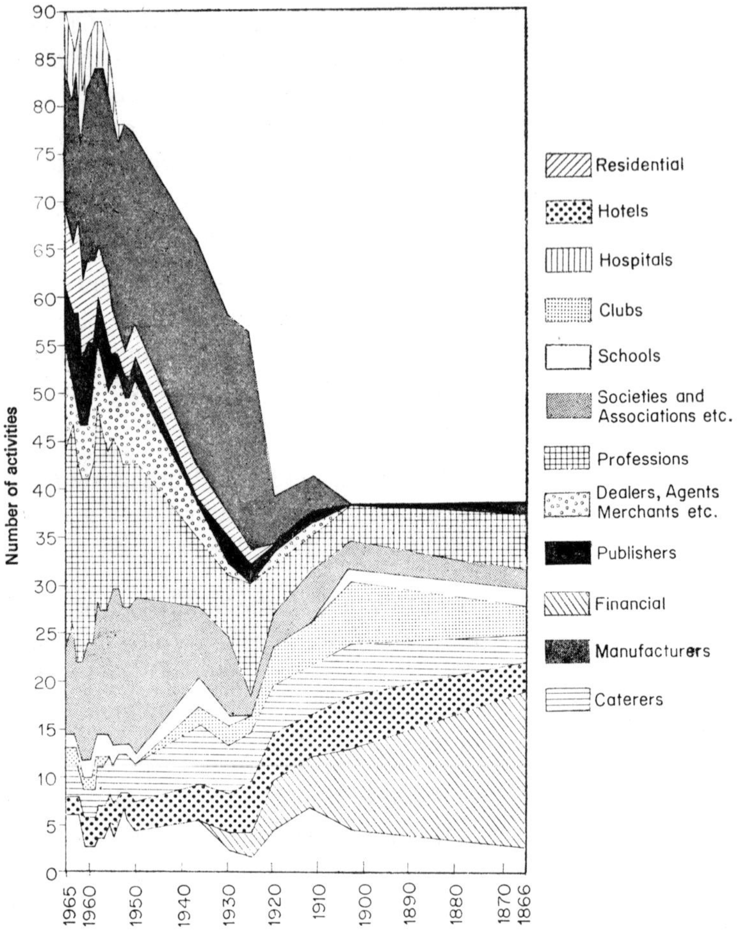

Fig. IV 1 Fitzroy Square 1886–1965.

A subsidiary exercise involved a closer examination of post-war changes in the Square. For each of the fifteen years 1950–1965, all occupants of Fitzroy Square were recorded, by street numbers and types of business. The years of arrival and departure were noted, and in addition movers' origins and destinations were recorded, where these addresses could be traced in the alphabetical list of firms.

Table IV 1 shows the general pattern of movement from 1950 to 1965.

One hundred and eighty-seven activities had been accommodated in the Square during the 15-year period; 11 of these moved to other addresses in the Square, giving a total of 198 'occupancies'. Of the 41 houses in the Square, several are combined with neighbouring houses, giving 35

Table IV 1 Movement of activities—Fitzroy Square, 1950–1965.

Date of Arrival	1952	1953	1954	1955	1956	1957	1958	1959	1960	1961	1962	1963	1964	1965	Total
Pre-1950	9	7	2	5	7	6		3			2	4	4	22	71
1952		1	1	3		1				2				1	9
1953			2	2					1					2	7
1954				2	1							1	2	5	11
1955					1	1	1	2			3	1	2	6	17
1956						2	2				1	3		2	10
1957								4	1	1		2	1	4	13
1958								1	2					1	4
1959									1	6				2	9
1960										1				1	2
1961											1			6	7
1962												1	3	7	11
1963													2	7	9
1965														18	18
Total	9	8	5	12	9	10	3	10	3	12	7	12	14	84	198

'units' of accommodation. Each of the 35 therefore accommodated on average 5·7 activities during the 15-year period. The number per house, however, varied a great deal:

Table IV 2

Number of Activities Accommodated 1950–1965	Number of Houses
1	9
2–5	10
6–10	11
Over 10	5
	35

Of the total of 198 activities, 36% were in the Square in 1950. The rest moved into the Square at an average rate of about 8·5 per year. The peak year was 1955, when 17 new activities moved in:

Table IV 3

Number of Activities moving into Fitzroy Square 1951–1965

1951/1952	9	
1953	7	
		44
1954	11	
1955	17	
1956	10	
1957	13	
		38
1958	4	
1959	9	
1960	2	
1961	7	
1962	11	
		47
1963	9	
1964/1965	18	
	127	

84 (42%) of the total number of activities recorded were still in the Square in 1965. Departures were at the rate of 7·6 p.a. (peak year 1965: 14):

Table IV 4

Number of Activities moving out of Fitzroy Square

1951–1955	34
1956–1960	35
1961–1965	45
	114

Of the 65 activities whose total length of stay in the Square is known (i.e. those who moved into and then out of the Square within the last 15 years) just over half (35) stayed less than two years:

Table IV 5

Length of stay	No. of activities	
Less than 1 year	15	
Less than 2 years	20	54%
Less than 3 years	7	
Less than 4 years	3	
Less than 5 years	1	
Less than 6 years	3	
Less than 7 years	8	
Less than 8 years	1	
Less than 9 years	5	
Less than 10 years	2	
Less than 11 years	—	
Less than 12 years	—	
	65	

In 1965 the largest group (40%) of activities in the Square were professional and other 'individual' services, predominantly accountants, solicitors and architects. The next largest group was manufacturing firms (20%) of various kinds:

Table IV 6

	No.	%
Professional and other 'individual' services	33	40
Manufacturing firms	16	20
Financial firms	10	12
Societies, associations, etc.	7	8
Catering firms	6	6
Publishing, printing firms	5	6
Hostels, colleges, halls, hospitals	7	8
	85	100

There does not appear to be much connection between length of stay and type of activity. Of those staying less than 2 years, 13 were professional and other individual services, 10 were societies and associations and 9 were financial companies. It does seem likely, however, that short-stay activities tend to be those occupying least space.

The addresses of many activities prior and subsequent to their stay in Fitzroy Square were traced. Eleven activities moved to other addresses in the Square within the period. Other locations were mainly very near the Square; of 78 previous addresses, 24 were in the same postal district (W.1.) and of 59 subsequent addresses, 24 were in W.1.:

Table IV 7

Postal District	Previous Addresses	Subsequent Addresses
W.1	24	24
W.C.1 & 2	19	8
E.C.1 & 4	20	13
N.W.1	4	2
Others (inner)	8	2
Very distant	3	10
	78	59

Comparing what was imagined to be a very much more stable area—Threadneedle Street, E.C.2—a considerable amount of movement was still evident, although of course, much less than in Fitzroy Square. 42% of the 1936 occupants were still there in 1963, compared with only 21% in Fitzroy Square.

The total number of occupants in Threadneedle Street has been falling since the war, from 44 in 1950 to 34 in 1963. Altogether 68 occupants had been in the street over the whole period, giving a much lower average number per building—2·6 compared with 5·7 in Fitzroy Square.

The turnover of occupants is shown below:

Table IV 8

	Moved Out	Moved In
1936–1950	12	18
1950–1955	9	6
1955–1960	6	8
1960–1963	6	1
	37	33

Occupants of post-war office buildings

Our second main study concerned the pattern of movement of firms occupying post-war office buildings in London.

Street directories were used to compile an inventory of occupants for over 300 post-war office buildings identified and located by a survey of planning permissions (see chapter VII). The occupants listed in the current Kelly's Directory were the firms which received postal questionnaires (see below).

Not only were current occupants identified, but the 'occupancy history' of each building was recorded, using the directories for each year in the building's life. We were able to measure the turnover of occupants, and the extent to which the building was subdivided from year to year.

We then attempted to trace the previous location of each firm which had occupied the building at any stage. These previous locations were also checked at earlier dates to establish the firm's length of stay, and again all earlier locations were recorded. Similarly, those firms which had occupied the new building but subsequently moved out were traced to their next addresses.

This study had to be restricted to new buildings within the London postal area. Even so, it was too big a task to deal with all buildings included in the planning permissions survey, and therefore only a 1:12 sample was taken of those in the 'central block'.

Because of our interest in decentralised offices, all the buildings which had been identified in the outer area were included in this study. We were aware that, because of the varying quality of the planning permissions data, the inventory of suburban office buildings was incomplete, and it was inadvisable to sample when the real population was unknown.

Another factor reducing the total number of buildings which could be examined was that planning permissions frequently could not be related to a building in the street directory. This happened where its location was inadequately described or where the exact location of a building listed in the directory was impossible to establish.

Planning permissions for extensions were excluded from the study, as it was concerned with the movement of firms into new accommodation. For the same reason, those for offices ancillary to factories were also excluded.

Having reduced the total number of planning permissions for these various reasons, there remained over 300 buildings for investigation, of which more than 200 were in the 'central block'.

The schedules of occupants referred to previously were used to provide the sample for the questionnaire survey. All firms listed in the current Kelly's Directory (1967) as occupying the selected buildings were sent a questionnaire, and also those firms which were traced to another address in the 1967 Directory, having moved out of the selected building.

The sample of new buildings for which schedules of occupants had been drawn up provided a total of 1,773 firms for the questionnaire survey. The only occupants excluded were government departments and local authorities.

The questionnaire was sent to 83 of the firms in April 1967 as a pilot investigation. The remaining 1,690 were approached in the following month. Alterations to the form were mainly in layout, and the results of the pilot survey are therefore not distinguishable in the following analysis. The only significant difference between the pilot and the main survey was that the response rate was considerably higher in the pilot survey, perhaps because the appeal made in the covering letter was more specific.

We had returned to us 641 completed questionnaires. (Of these, ten were returned by government departments and therefore were excluded from the analysis.) These 641 firms however provided information for 168 other firms which had received separate questionnaires but could not be treated separately because they shared in a single office organisation in terms of staff and accommodation. The total number of firms for which we received information was therefore 809—46% of the total.

Of the remaining firms approached, 83 could not complete the questionnaire for what was considered a valid reason, 30 were unco-operative and from the remaining 853 there was no response.

Table IV 9 gives a breakdown of the sample according to response.

Table IV 9 Questionnaire survey response.

	Number		%	
(1) Questionnaire returned completed	641		36·1	
(2) Questionnaire returned uncompleted		809		45·5
(i) Information included in (1) above	168		9·4	
(ii) No offices at the address, or accommodation address only	31		1·7	
(iii) Firm no longer at the address	28		1·4	
		83		4·7
(iv) Firm no longer in business	12		0·8	
(v) Unable to provide information—good reason	12		0·8	
(vi) Refused; uncooperative	30		1·7	
		883		49·8
(3) No response	853		48·1	
(1)–(3) Total	1,775*		100·0	

* Includes 2 firms double-counted because questionnaires were returned without reference numbers.

The 631 firms which answered the questionnaire together account for about 5½ million sq. ft. of London's office space, and about 40,000 of its office workers. This is about 3% of the total number of people employed in offices in the conurbation.

Ninety-six of the firms which replied had moved out of the building selected in the sample, and had either been traced to a new address in the current Kelly's directory or had had the questionnaire redirected from their previous address.

Forty-eight firms said they were in a pre-war building, mainly firms which had moved out of a building selected in the sample. The others we assume were either mistaken about the age of the building, or their building was wrongly included in the sample.

Five questionnaires were returned too late to be included in the analysis. The following sections relate, therefore, to information provided for 627 offices. (Firms were required to answer the questions only for the premises at the address the questionnaire was sent to.)

It had been the intention to exclude from the survey all office buildings which were ancillary to industrial premises. For most of the planning permissions from which we drew the sample of buildings, industrial offices were specified as such in the records and we were therefore able to exclude them. Others appeared in the street directories as factory premises, but it was inevitable that a certain number of factory offices remained in the sample and in fact 24 of the firms returning questionnaires stated that the firm also had industrial premises at the address.

Eight-two per cent of the premises in the sample, were however, solely offices. Of the rest (111) the offices were attached to one or more of the following uses:

Table IV 10 No. of firms with non-office accommodation at same address as office.

Factory	24
Warehouse	27
Shop	16
Showroom	66
Other (e.g. Labs.)	9

Most of the offices attached to shops and showrooms were in the West End. Most of those on factory sites were of course outside the central area.

Figs. IV 2 and IV 3 show the distribution of firms according to the type of office at the address to which the questionnaire referred; that is, whether it was the firm's only office, its head office, a branch or management service office.

Table IV 11

Type of Office	No. of Firms	%
Only office	258	41
Head office	178	28
Branch office	154	25
Other	37	6
All types	627	100

Fig. IV 2 Distribution of questionnaire returns: central area.

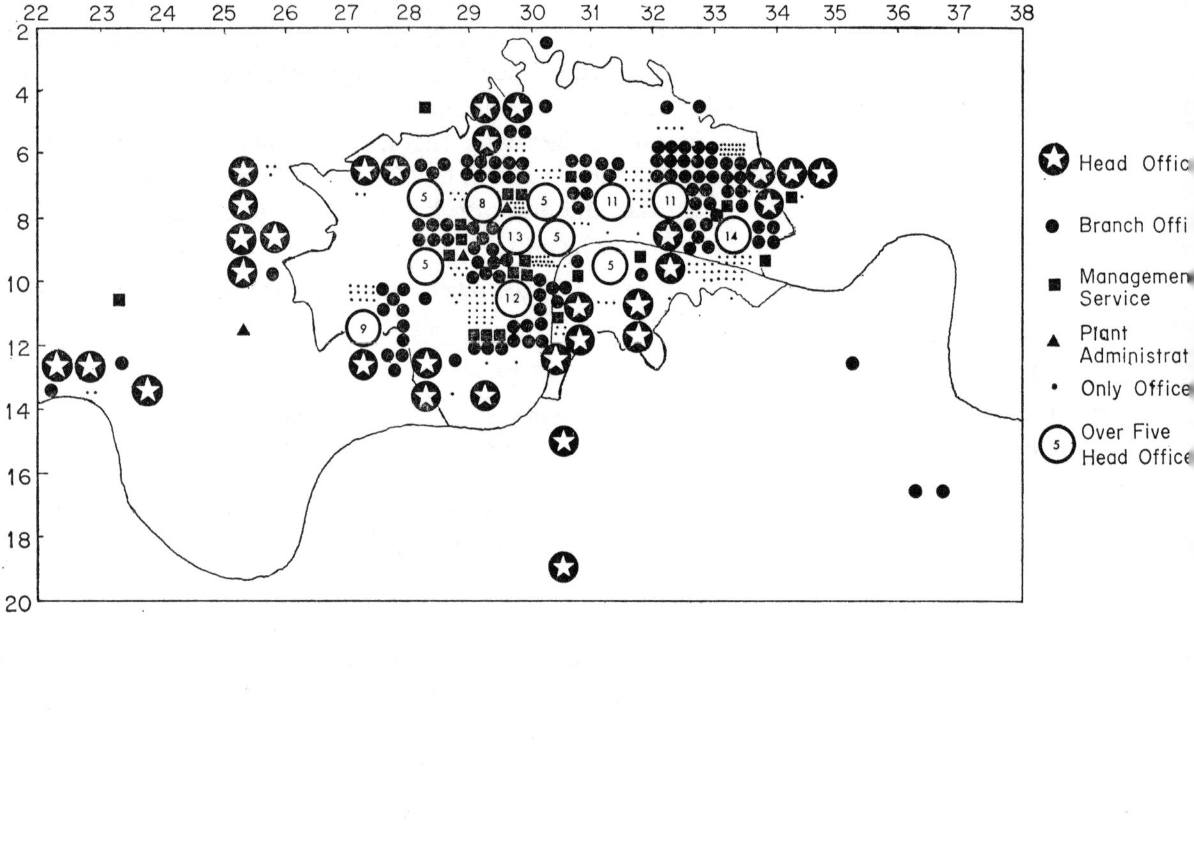

Fig. IV 3 Questionnaire returns: outer area.

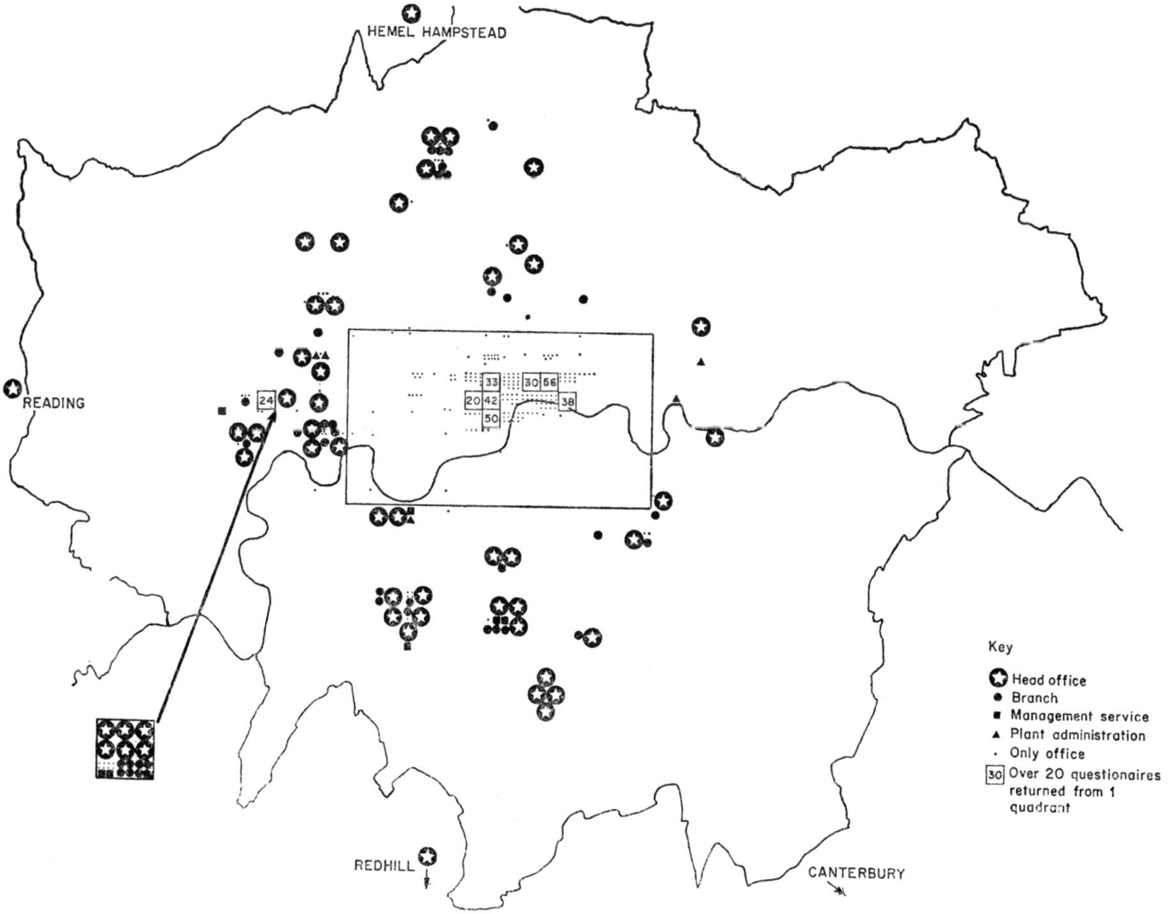

Of the total of 627 office premises, two-fifths were the firm's only office.

The type of office did not vary with location, as might have been expected.

Head offices were generally larger than other types of office, and, whereas only about 10% of other offices occupied the whole of a building rather than part of it, 20% of all head offices occupied the whole building. The size distribution of head offices compared to that of branch offices and firms with only one office is shown in Table IV 12.

Table IV 12 Type of office and employment.

No. of Office Workers	Head Offices	Branch Offices	Single Offices	Total all types
	%	%	%	%
0–5	1·7	24·2	17·4	15·4
6–15	15·8	32·0	34·9	28·1
16–35	17·5	19·6	24·8	21·6
36–55	12·4	6·5	7·4	8·8
56–75	10·7	3·3	4·7	6·3
76–175	19·2	4·6	5·8	9·6
176–275	9·0	2·0	0·8	3·6
more than 275	11·3	3·3	1·6	5·0
no information	2·4	4·5	2·6	1·6
Total	100·0	100·0	100·0	100·0

Although head offices were on the whole larger than other types of office, fewer of them had a high floor space per person ratio. Whereas only 22% of all head offices had an average of more than 175 sq. ft. per person, 30% of all branch offices and 41% of all single offices had occupancy ratios over 175 sq. ft. per person. This is perhaps to some extent explained by the fact that head offices appear to take generally longer leases, a fact which implies that they are less mobile and therefore perhaps are more likely than other firms to expand without extending their accommodation. This is borne out by the reasons given by head offices for moving; more gave expansion and the need for more space as reasons for moving than other types of offices.

Only 56 of all respondents owned rather than leased their accommodation, but 41% were head offices. Head offices also tended to have longer leases than other types of office. Only a third of the respondents had leases which expired after 1981, but 53% of the leases of head offices expired after this date (see Table IV 13).

Table IV 13 Type of firm and length of lease.

Date of Expiry of Lease	Head Offices	Branch Offices	Single Offices	Total all types
	%	%	%	%
1967–1971	10·9	18·6	22·8	18·4
1972–1976	10·3	14·5	15·2	14·0
1977–1981	14·1	17·9	21·1	17·7
1982–1986	25·0	13·8	14·8	17·5
1987–1995	10·3	6·9	5·5	7·0
After 1995	17·9	6·9	4·2	8·9
No information	11·5	21·4	16·4	16·5
All leaseholders	100·0	100·0	100·0	100·0

Rents will be discussed in more detail elsewhere, but it is worth repeating here that head office rents were generally lower than the rents paid by other types of offices. Only 8% of the head offices were paying over 50s. per sq. ft., whereas 18% of the branch offices and 14% of single offices were in this fairly high rent range. This is partly due to the fact that head offices were generally larger than other types.

It was not always possible to classify respondents satisfactorily into kinds of business categories, because the descriptions given to the firm in the street directories is frequently too general. These descriptions were entered on the questionnaires before they were sent out and, although respondents were asked to correct or expand them, very few did so. It would obviously have been more profitable to ask the firms to describe their activities without providing the information from the street directory.

The largest group was manufacturing firms, accounting for nearly a quarter of all respondents. Distribution was the only other group which had more than 15% of the total number of respondents. These categories, however, are both particularly open to doubt, at least in the way that they are used in the directories.

The numbers of firms in business groups of ten or more are shown in Table IV 14 with the proportions located in the City and the West End. (Location was coded by postal areas, 'the City' being E.C.1 2, 3 and 4 and the 'West End' including W.1, S.W.1., W.C.1. and W.C.2.) Most groups are very noticeably concentrated, whether in the City or the West End. Only two kinds of firm occurred more frequently outside the central postal districts—construction, with four-fifths of the firms outside the central area, and the miscellaneous services group (57%).

Table IV 14

Kind of Business	Total number all areas	City	West End	Elsewhere
	%	%	%	%
Manufacturing	141	11	41	48
Distribution	107	33	24	43
Professional	57	9	46	45
Insurance	45	53	11	36
Advertising, etc.	36	28	36	36
Financial	28	43	36	21
Trade associations	27	11	55	34
Publishing	23	22	65	14
Construction	23	—	17	83
Banking	22	55	18	27
Services (other)	21	—	43	57
Accountants	12	50	25	25
Solicitors	10	40	20	40
All respondents	627	23	36	41

In general there was little variation in the size distribution of firms in different business groups. Almost all groups had a similar proportion of very small firms—about 40% in each group employing 15 people or less.

Table IV 12 shows the size distribution of the firms by numbers of office workers. Just under two-thirds of respondents employed less than 36 people. The average size of the office premises for which floor space figures were provided was only 8,600 sq. ft. Table IV 15 shows occupancy ratios and locations of the 545 firms providing both employment and floor space figures.

Table IV 15 Floor space per person and location.

Square feet per Office Worker	No. of Firms	City	West End	Elsewhere
		%	%	%
less than 75	38	28	25	47
75–95	60	30	32	38
100–124	106	25	35	40
125–149	80	23	34	43
150–174	88	18	34	48
175–199	41	20	39	41
200–224	47	17	40	43
225–249	20	5	50	45
250–299	26	15	54	31
300 and over	39	21	41	38

The percentages in the last three columns show that the City firms have very few offices with a high floor area per person—only 29 had ratios of more than 175 sq. ft. per person, whereas 59 of the West End firms had ratios of this order.

Firms were asked why their address was a suitable location. It was thought preferable not to prompt answers to this question by listing possible reasons, although by asking an open-ended question, there was a risk of encouraging over-vague replies. Only 23 respondents (4%) gave prestige as a reason why their address was a suitable location. The Economist Intelligence Unit, in their survey for the L.O.B. (1964), asked firms how important prestige was as a location factor, and found that over 66% of their Central London respondents said it was either 'very important' or 'important'. The apparent discrepancy between this survey and that of the E.I.U. does not of course prove that either one or the other is right or wrong. But the fact that so few firms mentioned this factor when it was not actually suggested to them as a possibility implies that it is of less importance than has been commonly believed. The difference between 4% and 66% is perhaps too great to be completely discounted.

The interpretation of the replies to this question is, of course, open to debate. Some of the firms clearly felt it was an important issue and some apparently gave it little consideration. From the 571 firms who replied 983 reasons were provided, including 27 which simply stated that their location was not suitable. More than half gave only one reason, 175 firms gave two, 68 gave three and 29 gave more than three. It is relevant to the whole question of office location that firms located outside the central area appeared to have given the question much fuller treatment than central area firms. Only 9 of the 56 firms which did not reply were located outside the central area, and whereas nearly half of the central firms gave only one reason, four-fifths of the non-central area firms gave more than one reason. Among the single-reason replies, 'central' was particularly common, and most of the firms who claimed to be located in the 'traditional area' for their particular type of firm gave no other reason.

The reasons given, in order of frequency, are listed below, with the number of firms and the percentage of the total replying to the question. Reasons asterisked were given more frequently by non-central firms.

The firms which said they needed to be near a particular place (numbered 2 in the above list) were nearly all in Central London. Seventeen firms claimed they had to be near the Houses of Parliament or Ministries in the Whitehall area, another 17 near to Lloyds and 38 others specified particular markets in the City:

Table IV 16

Reason	No. of Firms	%
1. Proximity to clients	138	24
2. Near to a specified place	93	16
3. Central	83	15
4. 'Reasonably central'*	75	13
5. Good communications*	67	12
6. Near to parent or associated company	64	11
7. Proximity to suppliers or services	49	9
8. Suitable rent*	46	8
9. Traditional location for particular type of firm	44	8
10. Near to airport, railway terminals, motorway, etc.*	38	7
11. Accessibility for staff*	38	7
12. Tradition	34	6
13. Visitors from abroad	26	5
14. Labour availability*	25	4
15. Prestige	23	4
16. Car parking*	21	4
17. Good working conditions	21	4
18. Near director's home*	14	3
19. Modern new building	9	2
20. London telephone or postal area*	7	1
21. Available at the time	7	1

Of the total number of respondents, 97 said that their location was not ideal. This was in reply to a later question. A surprisingly large number of firms failed to answer this question.

Rent

Over 400 firms gave rents, the average rent being £1 12s., but this varied according to location as follows:

Table IV 17

Area	Average Rent per Square Foot		
Central Districts	£	s.	d.
E.C.1	1	2	6
E.C.2	2	5	6
E.C.3, 4	2	1	0
W.1	1	14	0
S.W.1	2	4	6
W.C.1, 2	1	15	0
S.E.1	1	7	6
S.W.3 and 7	2	1	0
Other Postal Districts			
West	0	18	6
South West	0	19	6
North West	1	2	6
South East	0	19	0
East	1	0	6
North	0	19	0
Elsewhere	1	0	0
All areas	£1	12	0

Of all rents quoted, only 2% were over 69s. and over half were under 30s. The following table gives rents and location.

Table IV 18

Rent (shillings)	Central	Non-Central	Total	No.
	%	%	%	
less than 19	11	39	21	86
19–29	25	46	31	134
29–39	17	6	13	54
39–49	21	4	15	62
49–69	22	5	16	69
over 69	4	—	4	10
Total	100	100	100	415

Most of the high rents in the non-central postal districts were in S.W.3 and S.W.7 which were similar in many respects to Central London.

There was a tendency towards larger units being let at lower rents; this was also true of buildings. In buildings with more than one respondent, we found a slight tendency for tenants with longer leases to be paying lower rents. In general, the newer the building, the higher the rent.

Past and Intended Moves

One hundred firms now located outside Central London had moved from Central London offices, mainly vacating them but in 13 cases retaining them when taking on the new accommodation. Most of these firms moved into the outer suburbs.

Of all the 222 non-central firms in the survey, therefore, 45% had moved from Central London. If those non-central firms are excluded which were newly established on taking their present accommodation, the proportion rises to 54%—i.e. 100 out of 186. Thus 54% of all moves into non-central offices premises were from Central London.

These 100 firms which have wholly or partially decentralised account for about 6,750 office workers.

As well as those which have already decentralised, the survey found 21 firms which although at present located in Central London, were actively contemplating moving out. These firms accounted for half of all the central firms considering a move and giving the proposed location (21 out of 44).

Thirty firms had moved from suburban locations to other parts of the suburbs. Of these only one moved nearer to Central London; the rest all moved further out, or in a few cases, moved 'across' the suburbs. These outward movements within the suburbs involved about 1,100 office workers. More than 500 firms gave their previous address; another 20 had vacated a previous address on taking their present accommodation but did not specify it.

Forty-three per cent of all previous addresses were in the same postal district as the present address.

Table IV 19

Previous Address in Relation to Present Address	No. of Firms
In same postal district	222
In adjacent postal district	118
Elsewhere in same area	61
In a different area; further in	95
In a different area; further out	17
Rest of South East	2
Elsewhere	3
Total	519

The most common reason for moving was that the previous accommodation was too small. The table below shows the number of firms stating various reasons for moving; as some firms gave more than one reason, the total exceeds the number of respondents.

Table IV 20

Reasons for Leaving Previous or Present Address	No. of Firms Leaving Previous Address	No. of Firms intending to Move
Too small	269	40
Expiry of lease	90	7
Inconveniently situated	63	15
Demolished; rebuilding	62	2
Too expensive	50	16
Reorganisation of firm	34	16
'Old-fashioned' building; inconvenient layout	21	—
Other	14	14

To sum up, it would appear that prestige is not as vital a factor in office location as has been suggested, e.g. by the E.I.U.'s survey for the Location of Offices Bureau. Asked to state the reasons why they thought their present address a suitable location, only 4% of respondents mentioned prestige (or 'good address'). Asked directly in the E.I.U. survey whether prestige was important, 66% of all firms in Central London claimed that it was. The discrepancy can prove nothing conclusively, but there is obviously a need for a much more careful study of this particular aspect of office location.

Decentralisation appears to have occurred at a significant rate. Over half of the firms occupying non-central offices (which had moved from

Plate 1
The office at the centre of the capitalist world: view of Manhattan Island looking south, with the Empire State Building in the right middle distance.

Plate 2
The office in a communist capital: The Palace of Culture in Warsaw.

other premises rather than being newly established) had moved there from Central London. These firms employed about 7,000 office workers.

Office occupants are extremely mobile. The main reason stated for having moved in the past or for proposing to move in the near future was that the accommodation was too small. Short stays and frequent moves appear to be the commonest way of coping with growth, and generally the longer a firm stays in a building the more crowded the accommodation becomes.

In general, the survey suggested that many firms appear to pay far less attention to locational requirements than might have been expected. This seems particularly true of small City firms. Although it is extremely dangerous to interpret a postal questionnaire in these terms, it does seem likely that tradition outweighs other considerations. This apparent lack of interest in location requirements can perhaps best be explained by assuming that the questions put to the firms could not reasonably be answered except by those responsible for policy decisions. The strongest conclusion should be, therefore, that the little evidence this survey provides needs to be tested by much closer examination of the problem it raises.

Chapter V
The Provision of Office Space

When a commodity is required in some quantity, it is often quicker and cheaper for specialists to produce it and sell for a profit than for each consumer to produce to his own requirements. This is happening today in the field of office development. The notion is not new to the building industry, but it is relatively new to office construction. This chapter studies the supply side of the office construction industry. We hope to discover how it is organised, the processes and characters involved, and how it differs from other production industries.

The Commodity

Mass production of offices is very rare. Each product is a unique item, individually constructed. Its production presents special problems of engineering, architecture and finance. Because buildings are fixed, the space which the building occupies is, in a sense, part of the raw material. Space, particularly in locations suitable for office building, is an invaluable raw material, and the supply is limited.

Office buildings are large, complex and expensive items. Even ignoring the problems of planning permission and building regulations, they take a long time to construct, and very large sums of money are involved. Hence the elaborate systems which have evolved for financing development.

Offices are usually built to last a long time. It generally suits both the developer and occupier if the latter rents instead of purchasing. This is perhaps one of the most important differences between offices and houses.

The other principal difference between offices and houses arises because offices are essentially capital goods, while houses have more of the nature of consumer goods. The kinds of risk involved in production are different, and they react differently to changing economic circumstances.

These characteristics are particularly important because they make necessary a measure of state control or participation in this industry, over and above the sort of participation the state has for reasons of safety or hygiene in any industry. In the office construction industry, the state must check on more than the mere safety of the buildings; it must check on the supply of land, and on the location of the product, and because of their position in the economy, the state checks on the supply of offices themselves, though the present system is far from perfect. The essential point is that because of certain peculiar characteristics of offices as a commodity, the industry as a whole requires an enlightened participation by the state.

Public Control

The details of control of development through the planning applications system is dealt with in Chapter VI. All that is needed here is to mention the main ways in which this system affects the structure of the industry.

Controls on development are intended to achieve two aims. First, they seek to control the form and plan of the building for reasons of safety, of aesthetics, or hygiene and of general environment. Second, they seek to control the use of land, particularly in congested, built-up areas of towns, so as to maintain a balance between activities and services in the area, and to provide space for those activities which are socially desirable but which may not be able to compete for space on free economic items.

Three items in the control of the form of buildings are important to us here; the daylighting code, height of buildings and plot ratio controls. The daylighting code controls the height of buildings immediately fronting on to streets and overlooking other buildings, while plot ratios control the total floor space that can be built on to a site of any given area. The combined effect of these controls is to make it extremely difficult to develop a small site, because the chances are that some, if not all, of the sides of the site will be subject to these restrictions. Small plot ratios, too, have made it uneconomic to carry out small redevelopments, where the maximum floor space permitted is not substantially greater than the existing floor space. It has become economically necessary to develop *groups* of sites, where enough space can be assembled to overcome these disadvantages. Hence the trend in recent years has been for redevelopment of offices to become more and more dominated by large-scale operations, usually consisting of whole street blocks. A discussion of this process is given by Llewelyn-Davies (1966). In London, it is rare for such large continuous parcels of land to come under the same ownership, and even where they do, existing leases and sub-leases cover very much smaller areas. All these interests in the land have to be acquired, or at least satisfied, before development is possible. In some of the larger block redevelopments, such as those at Broadway, Oxford Circus, Moorgate and the Euston Centre, as many as 1,000 interests had to be satisfied before old properties could be replaced by a single building.

Two important results ensue. First, the scale of development is often greater than the scale of the organisations which require office accommodation. This does not mean that there is any imbalance between total supply and demand, but most large office blocks built during the last few years have had to be let in parts. There are some organisations which require 300,000 sq. ft. or more floor space at one time (mainly government departments), but such figures as are available indicate that the main pressure of demand occurs for units of around 10,000 sq. ft., below that when investment is running at a high level, and above when conditions are stagnant. Of the total floorspace permitted by the L.C.C. for new buildings since 1948, only 28% is accounted for by buildings of under 50,000 sq. ft., and of the remaining 72% almost half (35%) was permitted in units of over 200,000 sq. ft. Since 1960, the proportion permitted in units of over 200,000 sq. ft. has risen to 41%. This means that offices are being produced en masse at certain locations, and it also means that a developer can produce one unit of 10,000 sq. ft. in conjunction with nineteen other similar units in the same building more cheaply than an individual firm can produce 10,000 sq. ft. for its own use.

The second main consequence of local authority control on office building has been to make the legal and preparatory work much more involved and time-consuming. Not only do all the channels of planning application procedure have to be followed, usually involving the alteration of a major scheme many times before work can be started. Even more important is the problem of acquiring all the interests necessary before a development company can begin to plan a major scheme. It appears to take about ten years for one of the larger office schemes in London to come to fruition, and most of this time is spent in satisfying all the existing interests in the property, and in seeking the approval of the local authority. Thus the whole process requires a high level of long-term planning and investment, and is particularly suited to firms with large resources and specialist knowledge of the work.

There is little doubt that the trend in the 1950's towards the production of larger units of accommodation by specialists was connected with the high level of demand for offices in certain specific locations within London. A lot of offices were needed quickly, and specialists could produce them more quickly and cheaply in bulk than non-specialists could produce them individually. But the factors outlined above indicate that when this high level of demand begins to fall off the trend towards fewer but larger producers will continue. Indeed the lower the profit margins on office production, the more activity will be concentrated in the hands of those companies who possess the financial resources and the expertise to produce in bulk.

The Producers

The increase in the number of size of property companies has been one of the outstanding features of the post-war development of London. According to Lean and Goodall (1966) there were, before the war, less than 25 such companies with shares quoted daily on the stock exchange.

Today the number has risen to over 150. Some 50 or so of these are listed, under the Trustee Investments Act, as having paid up capital of over £1,000,000. Some of these are merely property-holding companies (often subsidiaries of firms which use property as an investment, or subsidiaries of firms who need a regular supply of land for their main function), but the majority do engage in development and exist largely for that purpose. Most specialise in a particular field of development, such as Slough Estates Ltd. (industrial premises), Covent Garden Ltd. (shops), Daejan Holdings (residential) and the Rodwell Group (offices), although most of the very large companies are mainly involved with the comprehensive 'Central Area' type of development. There are about a dozen of these very large developers in London, and all of them have other interests elsewhere. No provincial firms compete with them for major schemes in regional centres and smaller towns, and more recently some of them have begun to acquire substantial interests in the cities of North America and Australasia. Many very large companies were in existence before the war, and already owned substantial sites in London at the start of the 'boom' period of the 1950's.

In 1952 Harold Macmillan said '. . . the people whom the government must help are those who do things: the developers, the people who create wealth . . .' As Marriott (1967) points out, the remark is revealing of governmental attitudes which started the property boom.[1]

None the less, the characteristics of the property development companies in this country are not well known. With the resources available to us it was not possible to undertake a very rigorous enquiry, but we did manage, by means of a very simple series of questions, to discover one or two interesting items.

Because of the nature of development companies and their particular need to safeguard their own interest, we did not expect a very high response from our enquiries, and indeed we found that the majority of the companies we approached were unable or unwilling to supply us with information. In fact 98 out of 204 firms replied; 31 of these gave outright refusals and 17 were holding companies. This left us with 50 companies who were engaged in property development, and we have used this group of 50 as a basis for the following comments. It should be remembered that these respondents did not represent a statistical sample of development companies; they are simply a group of firms who readily replied to our questions. And we are not sure what proportion of the total number of development companies our 50 respondents represent. There may be about twice this number all together but we cannot be sure because of problems of classification and so on.

Of the 50 firms 32 have addresses in the London postal district (see Table V 1); of these 10 are in W.1, 4 in S.W.1 and 11 in E.C.1, E.C.2 and E.C.4. Thus 25 of these firms are in the two main office districts which are outlined by Morgan (1961)—the City and the West End. It is fairly obvious that these two areas dominate the rest of the country in terms of density of property developers. Only 3 of the 50 firms were located in Birmingham and 2 in Manchester. No other city had more than one respondent. This heavy concentration is understandable, because London is where most of the transactions occur upon which development companies rely for loans and so on. Concentration of

[1] The research for this chapter was all carried out before the publication of Marriott, O., *The Property Boom*, Hamish Hamilton (1967). Anyone who wishes to enquire more deeply into this field is referred to this work.

banks, insurance companies and other financial enterprises, combined with the actual ripeness of post-war London for property development, is an obvious explanation for the tight clustering of property development companies in London. Not surprisingly the companies which are located outside London tend to be smaller than those in the capital.

Table V 1 Geographical distribution of the addresses of 50 property companies.

Area	No. of Firms	
W.1	10	14
S.W.1	4	
E.C.1	1	11
E.C.2	6	
E.C.3	2	
E.C.4	2	
N.W.2	1	7
N.W.10	1	
W.5	1	
W.10	1	
S.W.3	1	
W.C.2	2	
Total in London Postal District	32	
Rest of G.L.C. Area	2	
Total in G.L.C. Area	34	
Rest of South East	4	
Total in South East	38	
Birmingham	3	
Staffs.	1	
Manchester	2	
Leeds	1	
Bradford	1	
Edinburgh	1	
Glasgow	1	
Belfast	1	
Norwich	1	
Total in Rest of U.K.	12	

Table V 2 Total floor space constructed by firms by floor space groups.

Floor Space Groups (sq. ft.)	No. of Firms	Floor Space Built by Firms in each Group
Nil	16	0
1–49,999	5	34,300
50,000–99,999	4	245,000
100,000–499,999	5	810,000
500,000–999,999	5	2,980,000
1,000,000 upwards	2	2,516,570
No answer	13	
Total	50	6,585,870

Table V 3 Distribution of firms by floor space groups.

Floor Space Groups (sq. ft.)	No. of Firms
Nil	16
1–9,999	3
10,000–19,999	2
20,000–29,999	0
30,000–39,999	0
40,000–49,999	0
50,000–99,999	4
100,000–199,999	4
200,000–299,999	1
300,000–399,999	0
400,000–499,999	0
500,000–999,999	5
1,000,000 upwards	2
No answer	13
Total	50

Range: Lowest 1,700 sq. ft.
Highest 1,516,570 sq. ft.

We asked firms about the areas where their activity had been concentrated in the past ten years. Very few listed as their first preference any development abroad. Perhaps surprisingly, more listed development in 'the rest of the United Kingdom' than in either 'the rest of the G.L.C. area' or in 'the Central London area', although it is possible that our selection of these categories rather forced this conclusion. We made further enquiries about the possible location of further projected activity. Among the firms that envisaged some change, there was a slight tendency to switch from Central London development to development abroad rather than to other parts of the U.K., although it is difficult to draw firm conclusions from our data. This finding does not tie up with the more extensive investigation by Marriott (1967), which suggests that many development companies are turning their attention to provincial cities in the United Kingdom, where opportunities for office building outside the area covered by the 'Brown Ban' remain open.

We attempted to discover our respondents' production of office floor space in London (see Tables V 2 and V 3). Of the 50 firms, 13 did not answer this question and 16 had not built any offices. The remaining 21 firms appeared to fall into three quite distinct groups, according to their total floor space production. Five of the firms had each produced less than 20,000 sq. ft. in the last ten years, nine of the firms produced between 50,000 and 300,000 sq. ft., while seven of the firms produced from ½ million to 1½ million sq. ft. each. This distribution of office productivity is peculiar. It does seem that there must be some economic reason for the clustering around certain levels of output, although there does not seem to be any clear relationship between the size of the firm and its output of office space. Clearly those firms producing a small quantity of office space never really got into the major development process during the post-war years, while those at the top end of the scale were perhaps the companies which we all think of as participating in the post-war office boom. The remaining firms, with output levels in the middle range, are less easy to categorise. Perhaps they entered the process too late to build up a large amount of office space. It will be interesting to pursue this particular question further, given time and resources. These 21 firms between them, built a total of some 6,600,000 sq. ft. and it is thought that between 30 and 50 million sq. ft. was built in London in this period. Clearly our respondents on this issue do not contribute proportionally to the office development pattern of London, and their output figures must therefore be read with considerable caution, especially as some of them may have provided office space outside London.

We obtained data on the total property assets of each of the 50 companies from the Stock Exchange Year Book 1967 (see Table V 4).

Table V 4 Distribution of assets.

Assets (Million of Pounds)	No. of Firms
0,001–0,499	3
0,500–0,999	4
1,000–1,999	9
2,000–2,999	9
3,000–4,999	3
5,000–6,999	5
7,000–8,999	3
9,000–10,999	1
11,000–12,999	3
13,000–14,999	1
15,000–19,999	2
20,000–49,999	2
50,000–99,999	2
Over 100,000	1
No accounts	2
Total	50

Range: Lowest 000,232
Highest 147,448

The data on property assets were not strictly comparable, although we attempted to make them so by comparing a figure for total fixed assets. We checked on this by asking the firms about their total property assets. In most cases their figures confirmed those derived from the Stock Exchange Year Book. The distribution of assets is highly skewed. Half of the companies had assets of under £3 million, thirty-six of the companies had assets of under £9 million. Companies' assets ranged from a low of £1¼ million to a high of £147 million. It would be interesting to compare this concentration of such large assets in so few companies with other industries.

We attempted to find out the proportion of companies' total office production during the last ten years which had been built to the requirements of a specific occupant. Of the 41 firms who responded to the question 30 did not construct any offices for a particular occupant, and the remaining 11 tended either to build wholly for special clients, or to build only a very small amount of such accommodation. There seemed to be no middle way.

We enquired about the year in which the companies were registered. (See Table V 5.).

Table V 5 Year of registration of property development companies.

Year of Formation	No. of Companies
1860–1869	4
1870–1879	0
1880–1889	3
1890–1899	2
1900–1909	1
1910–1919	2
1920–1929	3
1930–1939	5
1940–1949	6
1950–1959	9
1960–1967	12
No date available	3
	50

We assumed that many of the companies would be of recent date. Of the 50 firms, we obtained data for 47. 27 of these were formed after 1940 and the total has risen in each decade since then; six of the older companies were formed to trade in some other commodity and were converted into property developers fairly recently. It might be of interest to note that seven firms were registered as Property Companies before 1900. Clearly the decades between the wars were not good years for the formation of development companies.

We thought that the number of subsidiary companies attached to each main company might give us a check on the size of each unit (see Table V 6).

Table V 6 Number of subsidiaries.

No. of Subsidiaries held by Companies	No. of Companies
0	6
1–4	14
5–9	11
10–14	9
15–19	2
20–29	2
30–39	3
40–49	1
50 upwards	1
No answer	1
Total	50

Range: Lowest 0
Highest 150

We therefore asked the firms how many subsidiaries they had. Just over half of those that responded had between one and nine subsidiaries. Six had no subsidiaries at all and one had over one hundred and fifty. As expected this largest company is also the one with the largest assets and clearly there is a difference in the mode of operation of such a company from those that have very few subsidiaries. We were not able to probe further into this aspect of organisation, and again it would be of interest for future study.

To sum up, this part of our study has thrown up in a very superficial way a whole batch of characteristics. First, a few companies held a great many of the assets. Second, the production of office space seems to fall into clearly defined groups, with a few companies producing a very large amount of space but a greater number of middle-size companies forming a steadily producing group during the past decade. Third, a great many of the companies have been formed during the 'boom' years of office development since the Second World War. Fourth, there is an overwhelming concentration of development companies in London. Fifth, no clear evidence is available concerning specialisation or possible changes in specialistion, despite the effect which we might have anticipated owing to the present government policies concerning office development in London and the south-east.

The Way Development Companies are Run

Few development companies employ large numbers of technical building staff. The head offices of one of the largest companies may have a staff of about fifty, the great majority of which are involved in purely routine administrative work, dealing with shareholders in the company and administering the property which that company owns. Unless the company is responsible for servicing and improvements in a large number of its own buildings (i.e., which it has built and let), the volume of work for such specialists as architects, engineers, valuers and surveyors fluctuates too much for it to be economic for the company to employ a large permanent staff in these fields. Most of this work is therefore given out on commission to specialists.

The function of the development company is to provide the raw materials (site capital) for development, and to bring together a team of professional technicians to carry out the work. The development company will raise the capital needed, will carry out the legal and other preparatory work involved in making the site available for development, will make broad fundamental decisions about the proposed use of the building, its size and how it will be let (as a whole, in separate floors, and so on) and will take the financial risk involved in the undertaking.

Since most development companies retain ownership either of the freehold or of a long building lease on their products, and since very few of these are let for long periods to a single occupant, the property company has a second main function of managing its estates. At least one major property company considers this to be its main function, and looks on the rebuilding of offices on those sites it already owns as being a 'servicing' operation on the site rather than the manufacture of a new product. This attitude is much more prevalent in the City, where the main property companies own large numbers of sites, mainly with out-of-date offices (built before about 1955) and have great difficulty in acquiring further property. In other parts of the central area, ownership of land is less fixed, and redevelopment of a site or block of sites often involves a change in the use of the buildings.

The attitude of the company towards their main function depends on their size and how they market their products. Generally the upkeep and management of buildings which are let as a whole or in a very large units (say of 1,000,000 sq. ft. and over) will be the responsibility of the lessee, while that of buildings let in small units will be the responsibility of the property company.

Certain companies prefer to let in large units, relieving themselves of the burden of estate management. For the smaller companies this often becomes necessary, because they do not own enough property to justify employing a large technical staff for periodical repairs and improvements. With one or two noticeable exceptions, therefore, the larger the companies, the more they become property management companies, rather than merely property development companies.

The Raw Materials (In this connection, see Chapter 3 of Marriott (1967). Four major raw materials are required in the production of any office building: (a) a site, (b) capital, (c) labour and (d) building materials.

The site

Most of the Central London area has been built up for at least two hundred years, and the square mile of the City for over four centuries. Different parts have, at some time or another, been covered by private dwellings or other very small units. We have already seen how, after the war, there was a need to develop or redevelop in large units, and therefore the main problem in acquiring sites is to piece together a sufficiently large block of these small units of ownership.

The owners of property in Central London fall mainly into four categories; the property companies themselves, institutions (such as livery companies and trusts), the local authority and the occupant or former occupant of the site. The attitude of each of these categories towards the land which they own differs.

Normally the development company will own part of the site at the outset, either because it erected the existing building or because part of the site was offered for sale. Ideally, it would hope to acquire the freehold of all the other sections of the site, for although this may take a long time, and the price may become very inflated, it leaves the property company with a free hand (within public controls) to do what it wants with the site, and to obtain all rent from the new buildings. However, neither local authorities nor institutions are normally prepared to part with their freehold interests at any price and, under these circumstances, the property company has to find alternative ways of making the parts of the site which it does not own available for development.

There are two ways in which this is normally done, one involving the local authority and the other involving institutions. If the local authority owns part of the site, and wishes to see it developed along the lines suggested by the development company, then the authority can acquire the entire site (including that part already owned by the development company) by compulsory purchase, and then grant the development company a long building lease on the whole site. This is very similar to the normal practice for central area redevelopment schemes for small towns, and will clearly lead to a position where a great deal of our urban land is publicly owned.

Where an institution (such as a livery company or university) owns part of the site, it will sometimes be happy to see the proposal for developing, but will not be prepared to part with the freehold. The institution often will demand an equity participation in the development.

Where this is the case a consortium will be formed between the development company and the institutions involved. The profits of such a consortium will be divided among the parties, according to the proportions of the site owned by each. The development will be carried out by the consortium, which will be granted a long building lease by each of the owners. In the City, where institutions are prolific owners of small sites, this is the most normal practice, but it has the disadvantage of perpetuating the unfortunate *parcellement* of the City.

The main difficulty faced by development companies is in acquiring sufficient interests in the sites to make schemes economic. One of the declared aims of the Land Commission Bill (1967) is to make sure that 'land will be more readily available for development when required'—largely through compulsory purchase procedures. But this is unlikely to affect the sale (or refusal to sell) of small parcels of land in the Central Area, where the proposal is to redevelop for offices. It is unlikely to solve the problem of institutional owners refusing to sell and therefore complicating the whole process greatly, and it is unlikely to solve the problem of individual owners holding out for vastly inflated prices when their plot is the last 'link' in a major redevelopment, unless the local authority has a specific interest in the development itself.

The capital

Capital is required for purchasing sites, and for covering the expenses of carrying out a project (mainly salaries and company expenses, fees to advisors and contractors and loss of rent during redevelopment) until it is complete and starts to yield a profit. These are known as 'purchasing funds' and 'bridging finance'.

Methods of raising bridging finance are substantially the same as those employed in any other industry, and of course, the problem of finding capital to run the business until it begins to yield a profit is not peculiar to the office-building industry. Short-term credit is normally available from the banks, and most of the companies can usually raise finance by a further issue of stocks and shares. A steady income is provided by a company's existing developments in any case, so it is only in the case of a particularly major scheme that it will need to go outside its own resources.

Purchasing funds involve much greater sums of money, and methods of raising it are necessarily more elaborate. The major source of finance on this scale is insurance and pension funds, and the expansion of these latter during the last two decades is intricately tied up with the expansion of development companies. Property has always been a secure investment, and after the war the insurance and pension funds started to provide fixed-income finance, generally by buying fixed-income debentures, by providing a mortgage against property already owned by the development company, or by buying the site itself and then granting a long building lease to the development company. More recently, however, these institutional investors have begun to demand an equity as well as a fixed-income participation in development, largely because of rapid inflation during the 1950's. There is a wide variety of ways in which this has been done.

One increasingly popular method is for the institution to purchase the site required for development (or at least that part not already owned by the development company), and then to participate in the sort of consortium arrangement that has already been outlined. In this way the investor has both a fixed-income investment (the ground rent charged to the consortium as a whole for the property it now owns) and an equity participation in the consortium. Alternatively, the investor may simply form a subsidiary with the development company to carry out a specific development, and in this arrangement the investor would hold the majority, if not all, the fixed-income shares, together with a proportion of the ordinary shares. The pension funds of large companies, such as Unilever, I.C.I. and the Imperial Tobacco Company, have been involved in many of the major office redevelopment schemes.

A further institutional investor whose importance is not often fully realised is the local authority. If the local authority is involved in the scheme, either because it already owns part of the site or because it agrees with the need for such a development, it may provide purchasing funds to gain participation in the development. Normally this will be done as outlined above by compulsory purchase and the granting of a long building lease to the development company. The local authority will then guarantee a fixed minimum yield to the development company. For example, it may be agreed that the development company should receive a minimum yield of 8% on its own capital (i.e., basically the bridging finance). Suppose this capital is £1,000, the first £80 p.a. of the rents charged to the tenants of the new building would then go to the development company. The excess over the £80 would be divided between the development company and the local authority, often in the ratio of 70% to the local authority and 30% to the development company. The proportion due to the local authority will be the ground rent charged to the development company for the building lease. This practice is clearly very popular among local authorities where the social need for new buildings outweighs any doubts about the economic viability of the scheme. In certain cases the local authority will be prepared to guarantee a minimum income to the development company above the total rents obtained from the tenants. But it is clear that these special cases are less likely to apply to new office building than to certain other proposed uses.

Obtaining finance for development itself is probably among the least of the property company's worries. Only the smaller companies have to raise bridging finance from outside the existing resources of the company, and even this is a relatively simple matter. Many of the larger companies are now concentrating on the redevelopment of sites which they already own and therefore do not have to raise purchasing funds, and even when this is not the case, they usually own substantial capital assets, in the form of property, against which large sums can easily be raised. Generally speaking those firms which consider their management functions to be most important, work at a 'low gear' in terms of investment; that is to say they keep as little as possible of their property mortgaged or otherwise tied. On the other hand, those firms who consider themselves primarily development companies are generally prepared to see a high proportion of their previous developments used to raise funds for future ones.

Labour

The third major raw material which the development company has to bring together is the labour required and, as pointed out earlier, only a small part of this is permanently employed within the development company. Instead, various consultants and professional firms are brought together into a development team, under the captainship of the development company.

Of other members of the team, the most important are the estate agent and the architect, and both will be brought in at a very early stage. The estate agent may have drawn attention to the site, or part of it, in the very first place, and will be retained throughout the whole course of the development. Since he will probably be responsible for finding tenants, and will have a great deal of knowledge about the requirements of the market at that moment, and for advice on the form of the building, the size of units and rooms, the use of certain materials and other factors which may be of importance to a firm requiring accommodation. There are about a dozen of these agents in Central London who deal with nearly all the major developments (i.e., nearly all offices) in Central London, in the suburbs, and most provincial centres. A few of these agents have special ties with one of the property companies, though most are completely independent.

The architect will also be introduced to the project at an early stage because the whole operation has to be costed very carefully at the outset, and certain economic limits must be laid down. If the architect is able to advise on these matters before final decisions are made (with regard to materials, form, etc.) he will partly be able to decide his own terms of reference in the design. The architect is often responsible for presenting an outline scheme to the local authority before the main interests have been acquired.

All this is not to say that the developer himself will not have a high degree of knowledge and experience of both the job of the agent and the job of the architect. He will have a highly developed 'feel' of certain locations, types of buildings, fluctuations in demand, and so on, and he will have to be competent enough in all spheres of the operation to compromise between the various sectional interests.

The other labour required enters only a much more limited section of the operation. A solicitor will, of course, be needed for all transactions, but unlike the agent, he will not be required to give technical advice on the actual structure of the building. The actual construction work will be undertaken by a firm of main contractors and a number of sub-contractors. The main contractor will be appointed after a tender has been submitted on the basis of the architect's design. This will not normally happen until work is ready to start. That is when all the legal and preparatory work is complete, and planning permission has been granted. For a large office building, the main contractor is likely to employ at least thirty subcontractors, each specialising in one small sector of the building process.

Building materials

Although decisions regarding the types of materials used are all in the hands of the development companies, it is the contractors who are responsible for bringing them together at the site. The processes involved in this are exactly the same as for any other sector of the construction industry.

Demand and Marketing

Only rarely is a tenant found for an office building in London before the building is completed. The situation may be a little different in the provinces and in some of the less successful locations in the suburbs, where the development company would hesitate before risking its capital without an assurance of some return fairly quickly. But the normal practice is for a site to be assessed on its own merits in the first place. Even though potential tenants may express interest, the company will not build unless it is sure that there will be a general pressure to occupy the site.

This state of affairs suits both the potential occupants and the development companies. Very few organisations can forecast their office requirements so far in advance that they can commission a building which may take anything up to ten years to complete. Much better for them to be able to select their accommodation as they require it from among a number of buildings which may all be ready for letting within a reasonably short time. On the other hand if the development company produces a building to the requirements of one specific organisation, the pressure of demand on that building is low, and alternative tenants, if required, may be hard to come by. The development company prefers to produce a building which is potentially suitable for a wide range of occupants, though in the Central Area, and particularly in the City, where certain types of business are grouped together, the developer will probably have a particular type of business in mind as his market.

Of course, there are some organisations, particularly government organisations, public bodies, and certain specialised departments of large firms, which require unusual 'built in' features in their accommodation, and these have to be catered for. In many instances, however, such bodies prefer to take a completed building or unit and to have it altered than to commission an entirely new building. On other occasions, these special requirements are met by adapting a half-completed building, when enough has been built for the potential occupant to decide whether he likes the building, and when subtle alterations to the internal details can accommodate particular departments. The new Scotland Yard building, off Victoria Street, was an example of this practice.

It is difficult to say exactly how much new office accommodation is built by potential occupants and how much is built by specialist development companies; and how much is built for a particular tenant in mind and how much is purely speculative. Today it is unlikely that more than 15–20% of all new accommodation is built by potential occupants, and the actual figure may be much lower than this. Of the remainder built by specialist development companies, only a very small proportion is purpose built. The great majority of all new office buildings in London (possibly as much as three-quarters) is speculative development by property companies.

As we have already seen, an important and unusual characteristic of the office development industry is the fact that the products are let rather than sold. Normally, average sized or small units of accommodation are let for periods of 21 or 42 years, with rent revision clauses after every seven or 14 years. Under this sort of arrangement the development company will be responsible for the upkeep and management of the building. Larger units, such as entire street blocks, may be let for rather longer periods, and are more likely to be subject to an arrangement where the tenant is responsible for the upkeep. Large organisations often prefer to take entire buildings under this arrangement, even when they do not require so much accommodation immediately, because they can always sub-let small units for short periods, and this will give them room to expand later.

Only on very rare occasions, however, will the property company contemplate selling the freehold of a new building rather than letting it. Not only is a steady annual income preferable to a quick, lump-sum profit, but the capital assets of the property under its ownership are the main instrument by which the company raises any large purchasing funds that may be required in the future. The main exception to this is when a small development company raises its initial capital by short-term credit, and then needs to sell the freehold of the developed property in order to pay off debt. In any case, organisations prefer to rent their office accommodation for a number of reasons. Firstly, if it is an industrial concern it can usually get a better return on its capital by investing in the product it manufactures than by investing in property, to which it is a comparative stranger. Secondly, a firm will often prefer to retain the freedom to move premises at quite frequent intervals, because it needs the most modern accommodation available, or because it is expanding rapidly, requiring extra space. There have even been cases of firms building their own premises, and then selling to a property company, because they have found that 'amateur' management of their own premises is more expensive than the normal rent which would be charged by a property company.

Conclusion

A number of important points about the office construction industry seem to emerge from this brief survey.

Although the unique nature of each product prohibits mass production, some economies have been achieved by building large blocks which contain many units of accommodation, where previously each unit had been provided separately.

Public control over the industry has put an end to simple 'building replacement' and now demands that all redevelopment shall be on the 'street block' scale.

The scale of redevelopment called for in cities today demands a specialist industry which can cope efficiently with the scale of investment this involves.

The property companies have a dual function of producing and managing office accommodation, though the latter is a more important function to some than it is to others.

The actual production of accommodation is carried out by a team of specialists commissioned by the development company, and the company has the role of chairman in this team.

The main resources problem is that of acquiring sites, not because these are unavailable, but because the units of ownership are much smaller than the units of development, and existing owners require a benefit from development, either through a share participation or through an inflated price for their interests.

This problem, plus the need to satisfy existing leases and sub-leases, has substantially extended the time required to carry through a development.

Since property is always an assured investment, finance is not a great problem for development companies, though more recently the trend in which the main investors (insurance firms and pension funds) have sought more equity participation has cut into the development companies' profits.

It also appears to suit most users if accommodation is leased rather than bought. This is rather an academic argument, when accommodation is very rarely available on anything other than a lease, and it is usually too expensive for firms to build their own.

Over the past two decades, when the amount and scale of development work in London has increased greatly, the industry has rapidly become highly specialised and departmentalised, with an increasing number of firms dealing in one small stage of the overall process. This disintegration is normally a sign of great confidence within an industry, but it necessarily makes these small firms and departments highly sensitive to any abrupt slackening of demand. If there are further restrictions on developments, there is likely to be a period of integration in the industry.

Chapter VI
The Legislative Background to Controls of Office Development in London since 1939

Previous chapters have dealt with some of the 'actors' in the urban scene—the providers and occupiers of office space. We have seen something of their behaviour, both in aggregate and in a few individual cases. We must now consider the framework within which these firms and individuals operate. A most important part of this framework consists in the rules of the game—the controls and laws which govern the process of providing office space, and which indirectly affect the decisions of occupiers of this space. There has grown up in Britain a most elaborate system of planning legislation, and the growth of London and the south-east has been one of the main foci of controls. This chapter tells the story of the evolution of this framework. It is divided into two sections. The first describes planning policy in London during and immediately after the war, and the basic legislation enacted to put policy into practice. The second part discusses planning in London since then, and the changes that have been made to the original plans and controls.

First of all it is necessary to make clear what we mean by 'controls', and to say a little about their nature. Public controls on private development can be divided into three categories. First there are controls on the *form* of the building, usually aimed at safeguarding the health and welfare of the people working in or around it. Second, there are controls on the *location and size* of the building, protecting existing uses and avoiding too great a concentration either of workers or of concrete. Third, there are various indirect controls, when a public authority makes some *adjustment to market forces,* though leaving the individual free to choose whether or not he takes advantage of the adjustment.

The division between these three categories is blurred, but the distinction is useful because the effects of each are somewhat different.

Controls on the form of buildings have been in operation for centuries. In London the first controls came in the twelfth and thirteenth centuries, when legislation was passed relating to the width of streets, the provision of sewers and the restriction of smoke-producing fuels. Since then a host of controls have been set on the sanitary arrangements of buildings, on precautions against fire and the need for fire escapes, on daylighting, and many similar social problems. By 1939 the practice of operating such controls was seldom opposed, since, in the great majority of cases, they affect all buildings, all sites, and all intending developers to the same extent. The additional expense of complying with such controls can be absorbed in rent or in selling price, without affecting the position of the development *vis-à-vis* its competitors, since they, too, will have to comply with the same controls applied in the same degree.

Controls of the second category were new in 1939, and were hotly opposed by influential sectors of the community. The Town and Country Planning Act of 1932 had empowered local authorities (county districts) to draw up simple zoning plans as a framework for controlling development, but for various reasons these were virtually impossible to put into effect. The system was optional, both on local authorities and on developers, who were not required to apply for planning permission. As Cullingworth (1964) says, 'all too often, developers preferred to take a chance that no scheme would ever come into force, or that if it did no local authority would face pulling down existing buildings'. Local authorities themselves were too small to have other than local interests, and would seldom entertain the idea of refusing permission for any employment-giving enterprise, and there was no central authority or guide to counteract this pattern. Planning refusals were likely to involve local authorities in compensation payments they could ill afford, so that one way and another the whole system was reduced to impotence.

The 1930's had seen attempts by the government to counter undesirable market forces, with some success, largely through the Special Areas Act of 1934. This designated a number of special depressed areas, and *inter alia*, made provisions for government aid to firms prepared to set up factories or plants there. A Commissioner for the Special Areas was appointed, but although some £21 million was spent in the scheme by

1938, largely on the improvement of local infrastructure and amenity, very little completely new industry had been attracted. This sort of system has appeals to the private developer, and, when applied to production industry, has the great advantage that it encourages rather than restricts growth. The main disadvantage arises from the strain on public economy. If applied effectively, it inevitably involves some levy on another sector or region in the economy.

The Development of the Planning Structure

The first step in the formulation of a policy for planning controls in London came with the publication of the Royal Commission on the Distribution of the Industrial Population, the 'Barlow Report' in 1939. The Barlow Commission was requested to 'inquire into the causes which have influenced the present geographical distribution of the industrial population, and the probable direction of any change in the future; to consider what social, economic or strategical disadvantages arise from the concentration of industries in large towns or in particular areas of the country; and to report what remedial measures should be taken in the national interest'. Its real value lay not in the remedial measures it proposed, but in its analysis of the causes and disadvantages of industrial concentration. Broadly it defined three problems: first, that of improving living conditions in the major urban areas; second, that of improving the economic organisation of the London Region; and third, that of national planning concerned largely with the maintenance of full employment and the prevention of regional economic depression. The report proposed re-development of sub-standard housing, reinforcement to the control of 'suburban sprawl' and minimum standards for recreational and other open space. All these required some reduction of population density, and eventually a reduction in population of the conurbation.

The national problem was the uneven distribution of specific industries. In pre-war years, the London and Birmingham regions had attracted a dominant proportion of growth industries (vehicles, plastics, electrical goods, light engineering, etc.) which had failed to offset the contraction of older industries (mainly ship-building, coal, ironworking and—in other regions—textiles). In order to prevent repetition of widespread unemployment in these regions, it was necessary to direct a high proportion of growth industries to them, and this involved a restriction on the attractiveness of the South East and the Midlands.

Plate 3
Late Regency terraces housing a variety of offices: general view of the west side of Fitzroy Square.

Plate 4
Diversity of offices housed in one building: nameplates in doorway of 24 Fitzroy Square. One space is vacant.

In setting out the problems, and enquiring into their causes, the report outlined a strategy for tackling them. The main points of the majority report were as follows.

1. 'National action' was necessary, involving a 'Central Authority whose activities should be distinct from and should extend beyond those within the powers of any existing government department.'

2. 'Continued and further re-development of congested urban areas.'

3. 'Decentralisation and dispersal both of industry and industrial population from such areas.'

4. 'Encouragement of a reasonable balance of industrial development so far as possible throughout the various regions . . . coupled with appropriate diversification of industry in each.'

5. The Central Authority should be either 'advisory or executive' and should 'formulate a policy . . . in relation to decentralisation or dispersal from congested urban areas.'

Three members of the commission (including Sir Patrick Abercrombie) did not sign the majority report, and submitted instead their proposals, in which the most significant departure was in the form and powers of the Central Authority. They felt that 'action implies the existence of a body with wide executive powers and failing such a body, no means exist for translating words into deeds', and later that the 'new Ministry (should be) charged with control over the location of industry and territorial planning on a national scale'.

As a result three advisory plans were prepared, one for the County of London, one for the Greater London Region, and one for the City of London. These were to provide the tactics for putting the 'Barlow strategy' into practice.

The County of London Plan and the Greater London Plan were both prepared by Sir Patrick Abercrombie (the former one with J. H. Forshaw) and appeared in 1943 and 1944 respectively.

At the outset a number of assumptions were made, which provided the framework around which the plans were built. Although not spelt out in exactly this form, these assumptions were:

1. That the recommendation contained in the Barlow Report, that 'no new industry shall be admitted to London and the Home Counties, except in special cases', would be accepted by the government;

2. 'that new powers for planning would be available, including powers for the control of land values' and including powers for the control of new development;

3. 'that as a result of the Barlow recommendations, and in consonance with the national trends, the total population of the area would not increase, but on the contrary, would be somewhat reduced;

4. 'that the Port of London would continue to be one of the world's great ports.'

The validity of the plans is clearly very much affected by the validity of these assumptions and there is one point at which they have proved to be very wide of the mark. Population growth had tended to slow down in the pre-war years and there was a widespread belief among demographers such as Carr Saunders (1935) that many developed countries were rapidly approaching a point of population stability, after which there would tend to be reductions rather than increases in the total population. Population projections on which both the Barlow Report and the Abercrombie Plans were based tended to assume that this point would have been reached by 1970, when the total for England and Wales would have fallen to just below the 1937 figure. Another projection, calculated on a different basis, forecast a population for 1970 nearly 8 million (15%) below that for 1937.

Thus the plans assumed that without large-scale migration, the population of the Greater London Region would remain stable, and as a result, employment too would not increase.

Within this framework of demographic and economic stability, the problem was to redistribute the population in better living conditions, and to disperse industry to achieve a better balance between and within regions. The advisory plans were plans for London within a stable Britain; yet the post-war years have seen increasingly rapid rates of population growth, accompanied by an expanding economy and increasing employment. Because of this it is tempting to dismiss the advisory plans as well-thought-out and well-produced exercises, which were nevertheless inapplicable, being falsely based. It would be wrong to reject them. First, national and local governments have not rejected them, but have based their policies firmly on these plans; and second, the assumption that the population of the Greater London Region would not increase above its 1938 level has become an objective of planning in the area, so that, in this respect, at least, it has been a case of changing the circumstances to suit the Greater London plans, rather than changing the plans to suit the circumstances. Abercrombie proposed to allow London to absorb all the growth that he foresaw, but to channel it along defined lines within London. This is emphasised by the criticism the plans received from Purdom (1945), who said 'that London contains too many people is something the authors admit by implication, but not explicitly . . . it would have been better for their plan had they acknowledged the fact which is known to everybody, of London's over-population.'

The major features of the plan were concerned with maintaining the form of London as it had evolved, but providing for an efficient urban organisation within that form, and within congenial surroundings. None of the proposals could really have been termed radical, although the idea of applying them all together in one big master-plan for an urban region of 10 million was new.

The dominant feature of the plans was the arrangement for redistribution of population. For this purpose the Greater London Region was conceived in terms of three concentric rings, an inner ring (including the County of London as constituted in 1944) of declining population, a middle (suburban) ring of static population and an outer ring of expanding population. Maximum densities were set over the whole area, providing, as Foley (1963) puts it, 'a simple-concentric ring pattern of residential densities with a low plateau in the centre, falling off to much lower densities in most of the suburban areas'. Such densities in the congested parts of the inner ring involved the decentralisation of about 1¼ million people.

The increases in the outer ring, which was to receive the great majority of these 1¼ million were to be provided for in 'planned' developments only, mainly by new towns and the expansion of existing industrial towns, as recommended in the Barlow Report. A Green Belt around the limits of the middle belt of static population was to control the spread of 'unplanned' development in this country ring. In this framework of maximum residential densities the plan provided for a great increase in open space, for comprehensive schemes by local authorities, and for integral 'neighbourhood' planning.

Much of the remainder of the plans was concerned with traffic improvements, or (in the case of the County of London Plan) with zoning.

The pattern of road routes was dominated by two ring roads (one around the central area and one around the edge of the then built-up area) together with a series of radicals of a rather higher standard outside the outer ring. The zoning schemes were broadly based and paid a great deal of respect to the *status quo*, although they involved a number of long-term changes. The schemes formed the basis for the County of London development plan which appeared in 1951.

In many respects the plans were a tremendous tribute to London as it then existed. The monocentric form of London was emphasised, both by traffic proposals which orientated the whole region towards the Central Area and by density proposals which restricted the power of suburban service centres to grow, because the size of the population they served was restricted. The new town and town expansion proposals did not involve the creation of competing centres, because they were small, and there were no proposals for suburban new towns. The formulators of the plan were aware that many of London's problems came from its monocentric form, which necessarily involves concentration both of the traffic generating forces and of investment. Why, therefore, did the plan give so little consideration to the idea of major competing centres in or near Greater London? The answer is once again that the plan was essentially for a stable London, and the authors felt that it was possible to deal with the problems associated with population and activity levels of 1943 by the conventional means of central redevelopment—new towns, a green belt to control lateral spread, and density maximums to control concentration. Indeed the creation of competing centres was hardly practicable in view of the fact that there was to be little new growth. This was, perhaps, the most serious consequence of the false population projections on which the plans were based, and it is possible that, if Abercrombie had been aware of the economic expansion that was to follow the war, the plans would have looked different.

Although the plans were not immediately accepted by the L.C.C., a number of the major points were taken, and in 1945 the Council approved the essence of the traffic proposals, the setting of standards for maximum densities and for open space, and the broad proposals relating to industrial location.

Subsequent approval was given, by the newly formed Ministry of Town and Country Planning and by the government. It was then a matter of devising legislative measures to make these and other plans work.

The series of Acts from 1943 to 1952 built up a structure of interrelated and inter-dependent government activity. Where previously these measures had been isolated, they now derived strength from their inter-dependence.

The first official legislation was the Ministry of Town and Country Planning Act of 1943. Ever since the 1919 Act, which had provided the means for development control by local authorities, day to day central control of town planning schemes had been carried out by the Ministry of Health, while, during the war, advisory or executive functions associated with town planning had gradually been accumulated by various other government departments. This Act created a Minister and a Ministry which would eventually group these activities under one umbrella, although the detailed workings of the new Ministry were left to be decided later.

Many of the functions were first set out in the Town and Country Planning Act of 1944. It re-emphasised most of the provisions of the 1932 Act, particularly that all development was subject to planning permission. It also introduced financial measures to ensure that the provisions were more effective than they had been during the 1930's. A development charge of 80% of the difference between the value of the property with a planning permission and that with a refusal was introduced, and compensation for a refusal was now to be payable on any loss of value since 31st March 1939. The Act also gave local authorities greater powers to purchase war-damaged or obsolete property for redevelopment, and provided Exchequer assistance.

In 1945 the Distribution of Industries Act was passed more or less following the recommendations of the Barlow Report. The first part of this Act gave the government (and in particular the Board of Trade) powers in the Development Areas similar to those which had been in operation from the Special Areas Acts of the 1930's, including powers to construct factories, to make loans to firms, to make compulsory purchase of land and to improve infrastructure and basic services. The second part required industrialists to register the location of any new building over 10,000 sq. ft., and originally included a clause giving the government powers to ban industry in the London area, though the latter was subsequently withdrawn.

The New Towns Act of 1946 was based on the report of the Reith Committee on New Towns, and provided for the setting up of development corporations for these. The Act outlined the difficult distinction of functions and powers between these development corporations and the existing local authorities. The former were to be financed and appointed by the Ministry of Town and Country Planning which, therefore, retained control over general policy and problems of individual new towns.

In 1946 a second Act made the process of compulsory acquisition easier, reducing the time involved in view of the increasingly heavy use which was being made of this procedure.

Thus by the beginning of 1947 an impressive volume of legislation had taken effect, largely based on the recommendations of the Barlow Report and the more detailed proposals contained in advisory plans such as those prepared for London by Professor Abercrombie. A 'Central Authority' with executive, rather than advisory powers had been created, headed by a Minister of Cabinet rank, and some of the cumbersome arrangements for inter-departmental co-operation which had existed before the war were now redundant. The optional nature of much of pre-war planning had been abolished by the temporary 1944 Act, as had the unmanageable financial provisions relating to compensation. Further recognition was given to the need for governmental control over the location of industry and for governmental interference in the powers of attraction of the various regions. Progressively easier powers of compulsory purchase were intended to implement recommendations for public reconstruction and redevelopment, particularly in the central areas of towns and large conurbations. Lastly, the government had taken powers to build new towns, and in December 1946 the first corporation (that of Stevenage) was appointed. This was followed within the next eight months by five others, Crawley, Hemel Hempstead, Harlow, Newton Aycliffe and East Kilbride.

Thus the Town and Country Planning Act of 1947 came with a firm basis of accepted legislation and containing the majority of the points on which planning policy after the war was to be based. The main function of this massive document was to relate this legislation to the central theme of post-war policy, to fill in the gaps to provide a comprehensive 'handbook' for town planning procedure.

It introduced four further measures. The first of these detailed the procedure under which local authorities would consider applications for planning permission. All local planning authorities were instructed to prepare development plans, consisting of zoning maps, programme maps (concerned largely with proposed local authority development or redevelopment), and a written statement of policy. Permission was to be granted or refused, depending on whether the proposed development conformed with these plans. Development plans were to be revised every five years, and it was intended that this review should be a continuous process. The Ministry would be responsible for the final approval of plans. This ensured that the plans would be 'consistent with the national interest'. It also had powers to deal with appeals against planning refusals or conditions the Ministry attached to a permission, and to deal with particular applications in which national policy was affected. Development control was now obligatory on all local planning authorities.

The second major innovation of the 1947 Act was the substitution of County Districts as local planning authorities by Counties and County Boroughs. Although clearly a step in the right direction, this was one of the least satisfactory elements of the 1947 Act, because it left many problems unaffected. The radical proposals of the 1944 Boundary Commission, which recommended an entirely new, three-tier system of local government, had not been accepted and this left the government very little alternative. This provision allowed little scope for regional planning, and in no way related the planning authorities with many of the public services and utilities, which thus had to be treated in the same way as non-public bodies. A specific advantage of the change, however, was a reduction of some 90%—145 compared with 1,441—in the total number of planning authorities.

The 1947 Act extended the powers of the government over industrial location, going further than the 1945 Act. A system of Industrial Development Certificates (I.D.C.'s) was to be administered by the Board of Trade, in which an industrialist wishing to build a new factory (or an extension to an existing factory) involving 5,000 sq. ft. or more additional floorspace had first to apply for an I.D.C. from the Board of Trade.

Lastly, the government proposed to clear up once and for all the problems of compensation and betterment which had plagued attempts to control development in areas characterised by a high concentration of capital investment and high value property. The proposal was to tax all increases in the value of property accruing from planning measures (all property was now subject to planning control) and to pay a lump sum in compensation to the owners of all property whose value had fallen as a result of planning measures. Compensation was to be paid from a central fund of £300 million, and when the fund had been completely used no further compensation was payable.

The main results of the 1947 Act were to complete the nationalisation of the *right* to develop land and to complete public control of the land values associated with development or the potential for development. Apart from having public control over land use and land values, the state was now in a position to build new towns, and to designate green belts. Through the I.D.C. scheme, central government had control over the location of new industry, which could be banned from the London region. Finally it was hoped that as the state was to have control over land values, fiscal measures to attract industry and employment to the depressed regions would have a more marked effect.

Planning powers were now split between the various tiers of government. The lowest tier—urban and rural districts and boroughs—were shorn of their powers of development control, and were to do only what was delegated by the county authorities. In London, where the boroughs were large, this delegation was sometimes considerable, but elsewhere this was not the case. These lowest-tier authorities were development agencies in their own right, producing schemes for housing and local services so that development control was not divorced from state-planned development. The main responsibility for day to day development control fell on the middle-tier authorities, the counties and county boroughs. Except in the special case of industrial development, these authorities carried out the planning application procedure within the framework of a development plan which they had prepared.

The highest tier, the national government, had a much more important say in the preparation of plans, and could impose aspects of national policy (green belts, transport improvement etc.) on the development plans as well as ensuring that the more local aspects were 'in the national interest'. Less satisfactory was the fact that since there was no statutory basis for regional planning, it was now up to the central authority to carry this out, or organise voluntary co-operation between county authorities. Finally, the functions of the central government with regard to town planning were spread out among departments; the Ministry of Town and Country Planning was responsible for the mechanics of development control, the Board of Trade for the administration of the I.D.C. scheme, the Ministry of Transport for new major road construction and for general transport policy, the Ministry of Health for housing construction, the Ministry of Works for government and public construction, and various other Ministries for such building as schools, universities, hospitals and so on.

Two further acts can be included under the heading of 'basic legislation'. The National Parks and Access to the Countryside Act of 1949, set up the National Parks Commission—a purely advisory body—and outlined the distinction between its functions and those of the departments of the local authorities which were to co-operate in administering the National Parks and 'areas of outstanding natural beauty'. This act also allowed planning permission to be conditional on the provision of trees, green spaces, etc. thus introducing the element of landscaping into the process of development control. The Town Development Act of 1952 was left until this date because, as Cullingworth (1964) puts it, 'it was contrary to the facts of potential life to expect local authorities to build houses for families from other areas, while they still had severe housing problems of their own'.

The expansion of existing towns was to be carried out by the existing local authority, rather than by development corporations, and was to be essentially an agreement between this and the exporting authority, rather than an imposition from above. Subsidy both from the treasury and from the exporting authority was to be available for expanding towns.

Financial Problems

The kind of restrictions that the 1947 Act brought into practice play havoc with the existing patterns of land values, and with the profit margins of development companies and property owners. Property values have two essential components; a *use value*, determined by the existing use to which the property is being put, and a *development value*, determined by the property's potential for development for a new, more profitable use. It is only very rarely that controls on the form of the building affect these values, so that before the war they were largely determined by market forces. On the other hand *zoning* and *development* control have a very dominant effect on the development values of property. Many lose the major component in their value by the planning process, while other sites, where development plans allow high-value development, will have values augmented because of scarcity elsewhere. Understandably the property owner who suffers a loss from this system feels entitled to claim compensation from the state, while the state itself feels equally entitled to recoup other property owners' gains due to planning measures, as Parker (1959) says, 'partly in order to reduce the charge on the public purse, but partly also as a matter of equity'. Unless planning controls restrict the total amount of development, then property owners' gains and losses ought to be approximately equal, and it is merely the task of the state to redistribute the values to offset the effect of planning control on the individual owner.

In practice this is less easy than it sounds, and the main problems arise from the phenomenon of 'floating values'. When a particular development is expected in a locality, all potentially suitable sites attract a certain development value. Once the development actually takes place, the development value 'crystallises' on the site chosen and the other sites which had seemed potentially suitable then lose the 'floating value' attached to them. If, through planning controls, the development is prohibited, these floating values are frozen, and since the development will not now take place, all property owners feel entitled to seek compensation for the prohibition of a development which might have taken place on their property. The claims of the owners, according to Parker (1959), *in toto* tend 'to exceed the true amount of the development value that would have crystallised through an inherent tendency to optimism amongst speculators'. Therefore it would be neither just nor practical for the state to pay these in full.

A second problem is that of 'shifting values', which relates to the fact that if development is refused in one locality it will probably take place elsewhere. In this case the development values are not lost but merely shifted from one site to another. A number of problems arise out of this, including the fact that the development which is refused by one planning authority may be finally approved by a different one. Thus if local planning authorities were to be responsible for compensation (the otherwise obvious course), one might be liable for compensation, while another was recouping betterment for the same development. Further, if the effect of planning control is to allow some development to crystallise on sites which formerly had some floating value for that development, and to cause other development to shift to sites which formerly had no floating value, is it fair to tax both increases in value at the same rate?

Up to 1947, the right of the property owner to seek compensation for loss of value consequent on a planning refusal had never been seriously challenged. After all, the property owner may have bought the land at an inflated price due to the possibility of development there in the future. But for the state to be in a position to pay such compensation, it would clearly be necessary to tax at least those increases in value that come about directly from planning restrictions elsewhere. But previous experience with the collection of betterment had not been encouraging. The Acts of 1909 and 1932 had provided for the taxing of 50% (75% in the later Act) of all increases in property values as a result of planning schemes. In practice it had proved impossible to determine how much of the increases in value had arisen directly from planning measures, and how much was due to other causes, so that the 1932 Act introduced a clause deferring payment until the increased value had actually been realised. So cumbersome and ineffective was the legislation that in only three cases was betterment actually paid under these acts. If the betterment tax was ineffective, therefore, local authorities were hardly to be in a position to pay compensation for refusals, so that the whole planning was virtually nullified. This was the crux of the financial problem the government faced if it was to make the 1947 planning measures effective. The planning authorities had to be financially strong enough to pay out any compensation that, in the interests of equity, was necessary, and this involved effective recouping of some, if not all, betterment.

The report of the Expert Committee on Compensation and Betterment, known as the Uthwatt Report (1942) was commissioned, as a result of the recommendations of the Barlow Commission, to look into the whole problem of compensation and betterment. Drawing the distinction between the different use values, the report concluded that if the *right* of development was now nationalised, and the state was thus responsible for increases and decreases in development values, then these too should logically be nationalised.

The major part of the recommendations of this report was, therefore, concerned with two things, (a) how the change-over to partial state ownership could be achieved without causing the individual property owner an immediate loss on his value, and (b) how the new system could be reconciled with those market forces which would continue to operate.

In practice the report recommended the division of all land in the country into three categories, developed land, undeveloped land and dead-ripe land. In the terms used above, these three categories may be described as (a) land with a low use value, and a low development value largely consisting of floating value, (b) land with a high use value and little or no development value, and (c) land with low or moderate use value and a high 'crystallised' development value. The solutions recommended for the three categories were briefly as follows.

(a) Undeveloped land included nearly all the land that had not yet been built on, and the right to develop it, along with any development values it might attract, was to be vested in the state. Any compensation for loss of floating value that the land might have had at the time of the enactment, was to be paid on a once-and-for-all basis, and was to be paid at the actual rather than the inflated value. When this category of land was needed for development, it was to be compulsorily acquired by the state at its existing use-value, and then re-leased to a developer at the new value.

(b) The second category of land was relatively stable because high existing use values made the land less likely to be developed (or redeveloped) in the near future. As the stock of buildings deteriorated, however, this existing use value would fall, and it would attract a certain development value. In this case, therefore, the total value fluctuated much less than the individual components of this value, so that here the report recommended that the total value was to be fixed at its market value at the time of the enactment, and, when required for redevelopment, it was to be compulsorily acquired at this price. In this category development values existing at the time of the enactment were to be compensated in full, but this was thought to be just since these development values largely referred to replacement of existing use, and were thus explicit, containing no floating values.

(c) For land of the third category, dead-ripe land, development plans had already been prepared, so that the nature and value of the proposed development was known. The value was 'crystallised' although the actual development had not yet taken place. Here the report recommended the paying of full compensation for loss of this development, and so that this compensation burden should not fall unequally on the local authorities concerned, this was to be paid from a separate fund. Finally the report recommeded a betterment levy for properties affected by other developments. It is, of course, not only those sites actually developed but also adjacent and dependent properties which gain additional values as a result of a planning action, and so all properties were to be assigned a datum value in 1947 which was to be reviewed every five years; the annual increment in those five years was then to be taxed at the rate of 75% in the following five years.

The Uthwatt solution to the problems of compensation and betterment was logical in that it recognised the difference between development values which had already crystallised on certain sites, and other development values which were inflated due to a large 'floating' component. Secondly it recognised that the compensation problem for the nationalisation of development rights was a once-and-for-all problem affecting only one generation of property owners, and accordingly proposed a once-and-for-all solution. Betterment was to be collected by the simple process of buying at the old price and then re-leasing at the new, or, in properties not actually developed themselves, by taxing 75% of the increase in total value.

The recommendations, however, proved unacceptable to the government of the day, partly for practical and partly for ideological reasons. In the first place the task of dividing all land in the country into three categories was clearly enormous, and although largely a once-and-for-all task, it was tailor-made to secure the objection of a vast number of interested parties. The proposed solution for the two of the categories too, it will be noted, ensured the 'creeping nationalisation of urban land' through the process of compulsory purchase and re-leasing, and this was a step the government was unable or unwilling to take. Accordingly, the financial provisions of the 1947 Act were based on the analysis and the principles contained in the Uthwatt Report, but were very different in practice, and contained a number of obvious faults.

The basis of these provisions was in the Uthwatt proposals for *one* of the categories, undeveloped land. But the 1947 Act applied the proposals to *all* of the categories, and made one important change in them. All development rights and all development values were to belong to the state, but the latter were to be recoverable not by the process of buying and re-leasing, as in the Uthwatt proposals, but by a development charge. This charge was to equal the difference between the old, restricted use value, and the new, permitted use value, and was to be payable when planning permission was granted. The principle that land owners were entitled to compensation for the loss of real development values was not accepted by the government completely, and instead, such compensation that was to be paid was to take account as much of the effect of the loss on the individual's resources as of the total value of the loss; in short, preference was to be given to cases where the loss was likely to induce hardship. The grand total of compensation to be paid out under this scheme was to be £300 million, and this fund was to be administered by the newly constituted Central Land Board. Lastly the idea of the betterment levy was also dropped by the government, partly perhaps for the practical reason that it would have involved a great deal of valuation work (though perhaps no more than is at present necessary for rate collection), and partly perhaps because it was inherent in the other provisions for collecting betterment (the development charge) that betterment was to be collected only when it was actually realised. There was an element of compromise in these provisions; compromise between, on the one hand, the property owners and speculators and their champions in the political sphere, and on the other, the warnings of the reports and plans which had been produce by the Barlow Commission, the Uthwatt Committee and others, emphasising that nothing would be possible without planning control, backed up by effective fiscal measures. On one important point these conflicting pressures managed to destroy the workings of the Act. In the Uthwatt proposals the fact that government fiscal measures would play havoc with the existing patterns of supply and demand for land did not matter. As Parker (1959) says, 'existing patterns of supply and demand for land did not matter, because there was to be no conflict between the collection of betterment and the operation of the market mechanism because the market was not relied upon to work on the supply side. When the land was wanted the local authority simply acquired it'. By rejecting the Uthwatt proposals for compulsory acquisition whenever land was needed for redevelopment, the government was reverting to just such a reliance on market forces. The property owner now had no incentive to sell to the developer because the price he could now get would be no greater than the existing use value. Thus the Act put a brake on the whole process of development at a time when a great deal of reconstruction and redevelopment was needed. This has always been the major criticism of the 1947 Act, and many of the changes that have since been made to it were directed specifically at this fault.

In spite of these criticisms, however, it would certainly be true to say that the 'great plan' for development control inherent in the Act itself, was never really given a chance to work, for it was only in operation for less than five years of abnormal economic conditions before subsequent governments began to erode some of its major features.

The Development of Controls since 1951

This chapter has concentrated upon the background of planning legislation, against which the growth and development of offices took place. For until 1951 the development of offices was not seen as a major problem, and their increase was not regarded as separate from many other land uses.

The official interpretation of the economic problems of London has slowly changed since 1951. Uneven distribution of 'growth' industry in the country is still looked on as dangerous, leaving some peripheral regions precariously subject to local depression. But it is the growth of office accommodation which poses the greatest threat, strangling London's public transport system, and threatening to banish from the central area all those other uses which cannot compete on capital investment terms. The basic planning machinery, pieced together in the 1940's, was never drawn up with this particular problem in mind. Further, the problem was peculiar to one area, Greater London, so that there was less need for standardisation of the practice for dealing with offices than in the case of industry, where the problems were nation wide. The development of controls on offices since 1951 has been fairly independent of other developments, both in changes to national planning policy and in amendments to the 1947 Act.

Briefly, the period since 1951 can be divided into four phases. In the first—up to about 1954—the abnormal economic conditions which followed the war in Britain dominated new office building in London, although the effects were accentuated by the financial provisions of the 1947 Act which discouraged selling land to developers. It was under these conditions that the 1951 L.C.C. Development Plan was drawn up. The second phase, lasting only two or three years, followed the repeal of part of the 1947 Act, and a return to more 'normal' economic conditions. It was characterised by a sudden office boom. The third phase followed from 1956 onwards in which the L.C.C. took strong measures to restrict the growth of offices within the existing legislation, holding the total permitted floorspace to about 4 million sq. ft. per annum, but gradually reducing the proportion of this which was new (as opposed to replacement) building. In the last phase, starting about 1963, the central government has begun to pass a series of legislative measures specifically directed at office development, culminating in the total ban of 1965. These phases are dealt with in some detail in the next chapter, and we will not dwell on them here. We can, nevertheless, make out a few of the main issues which have been involved in the control of office development in London since the war. As we shall see, these issues go beyond the immediate task of controlling office growth, and pose problems which one bound up with the future of the nation as a whole.

Conclusion

Recent developments in the control of office growth refocused attention on two most fundamental issues; first, the amount of containment applicable to central area offices under the sort of economic conditions Britain has experienced since the war, and second, the amount of state interference in the finance of valuable city centre development acceptable in a society which still puts its faith in private enterprise as the main element in economic development.

Although the South-East Study of 1964 reappraised the projections for economic and population growth which had been used for the London Advisory Plans, it did not reconsider the policy of these plans in all its aspects. It did not discuss in any detail the merits of attempting to restrain the economic growth of the London region in the light of these projections. As Westergaard (1964) says, 'The need for a rational reappraisal of inherited assumptions should not be obscured by a belief that abandonment of some traditional "anti-megalopolitan" formulations of planning aims must mean the abandonment of planning or by a suspicion . . . that a revision of urban ideals can only be inspired by *laissez-faire* inclinations.' Satisfactory economic growth of London involves a great deal more planning than the mere imposition of minimum controls and the use of restrictions that have been in operation since the war. In many respects we abandoned planning when we accepted the idea of containment and the Abercrombie proposals of 1944. These said in effect, that there was nothing wrong with London, except that it needed polishing up in a few places and contained rather too many people. This would have worked if economic conditions had remained stable; but they did not, with the result that industry, the government economic departments and the rest of the country generally have been planning for growth while London has been planning against growth. Perhaps the most unsatisfying thing has been the failure to fit into any plan—or even policy—for national economic growth. The Central London office function is one of the keys to economic growth in Britain; its financial and banking sectors provide the bulk of our 'invisible' exports, while the prestige commercial offices of the West End are the headquarters of the marketing, advertising and after-sales services which are so vital in competing for industrial and service orders both at home and abroad. If Britain joins the Common Market these functions will have to expand many times. Yet growth in this sector is being stunted, surely without adequate knowledge of the effects, particularly on the peripheral industrial regions of the country which we have been so keen to protect.

The principle of containment in London as originally conceived by Barlow and Abercrombie in the 1930's and 1940's was part of a nation-wide plan. Amid conditions of economic and demographic stability, London threatened to grow, taking people and activity away from peripheral regions. If those regions were to be protected then London's capacity to harm them had to be curtailed. London has continued to grow, and it has to some extent absorbed activity from other areas, but because there has been rapid economic growth, these other regions have also been protected from depression and to some extent from unemployment.

But should we check this centralisation of economic life, if its effects on peripheral regions can be dealt with another way? If the Barlow Report had been commissioned in 1839 instead of 1939, it might well have concluded that the concentration of manufacturing into large-scale operations involving the breakdown of the cottage industries 'was a social and economic problem demanding immediate attention'. Yet this change to large-scale operations was not inherently evil. Its side effects on housing, health and congestion were what was wrong. The same is true of the concentration of office work in the London area; the problem is that we have yet to adapt our way of city life to accommodate them. This is not to say that we should return to *laissez faire*, allowing Soho, Hampstead and the 'precincts' of the central area to be built over with offices, or allowing residential accommodation to be converted wholesale to commercial use, but we should make provision for office growth, either in London, or somewhere where facilities can be made comparable. After all, the economies of the 'industrial' regions depend on their products being efficiently marketed, their organisation being efficiently run, and their firms being properly advertised. If, as appears to be the case, no other location can accommodate these functions as efficiently as London, then we must allow them to grow there, or we must provide a reasonable alternative which certainly does not at present exist.

Recent developments in the financial aspects of planning controls have emphasised the reluctance with which lasting changes are made. The net effect of a series of major financial planning acts in 1944, 1947, 1952, 1954, 1959 and 1965 has been to make a series of tests as to what is the minimum state of interference in property values which will allow effective development control, and what is the maximum interference that public opinion will allow. Finally in 1965, we returned to virtually the same (maximum) degree that we achieved in 1947. There is, however, one important departure in the more recent Act. One of the reasons the Uthwatt Report was originally rejected by the government in 1947, was that its proposals were open to the charge that they led to a complete land nationalisation. The 1965 Act, however, has produced a scheme very similar to the Uthwatt proposals, and in this case, with absolutely no safeguards against the 'creeping' nationalisation of land. This is the one place where the new Act goes further than its predecessor.

In other features, the degree of state control has tended to lessen, up to the publication of this Bill. In the Uthwatt Report, importance was attached to the connection between the different development values, and the point was made that, if the former were to be nationalised, then so should the latter. This was duly done in 1947. Within five years, however, they were denationalised, and, although the vesting of development rights in the state has evolved unquestioned from strength to strength, the state's control over land values gradually decreased up to 1964.

Nor have we accepted the right of the state to control the location of economic activity in a positive way. The initiative for the siting of private activity has to come from the developer or the proposed occupant; the state then either accepts the initiative or rejects it.

The positive contribution of the state towards locating activity is confined to an advisory rather than an executive function. It announces locations that will be encouraged to grow and those that will be discouraged; through bodies such as the L.O.B. and the information departments of the B.O.T., private entrepreneurs are advised where they can get state approval or even assistance, and where conditions will be made favourable by government interference. Other than in the case of nationalised industries, there is still no possibility of the state instructing the developer where to build—only where not to build.

One of the problems is that the whole process of town planning and development control has been something of a test in Britain's evolution from a free to a mixed economy. Where this has happened in other sectors of the economy, notably in the fields of industrial organisation, labour relations, and public transport, the state has always been at pains to demonstrate that the industrialist and the entrepreneur have a great deal to gain by public interference in their work, and the idea of 'partnership' between the state and the private industrialist has gained more than lip-service. In the field of city planning, however, this has not been the case. The property owner and the developer are looked on as enemies of the people, to be controlled, restricted, and finally banished from the central area. This is partly because the providers of accommodation in the central area are distinct from the users, and the state sees the speculator as an unnecessary middle-man in the process of urban development. Partly, perhaps, it is because the state cannot yet accept that offices, and the functions they provide, are an inherent part of the productive process—a non-acceptance implied in the Selective Employment Tax. Whatever the reason, it seems clear that the idea of a mixed economy in city development is not based on the idea of a partnership between the similar interests of the state and the entrepreneur, but on that of a balance between their conflicting interests.

Chapter VII
London's Growth and the Post-War Office Problem

Unlike the growth of most other things, the growth of London worries people. It seems to have given rise to dismay and concern for almost as long as it has been growing. We are no longer afraid of metropolitan growth bringing food shortages or the plague, and nobody seriously sees the City or even the G.L.C. as a real threat to Parliament or the Crown. Nevertheless, the source of current anxieties is still that London's size and growth are a *threat*, a threat both to London itself and to the rest of the country.

How real are these threats? What evidence is there that the constantly repeated fears have substance—that congestion will eventually bring London to a standstill, and that the metropolis will eventually drain the life-blood from the provinces? One piece of evidence against these convictions serves at least to put them into perspective; neither thing has yet happened, despite the fact that the warnings have been repeatedly given for a very long time. The traffic is still moving and the provinces are still alive. And it is surely doubtful that it is only the planners' restrictions that have prevented either of these catastrophes from taking place. They have obviously had some effect; precisely how much effect they have had is not known.

These fears about London's growth and influence may be to some extent exaggerated, but we are still a long way from answering the crucial question: what is the proper role of the metropolis, or the metropolitan region, in a small country like Britain, where the provincial cities are all within relatively easy reach of the capital? This question is basic to many others which are of current concern. How much of Central London's activity could be more efficiently carried on elsewhere? How wasteful of energy resources is the present travel to work pattern in the London region? How inefficient is the existing regional distribution of employment? Could regional centres contribute more to national growth if they had a larger share of those activities which are still mainly confined to London?

London's Growth

That growth causes chaos and congestion and that the chaos will get worse unless growth is restricted are views which are by no means confined to modern London. The argument was used to justify the latest of the official restrictions on London's growth—the 'Brown Ban' on office development—and also resulted in the green belt just after the war. But the same thesis was put forward as long as 400 years ago. In a Royal Proclamation issued by Elizabeth I in 1580, Her Majesty, perceiving that the daily increase of population in the City and suburbs was causing 'many inconveniences', judged that many even greater inconveniences were likely to follow if nothing was done to stop London spreading. She therefore imposed a ban on all development within 3 miles of the City gates. In the next century, under the Commonwealth, a law was passed prohibiting development within 10 miles of the City. By the time the green belt barricade was put up, the built-up area had extended far beyond these earlier limits, to over 20 miles from the centre of London. The 3-mile and the 10-mile limits had simply lapsed. The green belt did effectively stop further continuous spread, but its only influence on London's *growth* was to keep it at a distance; development simply leap-frogged the green belt and flourished in what is now known as the Outer Metropolitan Area, thereby considerably lengthening the average journey to work. The ban on office development will require something more than a leap-frog, as it extends over more or less the whole of south-east England. What its effect will be is not yet clear; but it seems possible that, like other bans imposed in the past, it will be relaxed. Already, after only 2½ years, there has been a slight relaxation—in July 1967 the President of the Board of Trade announced that the exemption limit of 3,000 sq. ft was being raised to 10,000 sq. ft. outside the Metropolitan Region, i.e. beyond about 40–50 miles from the centre of London. There was also a hint that office development permits might be given more generously. He would, he said, 'give greater weight to the needs of physical planning and the efficient use of labour put forward by employers unable to move from the South East'. Some relaxation is also recommended by South East

Economic Planning Council in its first report, published in November 1967. Raising the exemption limit to 10,000 sq. ft. in the Outer Metropolitan Area would help smaller firms to decentralise from London, and O.D.P.'s should be given to allow a considerable scale of modernisation of Central London Offices. The council also recommends emphatically that the control policy must be flexible, particularly in relation to international firms wishing to establish offices in London. It also finds it necessary to remind us that 'the City is the natural office centre of the capital', and that it is therefore desirable to give permission to build some offices there for more general reasons (e.g. in the completion of the Barbican scheme and in the development of the London Museum site).

In the long series of bans, therefore (with the exception of the latest, the effectiveness of which cannot yet be judged), one particular feature has been common to each measure—none of them has had the effect initially intended. This is possibly because there is a fundamental resistance to the idea of a static or declining London. It is one thing to say that London's influence is growing too fast; it is a completely different thing to happily accept its decline. There was a great outcry against the drift to the south-east. Now that this drift is discovered to have been 'a very minor and diminishing facet of the country and the region's population experience', anxiety is being expressed about the fact that London will experience an increasingly acute labour shortage in the future. We have not yet come to the point where anybody is advocating the encouragement of migration to the south-east, but the fears that are now being voiced may perhaps indicate some basic doubts about the wisdom of anti-growth attitudes to London.

The two main anti-growth arguments bear further examination—that the resulting congestion is expensive and unpleasant, and that the rest of the country suffers. As Peter Hall points out in *London 2000* (1963), the Barlow Report, attacking in 1940 the whole concept of the giant metropolis, 'became the basis of official post-war planning policy, and . . . then passed almost into the folk-consciousness of a whole generation of planners, so that its precepts have become accepted virtually as tablets of planning law'. But the reality of the social, economic and strategical problem which Barlow claimed that the growth concentration in the London region gave rise to can now be seriously questioned. The strategic disadvantage, though of obvious importance at the time, is of doubtful significance now. Similarly, the harmful social effects of large concentrations of people and industry were much more of a reality at the time the Barlow Commission reported than they are now. Clearly, if it could be proved conclusively that unrestrained metropolitan growth was economically essential for national growth, there would be little question about allowing free expansion. But the fact is that we are a long way from being able to measure the benefits or the costs of metropolitan concentration. There cannot be much doubt that the rest of the country suffers, or at least that other cities would benefit from a spread of metropolitan functions. But the costs of such a redistribution cannot yet be measured.

The problem seems to involve two apparently simple questions which are as yet unanswered.

(i) Do people really prefer London, or do they want to stay there only because it offers them opportunities that do not exist elsewhere? A recent survey of commuters by the L.O.B. (1967) suggested that, for something like half of the office workers interviewed, London's disadvantages are outweighed only by its material benefits.

(ii) Is a London location economically more advantageous to London firms than any other location; and if so, can the advantages be more widely dispersed or are they a function of concentration?

Historical Development

The historical development of London is well-documented and widely known. Certain features, however, are worth brief discussion in connection with this particular study before the more recent developments are described in more detail. The two aspects of London's growth which are fundamental to an understanding of the present-day structure of the central area are, first, the sharp distinction between the City and the West End, and, second, the grouping of certain kinds of activities which is such a marked and persistent feature of central London's internal structure.

It is commonly appreciated that London has grown from two nuclei, the original London being what is now the City, with the small settlement of Westminister upstream grouped round the Abbey and the royal palace. There is little illogical or unexpected in what subsequently happened to London, given this initial situation of twin growth points on the north bank of the river. Once the nobility was settled to the west, trade and commerce had to extend downstream from the original riverside wharves, and the very persistent east-west division of London was therefore established from the outset. This basic class division of London is still quite plain, particularly in inner London, but also to a considerable extent even in the later suburbs. Its latest manifestation is in the distribution of 'decentralised' offices, which are found mainly in the western half of suburban London. The fact that the central area has shown no tendency to extend to the east or south is also the result of the original situation; the river provided a barrier to the south for too long, while to the east the spread of the city's port functions with its associated working-class housing discouraged the invasion of central area activities. These, however, found it easy to adapt to their use the large houses of the well-to-do on the western fringe of the city.

The Development of the City

The fire of 1666 destroyed about three-quarters of the City—over 400 acres, compared with just over 200 acres destroyed by bombing in the Second World War. By the end of the seventeenth century its reconstruction was complete, world trade was rapidly expanding, and improved inland transport was also increasing the volume of internal trade, leading to a need for financial and commercial operations on a national scale—a need met primarily by London. It was in this period particularly that the City, in becoming a specialised commercial centre, began to lose many of its original functions. Its residents were the first to go, the well-to-do to the west, and the poorer to the north and east. Then those activities which existed primarily to serve the wealthy followed their clients west and established the West End as London's shopping and entertainment quarter.

By the middle of the eighteenth century many of the institutions of the City and various of its activity groupings had become established in the locations they still occupy. From then on, these institutions and the more powerful and wealthy private firms gradually rebuilt their premises. Then, as now, the acquisition of enough land to embark on a big building project often took many years. The best-known example of this gradual accumulation of small sites to allow a large building scheme is the Bank Corner. The Governor and the Court of the Bank of England acquired in 1724 a small property in Threadneedle Street, to which they then began to add small adjacent plots until they had a site large enough to build the first Bank of England, which was completed in 1734. This was again gradually extended as more plots were bought up, until finally in 1792 the whole of the island site on which the present Bank of England stands was acquired, and the financial centre was firmly established.

The rapid growth of the Victorian period, resulting from suddenly improved communications and the associated increase in trade, added about 100 square miles to the built-up area of London. In the same period the population of London grew from just over a million to over 4 million by the 1891 Census. The demand for land in the city increased its value, forcing less profitable uses to move out—the resident population in the City dropped from about 125,000 in 1831 to only 30,000 in 1891.

The Victorian period was one of massive rebuilding operations in the City. Of all those buildings existing in 1855, it has been estimated that no less than four-fifths had been rebuilt by 1905. Higher densities were, of course, achieved on redevelopment, and the total amount of floor-space in the City is thought to have increased by at least half by the turn of the century, perhaps from 50 million to about 75 million square feet. It was in the Victorian period that the office block appeared for the first time, offices having previously been accommodated in the lower floors of dwelling houses. At first these were primarily purpose-built for the occupier, but by the 1880's large office blocks built to accommodate many occupiers began to appear.

By the end of the Victorian period the City had become essentially what it was in 1939. There was more rebuilding after the turn of the century but at a much less rapid rate; about a fifth of the buildings which existed in 1900 had been rebuilt by 1939. The total effect of changes between 1900 and 1939 was to increase the number of people who worked in the City to about ½ million, and also, vastly to improve working conditions. Rightly or wrongly, this improvement has been attributed partly to the great increase in the number of women employed in the City. By 1939 about a third of the City's office workforce was female, compared with less than 1% in 1851. Census data, although not strictly comparable, suggests the following trend:

	Clerks as % of Total Labour Force	Female Clerks as % of all Clerks
1851	0·8	0·1
1901	4·0	13·4
1951	10·5	59·6

The West End

The growth of the City as London's business centre was achieved by the squeezing out of other uses originally contained within the city walls. The first to go were the houses of the rich. The rich moved west probably for two reasons; the palace was at Westminister, and also by going westwards they escaped what William Petty in the seventeenth century described as the 'fumes, steams and stinks of the whole easterly pyle'—the growing port of London and its associated functions. Once the West End's upper-class residential character was established, the City's service functions moved west to follow their clients. In the seventeenth century, just before the Fire, John Graunt wrote that the woollen drapery and other clothing trades were moving west, into Ludgate Hill and Fleet Street, and particularly to St. Paul's Churchyard, from which district in fact the rag-trade was only finally ousted by bombing in the war, when it moved west again into the area north of Oxford Street. The reasons for this early westward movement, Graunt (1662) observed, were that 'the King's Court is now almost at Westminister', and also that 'where the Consumption of the Commodity is, viz among the Gentry, the vendors of the same must seat themselves.'

The commercialisation of what we now know as the West End took place mainly after the middle of the nineteenth century and was firmly established by 1939. The earliest penetration of offices into the West End was by the conversion of large houses and hotels. Purpose-built office blocks began to appear in the West End only after 1900, the earliest being associated with the building of Kingsway, finished in 1905 and then lined by office blocks by 1915. But the main phase of large-scale office development outside the City was between the wars—e.g., the I.C.I. building in 1928, Shell Mex House in 1930, Brettenham House in 1932 and the New Adelphi block in 1938.

The eastern half of the West End, as far as Bond Street, appears to have been almost completely taken over by commercial uses by the beginning of this century. By the 1930's there had been a noticeable extension into Bloomsbury and also immediately north of Oxford Street. By this time also the commercialisation of the Victoria Street area was beginning with the conversion of Grosvenor Place and Gardens to office use.

Mayfair and the district north of Wigmore Street persisted longer as residential areas, largely because of the policies of large estates, e.g., the Grosvenor and Bedford estates. The leases they granted were controlled by restrictive covenants which generally ruled out any commercial use.

The war brought another phase of movement from the City to the West End, as many firms who had been bombed out of their City premises moved into what was thought of as temporary accommodation in the West End, where bombing was less intense and where large houses were being requisitioned to provide emergency office space. Many of these firms never returned to their City locations.

The Clustering of Activities in Central London

Morgan (1960) has defined eleven areas in the West End's 'General Office District'. Figs. VII 1 and VII 3 show these areas and the grouping of activities in the City as shown by pre-war land use surveys. Very little beyond the trite and obvious is known about the factors which hold together these groupings, many of which show as yet no sign of dispersion. To what extent the apparently close links between grouped activities are based on still active business networks and to what extent

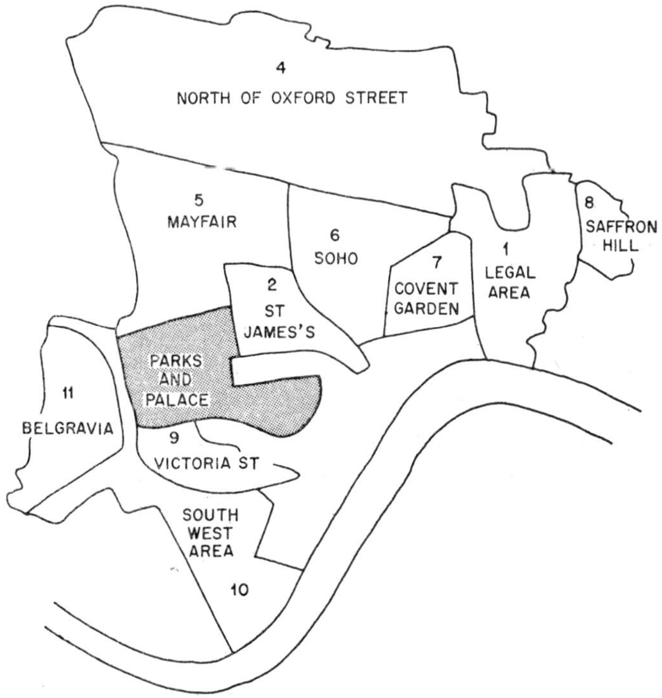

Fig. VII 1 Regions of the West End general office district.

merely on tradition can only be guessed at, in the present state of knowledge. Similarly, although prestige is widely acknowledged as a factor influencing choice of location, it is not known to what extent it is secondary to other factors (see Chapter IV).

Morgan identifies three factors leading to the concentration of office activities.

(i) It is functionally convenient for some offices to be near a particular organisation. Chains of this kind of dependence lead, in the West End General Office District, to two fundamental 'localising bodies', Parliament and the Inns of Court.

(ii) 'Functional prestige areas' exist for certain kinds of offices, e.g., Wardour Street for the film industry. These are based on functional inter-relationships which cause similar firms to want to be near each other.

KEY TO *VII 3*

1. Law Chambers Precinct
2. Press and printing
3. Law
4. Meat and poultry market
5. Hospital
6. G.P.O.
7. Commercial and light industrial
8. Textiles
9. Guildhall
10. Wool Exchange
11. St. Paul's Precinct
12. Commercial
13. Banking
14. Financial
15. Stock Exchange
16. Insurance
17. Shipping
18. Furs and skins
19. Liverpool Street Station
20. Clothing warehouses
21. Railway warehouses
22. Wines and spirits
23. Commodity markets
24. Corn Exchange
25. P.L.A.
26. Wharves
27. Tower Precinct

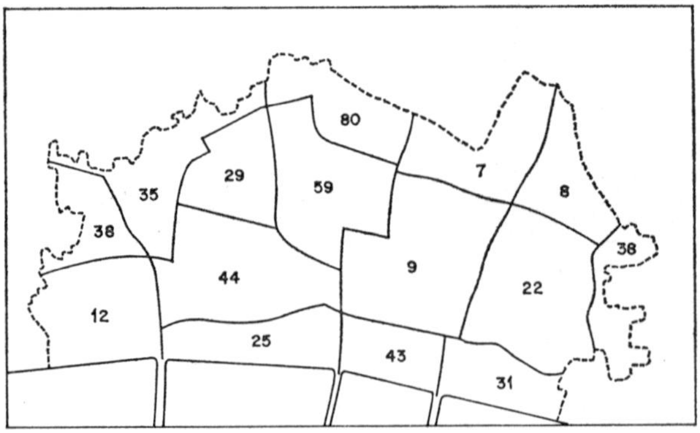

VII 2 Percentage of 1939 floor space lost by war damage in the City.

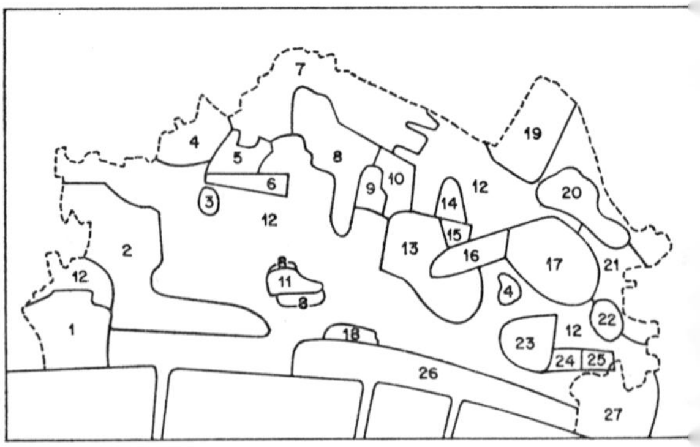

VII 3 Pre-war grouping of activities in the City

(iii) 'Social prestige areas' exist for certain kinds of office activity, e.g., Embassies.

Although (i) and (iii) are, at the superficial level, obviously in operation for what appears to be obvious reasons, it is difficult to do more than merely observe the existence of (ii)—the 'functional prestige areas'. Why they exist and whether they are necessary to the functioning of the firms within them is very uncertain.

The City is more completely an office district than the West End; over half of its commercial floorspace is in offices, compared with considerably less than half in the West End. The City is also dominated by certain kinds of office; whereas banking, insurance, trade and transport firms account for over two-thirds of the City's office floorspace, these activities take up only about a fifth of the West End's office space.

The financial district of the City, its eastern half, is characterised by three main functions—commodity trading, shipping and finance. The Mincing Lane area is now the centre of the commodity markets, originally associated with the riverside wharves. Brokers' premises are closely grouped round the appropriate exchange to allow close and frequent contact. North of Mincing Lane lies the shipping district with the Baltic Exchange (the shipping market) in St. Mary Axe. This area also developed because of its proximity to London's port before it extended downstream with the building of the wet docks. The financial area is centred on three closely interdependent institutions, the Bank, the Stock Exchange and the Bankers' Clearing House.

Fig. VII 3 shows the grouping of activities within the City, based on land use surveys carried out in the mid-thirties. A report produced by the City in 1936 refers to this 'self-zoning' system within the City, observing that land use maps clearly showed that 'to a large extent the various commercial and industrial activities of the City congregated in well-defined areas, creating specific commercial markets or exchanges, and amounting substantially to a self-formed zoning system within the general market which is the City of London'.

Morgan's 11 office regions (Fig. VII 1) within his West End General Office District mainly contain a greater mixture of functions, and their characteristics arise in many cases more from the pre-commercial nature of the district than from the kinds of activities they now accommodate, e.g. Mayfair and Belgravia.

London Since the War

The following figures of office space approved in London since the War show the broad pattern of development over the period (Table VII 1).

Table VII 1 London County Council Area. Office space approved 1949–1963: New buildings and extensions (millions of square feet).

Central Area		Outside Central Area
1949	3·6	*No information*
1950	3·3	*No information*
1951	1·7	*No information*
1953	3·0	*No information*
1954	5·7	*No information*
1955	5·9	0·4
1956	3·7	0·3
1957	4·7	0·5
1958	4·2	0·4
1959	4·3	1·2
1960	4·3	1·0
1961	4·4	0·9
1962	2·9	0·6
1963	2·0	0·7
Total	59·9*	6·0

* Including space approved in part of 1948, and in Crown buildings not included in annual totals.

Source: London County Council.

The Immediate Post-War Years

It has been estimated that in the central area as a whole about 58 million sq. ft. of commercial and industrial floorspace was destroyed or damaged in the Second World War, i.e. a loss of 20%. Nearly 10 million sq. ft. was office floorspace, reducing the pre-war total of 87 million sq. ft. to less than 78 million. Rather more than half of the loss of office space was in the City of London, mainly in the western half of the district round St. Paul's, a district which in fact had contained most of the City's obsolete property.

Fig. VII 2 shows the relative amount of damage in the City of London. Nearly a third of the City's acreage was destroyed or badly damaged, compared with only about 8–9% of the West End, mainly in the Holborn area.

With the acute housing shortage of the early post-war years, the re-building of commercial property was severely restricted. By 1949 less than 1% of the damaged area in the City had been at least temporarily rebuilt, whereas in the County of London as a whole, the proportion of damage area rebuilt was up to nearly a third, mainly housing.

The replanning of the City was started during the war. It seems now incredible that a major concern in these early plans was to attract back enough commerce and trade to the City. There was certainly no hint that the growth of offices was soon to be treated as a problem. In fact the main aims of the 1944 plan (which was rejected) were to ensure that reconstruction could proceed rapidly in order to return the City to its pre-war level of activity. Far from being anxious that development might create problems, it was stated in this plan that 'the greatest pressure, *we hope and anticipate*, will come from commerce and trade'. It was also emphasised that new development 'will hold more persons per unit of site area than their predecessors, and rapidly counteract the early shortage of space'. Another indication that the speed of renewal was very much under-estimated was that it was proposed that residential development should take place in the backland behind the main street frontage—land that might remain derelict for too long if allocated for commercial purposes. Housing in such areas would be constructed with conversion to commercial use in mind, if at some later date 'demand exceeded anticipation'.

It was not then thought that the City's daytime population would grow much beyond the pre-war figure of $\frac{1}{2}$ million. Observing that, if re-building was carried out to maximum heights laid down for commercial properties, the daytime population might increase to about 800,000, the authority stated that this was most unlikely: 'our experience in the City does not lead us to confirm this'. As was later the case with plot ratio controls, maximum permitted densities were regarded as unlikely to be achieved, owners 'not everywhere exercising their full rights'. It was clearly not anticipated that such limitations would soon become the minimum that owners and developers would accept, rather than a maximum they would rarely reach. The City went on to assert that the only and unlikely circumstances in which the City's daytime population was likely to exceed the pre-war figure would be if

'(1) the amount of business transacted and the methods of administration practised required the employment of such numbers in close proximity;

'(2) the public transport could convey such numbers speedily and cheaply from their widely distributed homes to the centre;

'(3) the ratio of persons in the London area employed in the City increased considerably against the general sense of the findings of the Barlow Report.'

Although the City of London gave no indication that congestion called for any reduction in its activities, the Greater London Plan (1944) advocated the decentralisation of 'business firms', but—as in the Barlow Report—the main emphasis was on the need to disperse industry from London and thereby reduce the concentration of employment.

Although the decentralisation of offices did not become official policy until ten years later, it is interesting to see that Abercrombie's Greater London Plan put forward the policy in exactly the same terms as it was later adopted. 'Whilst key business employees must remain in central London, in close contact with the financial and business market, much routine work can be done in the suburbs or outside London where rents are much lower than in the City and employees can live near their work. Decentralisation of business firms is very desirable, and, as far as is practicable, firms who have moved to the suburbs should be encouraged to stay there, at any rate for dealing with their routine work.' Little interest was shown in Abercrombie's early plea for office decentralisation; there was as yet no office problem.

In 1945 the New Towns Committee also gave passing mention to the desirability of moving some of London's offices to the new towns, though this was no doubt as much to benefit the new towns as to relieve London's problems. But ten years later virtually nothing had been achieved, and by the end of 1966 only 2 million sq. ft. of office space had been built in all new towns.

In 1951 the L.C.C. produced its first Development Plan. The need to reduce central area congestion was stressed, but nevertheless provision was made for an increase of offices within defined zones. (When the Minister finally approved the L.C.C. plan in 1955, the office allocation was reduced, as by then office development was being seen as a problem requiring attention.)

The control of office development was left solely to the development control powers of the 1947 Town and Country Planning Act, unlike industrial development for which the Act had made special provision, requiring the issue of Industrial Development Certificates from the Board of Trade before planning permission could be applied for. The first controls specifically for office development were however not enacted until 1964, long after the office problem had been recognised.

But, although few people appear to have anticipated the problem, it has been suggested that it was quite apparent at least by 1953 that there was a strong demand for offices in London. This might well, of course, have been more true of the developers than of the planners. Marriott maintains that this strong demand must have been evident for three obvious reasons. Ten million square feet of office space had been lost by war damage, and there had been relatively little rebuilding between the wars, leaving many obsolete Victorian buildings ripe for renewal, but the main reasons for the building up of demand for extra office space was the very rapid change of emphasis from making goods to designing them and marketing them, and the already established tendency of firms to amalgamate into bigger units, for whose headquarters Central London was the obvious prestige location. The south-east was in any case at this time already attracting the post-war 'growth' industries, and also London was becoming more and more an international city.

Second Phase—the Office Building Boom 1954–1956

Had the betterment provisions of the 1947 Act been retained, there can be little doubt that the boom would have been less dramatic. Presumably there would still have been plenty of office development, but developers would have been in a much less favourable position. Mr. Macmillan ushered in the office boom in December 1952 when he introduced the bill that became the 1953 Town and Country Planning Act, saying that 'the people whom the Government must help are those who do things: the developers, the people who create wealth whether they are humble or exalted. . . .' The government certainly did what they could to help the developers, deliberately in the case of the Conservatives with the 1953 Act, in which the 100% development charge was abandoned, and with the lifting of building licensing requirements the next year. Just as significant, however, was the unintentional gift of the 'Third Schedule' loophole in the 1947 Act, which made nonsense of the L.C.C.'s plot ratios aimed at controlling site densities. The Third Schedule laid down that a building could be enlarged by up to 10% of its cubic content, the purpose being to allow owners to make minor improvements to existing buildings without having to pay the development charge. These Third Schedule rights had a spectacular effect from about 1958 when re-development overtook the development of bombed sites. As Sir Keith Joseph said in 1963 when he announced the modification of the Third Schedule rights, 'the reference to cubic capacity in the schedule enabled a developer to drive a coach and horses through the original legislation'.

An example of the effect of this, quoted by Marriott, is the new Scotland Yard building in Victoria Street. The maximum plot ratio allowed for the area was 3·5:1, but by adding 10% to the cubic capacity of the buildings that were demolished, a building of 400,000 sq. ft. was achieved—giving a plot ratio of 7:1.

Once the building licences regulations were removed, on 2nd November 1954, there was little to hinder 'the people who create wealth', and they immediately got down to creating it. Values rose literally overnight (Marriott quotes an example of a 70% increase in site value); property became 'a paradise for gaining a tax-free profit', and Central London began its most dramatic transformation. The only restrictions left were the ordinary provisions of the Development Plan and development control which prevented the spread of offices out of zones allocated for office use, and imposed plot ratio limitations. As well as being able to get round the plot ratio control by claiming Third Schedule rights, developers quickly became talented in getting much more floor space on to sites than had been expected when plot ratios were introduced. They had been originally designed as imposing a set of theoretical limits on the density of workers in given areas. Nobody apparently thought that developers would ever want to build as much as the plot ratio allowed, and, of course, they attracted a great deal of criticism for treating as a minimum density what was intended as a maximum. This kind of criticism, as Marriott points out, is like criticising a giraffe for having a long neck.

By the end of 1955, approval had been given for no less than 27½ million sq. ft. of office space in Central London, nearly three times as much as had been lost through war damage. Of the total amount approved, 38% was in the City of London. The annual amount of office space approved almost doubled in 1954 and 1955 as the result of the lifting of building restrictions.

The Decentralisation Movement: 1956–1964

By 1955 the L.C.C. and the Ministry of Housing were worrying about the dangers of rapid office growth in Central London. But although concern grew more acute and more widespread as time went on, with growing pressure on the government to take prevention action, 'it took another nine years, a constant spate of planning approvals and office building, and a change of government from Conservative to Labour before the problem was finally stamped on. By then market forces had in any event run the boom dry. The market was ahead of the legislator.' (Marriott.)

Various attempts were made, between 1955 and the 'Brown Ban' of 1964, to control the unforeseen boom. In 1955 the Minister approved the L.C.C.'s first Development Plan (submitted four years earlier), reducing the amount of land allocated for office development. In his letter to the L.C.C. approving the plan he stressed the need to find out more about potential office development, e.g., the amount approved but not yet built, possible increases resulting from redevelopment etc. (A planning authority rarely knows the state of play in these terms; it usually knows how many approvals have been issued but does not normally keep records of actual development. Building Inspectors, employed by the boroughs, vet all building operations, but to find out about completions, i.e. whether an approval has been acted on or not, the planning authority usually has to carry out a special survey involving field inspection.) Soon after this, the L.C.C. began a series of surveys of office approvals and completions, carrying out each year a field survey of outstanding planning permissions to find out the amount of development which had been carried out and how much potential remained.

In 1957 the capacity of the areas allocated for offices was again reduced by revising plot ratios. At the same time, higher plot ratios were allowed in mixed schemes, if the extra space was used for residential accommodation.

It was in 1956 that the decentralisation solution was first given official backing, when the Middlesex County Development Plan was approved. Land was to be made available in the outer part of the county (beyond the North Circular Road) for offices 'which have a need to be in the Greater London Area, and in particular for offices transferred from the centre of London. It would afford considerable relief to the congested central areas of London if more business concerns could be persuaded to establish their offices in the outer parts of the county.'

In 1957 the L.C.C. launched the campaign to encourage decentralisation of offices with a publication, *A plan to combat congestion in Central London*. (Places as near to the centre as the Archway, Notting Hill Gate and the Elephant and Castle were suggested as suitable locations.) Later in 1957, a conference was held of all the London area planning authorities, at which the decentralisation policy was fully endorsed.

The next year the L.C.C. issued its propaganda pamphlet *Offices on the Move* and held an exhibition at County Hall. The Town and Country Planning Association joined the campaign, with a conference on 'Office location in the London Region'. The Minister of Housing, Henry Brooke, openly committed himself, sending a personal letter to 200 companies with Central London offices, suggesting that decentralisation should be considered.

In fact official policy was again trailing behind what was a natural movement. This has often been pointed out, particularly by developers. Marriott maintains that the trend was only 'fractionally influenced by official exhortation'. Some of the decentralisation moves described in Chapter IV took place in the early 1950's, and, although fairly rare until the second half of the decade, the fashion was obviously being established well before it really caught on. Often it was a firm building its own offices which started the ball rolling in a certain area. Obviously it required considerable courage for a developer to build an office block 'on spec' in some untried suburban location. Even Knightsbridge was thought risky until Bowaters took the whole of a 321,000 sq. ft. building before it was started. This scheme was announced in 1956. It established the fashion and more blocks soon followed.

In a surprisingly short time, the decentralisation movement sprinkled the outskirts of London with what has been considered to be a host of banal and unrelated office blocks, radically altering the townscape along the main roads and railway lines out of London. With the exception of a few marked concentrations, notably in Croydon and in Ealing along the Uxbridge Road, these blocks sprang up in virtual isolation. (See Fig. VII 10.)

Middlesex was the first authority to attract decentralised offices in any volume. Between 1955 and 1964, the county gave approvals totalling no less than 17½ million sq. ft. of office space.

In the late 1950's there was slightly more office space approved outside Central London than inside. This was obviously a success for the promoters of the policy, but planning authorities have been criticised for failing to relate their separate policies. Only in 1962 did they join together, forming the Standing Conference for London and the South East Regional Planning.

The most dramatic success story in the decentralisation movement is that of Croydon's office boom. Undoubtedly the main reason for

Croydon's success in attracting office firms from London is the fact that the rail journey from Victoria to East Croydon station takes only a quarter of an hour. Other factors helped considerably; Croydon's main shopping street is one of the busiest outside London, and the area contains a large pool of white collar workers.

In 1956, Croydon promoted its own private bill through Parliament, the Croydon Corporation Act, which gave it the power to acquire land compulsorily without having to get Ministry approval. The first office block was a by-product of a road widening scheme (George Street). Two more soon followed, and, when these first three blocks were quickly let, the developers and the council saw Croydon's potential. An immediate effect was a rise in site values. Marriott quotes a case of a site where Victorian houses selling for £5,000 rose to over £100,000 in three years. Rents of the new office space also rose sharply. In 1959, the first office block was let at about 9s. per sq. ft. By the end of 1960 another block was let at 14s., and the tenant two months later sub-let part at 20s.

From 1957 up to the ban in 1964, 2 million sq. ft. of office space had been built in Croydon, and another ¾ million sq. ft. was under construction. Added to this, another 3·3 million sq. ft. had planning permission, of which 2·3 million escaped the ban and is now completed or under construction. Another 1½ million sq. ft. of new office space is contained in developments outside the main centre. Croydon's total amount of new office space is therefore about 6½ million sq. ft., with another million held back by the present restrictions.

Increasing Restriction

Decentralisation was official L.C.C. policy up to 1964. In 1960 the First Review of the Development Plan allocated 73 acres outside the central area for offices intended mainly for local needs, and also earmarked office centres, e.g., Archway. But during this period, other planning authorities in the conurbation became increasingly doubtful about the policy's purpose. Middlesex, the first to encourage decentralisation, was also the first to lose faith in it. Even in 1958, its county planning officer had warned that, if employment continued to grow in the centre, suburban office development would only result in an overall increase in the conurbation as a whole. By 1959 Middlesex was pointing out that its speculative blocks were being let to firms outside the L.C.C. and Middlesex, and in 1961, having approved 9 million sq. ft., the county reversed its policy. Permissions for new offices dropped sharply. Plot ratios as low as $1\frac{1}{2}$:1 were imposed, and attempts were made to limit the occupation of new office buildings to firms already in the county or from the L.C.C. by imposing a condition to this effect on planning permission. These conditions were in fact not often used, and of course could apply only to the first tenancies.

In 1961 Essex followed Middlesex's lead, and in 1962 Surrey did the same. By 1961 Herts had also reversed its policy and Croydon showed reluctance to come into line.

Planning authorities were realising that the new developments were generating unexpected traffic congestion, on a scale that could only be dealt with by major road improvements schemes. (There is evidence that a very high proportion of people working in decentralised offices travel to work by car.)

Two principles increasingly dominated discussion of policy in the early 1960's. The idea of encouraging large office centres well beyond the conurbation gained considerable support, as a means of taking decentralised offices beyond or to the edge of the commuting area. Secondly, it became more widely accepted that the current planning legislation was inadequate. Decentralisation could be effective only if there was some way of restricting the reoccupation of vacated central area premises, and of ensuring that non-central office development was used only by firms for which it was intended, i.e., those moving from Central London. There were also various methods suggested to discourage firms from staying in Central London. The Surrey Town Planning Committee, for example, put forward in 1963 a proposal that a levy should be imposed on the owners of London offices to subsidise public transport. In 1964, the L.C.C. recommended that office blocks should be bought by planning authorities and used for other purposes. The complete abolition of Third Schedule rights was repeatedly advised, and the standing conference proposed that they should establish a joint fund to meet the costs of extinguishing office use rights, to which the government should contribute. It was also suggested that the 1963 Offices, Shops and Railway Premises Act should be amended to prevent any increase in the occupation density of offices.

The government persisted with the decentralisation solution for several years after the planning authorities had lost faith in it. The Standing Conference was quick to criticise the South East Study (1964) for still advocating suburban decentralisation despite the fact that the planning authorities had abandoned the policy.

In the wake of the decentralisation movement, the government's Location of Offices Bureau was set up in April 1964, to exhort and give practical help (by way of information) to firms wishing to move all or part of their offices out of London to any 'suitable' alternative location. By the end of March 1967 the L.O.B. had received 1,592 enquiries requesting 165,176 jobs, 419 firms had actually moved out of Central London, either wholly or partly, with a total of 29,119 jobs and, in addition, 55 firms representing 10,407 jobs had made definite decisions to move within the next two years.

The L.O.B. has been much more successful in encouraging short-distance moves to suburban locations than moves over longer distances, as shown in Table VII 2.

Table VII 2 Distance of moves by Location of Offices Bureau clients 1963–1967.

Distance	Percentage of Jobs* 1963–1966	1966–1967	Expressed Wish† New Clients 1966–1967
Inside G.L.C. area	46	54	32
Beyond G.L.C. area			
up to 19 miles	6	12	10
20–39 miles	17	22	21
40–59 miles	7	5	10
60–79 miles	10	3	11
over 80 miles	14	4	16
	100	100	100

* Number of jobs actually moved or to be moved from Central London by all L.O.B. clients who had taken a firm decision in the period.
† Expressed wish of new clients when first interviewed (by number of jobs).

Source: Location of Offices Bureau Annual Report 1966–1967.

The Location of Offices Bureau has been constantly criticised by the standing conference for its encouragement of short-distance decentralisation. The Chairman defended his policy in a reply published in the *Guardian* in 1964. 'The hard fact is that the great majority of firms are prepared to move only within a 50-mile radius of London. In these circumstances, 1,000 jobs in Southend are to be preferred to 1,000 jobs in Central London.' He defended this view by stating that he was confident that pressures in the central area had been relieved because new office space had not all been taken up.

In his report for 1965–1966, the Chairman of the L.O.B. again attempted to answer his still active critics. 'The problem of what happens to the empty office is in my opinion at present being solved by their either remaining empty or being occupied at lower overall density.' At this stage, he was able to reinforce this view by claiming that, 'the office population in Central London has not increased over the last three years'. (Recent employment trends are discussed in Chapter VIII.)

The total ban on office development was imposed on 4th November 1964 in a White Paper, *Offices: a statement by Her Majesty's Government*. The standstill was applied over an area of about forty miles radius. In 1965 the White Paper's contents were incorporated in the Control of Offices and Industrial Development Act, which had the following provisions.

(i) The Board of Trade was given powers to control office development in the whole country. In the first instance these were to be applied to the metropolitan area and also in Birmingham. Later, control was extended to cover the whole of south east England.

(ii) Control was to be exercised 'with particular regard to the need to promote a better distribution of office employment'.

(iii) Control was to be exercised by Office Development Permits, which were needed for any building, rebuilding or change of use providing office space of 3,000 sq. ft. or more.

(iv) The Act was retrospective; O.D.P.'s were required even for projects with planning permission, if contracts had not been signed by midnight on 4th November 1964.

(v) There could be no appeal against the Board of Trade's decision not to issue an O.D.P. and no compensation was payable on refusal.

Shortly after the office ban was imposed in November 1964 the Ministry of Housing, from information supplied by the planning authorities, estimated that at the end of 1964 there was, in the metropolitan region, about 48 million sq. ft. of office space 'in the pipeline', built but not yet occupied, under construction, or in projects which, although started, were covered by a valid planning approval. Of this area, 25–30 million sq. ft. was in the conurbation.

Of the total in the metropolitan region, something less than half was caught by the ban, but 6 million sq. ft. was already built and awaiting occupation, and another 18½ million sq. ft. was under construction.

There is some measure of agreement that the 1964 ban on office development came too late. This was the opinion of Mr. Costain even as early as the Second Reading of the Bill which became the 1965 Act. He said during the debate in the House of Commons that 'the office problem was solving itself. Too many offices were being built, and the fact that many remained vacant was proving a deterrent to further building.' This, he claimed, was much better than any form of control.

Marriott (1967) goes even further. The 'Brown Ban', he asserts, did most developers 'a power of good', because by artificially restricting supply it helped to fill up unlet blocks which, he maintains, were becoming more and more frequent in and around London. The ban, he claims, sent office rents soaring up. Whereas 50s. was common when it was imposed, the average for new buildings was nearer 70s. 2½ years later. 'The increase in rents,' he asserts, 'has been as sharp since November 1964 as in any period since the war; in some places much sharper.' Only a month after the ban was imposed the *Observer*'s business editor commented that 'every developer has his tale of the prime building let at 23s. which could now fetch 50s. or more with no bother at all'.

The view that demand for office space had started to fall off well before the ban was imposed is also held by many estate agents. In the 1966 Annual Report of the City Offices Company Ltd., for example, it was claimed that there had been 'a noticeable reduction in demands for additional space'.

In Brecker, Grossmith and Company's *Market Review 1964*, however, demand for Central London office space between 1963 and 1964 was said to have increased by 130% whereas the supply had remained almost at the same level. The Company gave the following figures, which are quoted by Mrs. Kirstin Williams (1965). On their own estimate, these agents handle about 70% of Central London lettings.

Size of office Premises (sq. ft.)	Demand		Supply	
	1963	1964	1963	1964
0–2,000	76,000	1,040,000	190,000	740,000
2–10,000	530,000	1,255,000	3,000,000	2,000,000
over 10,000	400,000	1,521,000	4,000,000	4,553,000
Total	1,006,000	3,816,000	7,190,000	7,293,000

But in general, property companies are complaining about the now considerable amount of legislation restricting their operations in the field of office development, and make no admission, at least in public, that they have benefited, as Marriott claims, from the tighter controls.

The Watney Mann Property Co. in their Annual Report 1965–1966 reacted very sharply to current legislation, which they said had 'utterly bemused' the whole property world. Listing the string of measures which had progressively limited their activities, they mentioned 'the controversial and largely incomprehensible Land Commission Bill', and 'the re-organisation of local authorities, the increased complexity of town planning, building licences, restriction of office development, high interest rates and general financial crisis'. 'You will see,' the Chairman's report concluded, 'that there is little scope at present for exciting manoeuvre.'

Some companies have made more constructive criticisms. The City of London Real Property Co. in their 1966 Annual Report pointed out that, under the 1965 Act controlling office development, there was no machinery for dealing with O.D.P. applications for new buildings which would be occupied by a number of different tenants, by far the commonest situation. 'It is clear that only those developers who can obtain the support of a large company to occupy the whole or a substantial part of the new building will have at the moment the slightest chance of obtaining a permit.'

Like many others, this Company also complained that a detrimental effect of the Act was that it prevented the replacement of old by new. Buildings with equal floor area should be permitted without restriction.

The Future

The most commonly held view now seems to be that long-distance decentralisation should be encouraged, to deal with what is left of the office problem or the next office boom period, which a number of commentators have suggested might occur in the 1970's. *The Economist*, reviewing Marriott's recent book, took the opportunity to suggest that 'the best and biggest developers are now counting on the necessity for any government to regionalise. They are not very hopeful that long-distance decentralisation would appeal to the firms themselves. 'The largest employers of semi-skilled clerical labour (e.g., the insurance companies and clearing banks) have not yet digested the obvious lesson; these days you move where the labour is. . . . few seem to have grasped that labour is less mobile than offices.'

The same point is made by Marriott, who criticizes the National Provincial and Lloyds Banks for installing computers in extremely expensive and modern City office buildings. These computers, he points out, could have been located more or less anywhere.

A Study of the Pattern of Office Development since the War

This section summarises the results of a detailed examination of planning permissions for office development. The original intention was to build up a complete picture of post-war office development in terms of its spatial distribution and the rate at which it was provided. The picture that has emerged is less than complete, the main defect being that the quality and quantity of information available for inner London was not matched by that obtained for the outer suburbs. Furthermore, information for the outer suburbs varies according to which planning authority collected it.

The information collected by the L.C.C. for their office surveys (made available to us by the G.L.C. and transferred to a 500-metre grid) was analysed in terms of boroughs, for the whole of the L.C.C. area. In the central area, as defined by the Registrar General for Census purposes, the total amount of office space approved since 1948 was over 60 million sq. ft. The L.C.C. estimated that if demolition of existing space was subtracted, the net permitted floorspace would be about 50 million sq. ft. The percentage of approved floorspace which was replacing previous floorspace rose from about 6% in 1957 to over 80% in recent years. The net amount of new floorspace approved was therefore rising much more slowly than the gross floorspace approved.

The peak year for office planning permission in the central area as a whole was 1955, whereas the rest of the L.C.C. area the peak was later—in 1959. But within the central area the peak reached in the mid-1950's was exceeded in the 1960's in the City of London (2 million sq. ft. approved in 1960), Westminster (1·7 million in 1961) and St. Pancras (1962).

The Central Block of Quadrants (see Fig. VII 4)

The distribution of office floorspace in the central block of quadrants was available for two dates, 1957 and 1962, these being the land use surveys which were carried out by the G.L.C. Because office floorspace as measured for the land use surveys includes various ancillary uses not included in the planning permissions floorspace data, the land use figures were reduced by one-third, on the advice of the G.L.C. These ancillary uses include canteens, and some loading, storage and car parking space.

By 1962 the total amount of office floorspace in the central block of quadrants had increased to about 125 million sq. ft., from about 116 million in 1957. The distribution in 1962 is shown in Fig. VII 5, and the 1957–1962 change in each quadrant is shown in Fig. VII 6.

Fig. VII 4 Central block of quadrants—reference map.

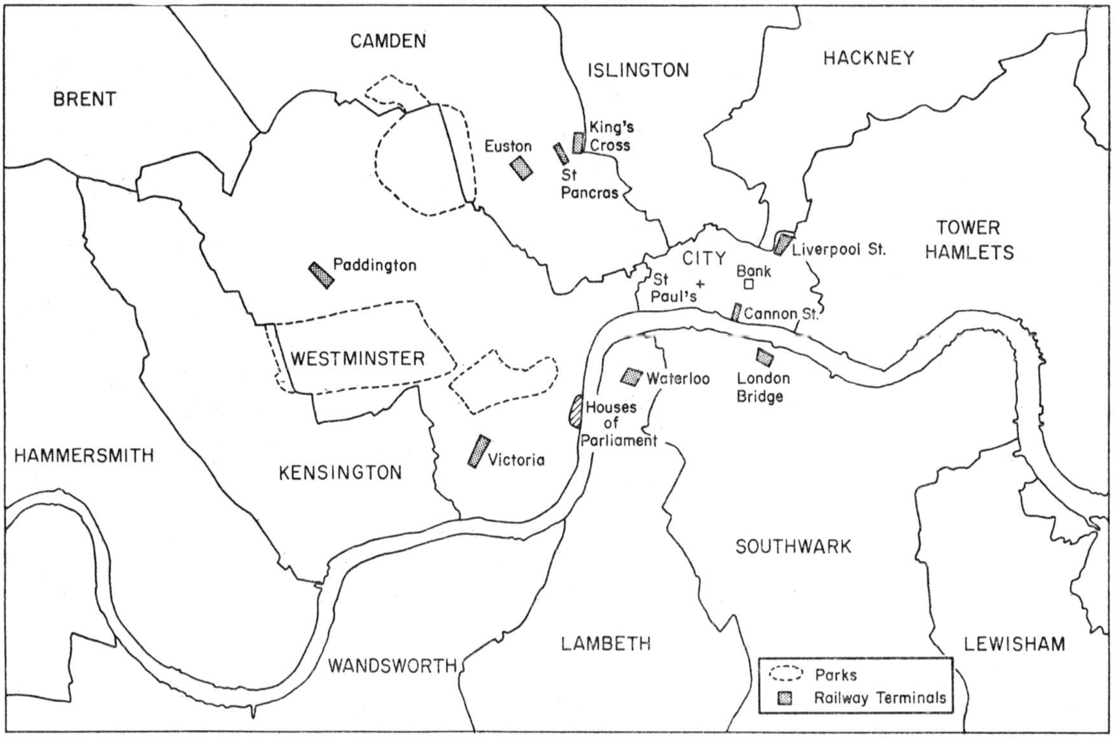

Fig. VII 5 Office floor space 1962.

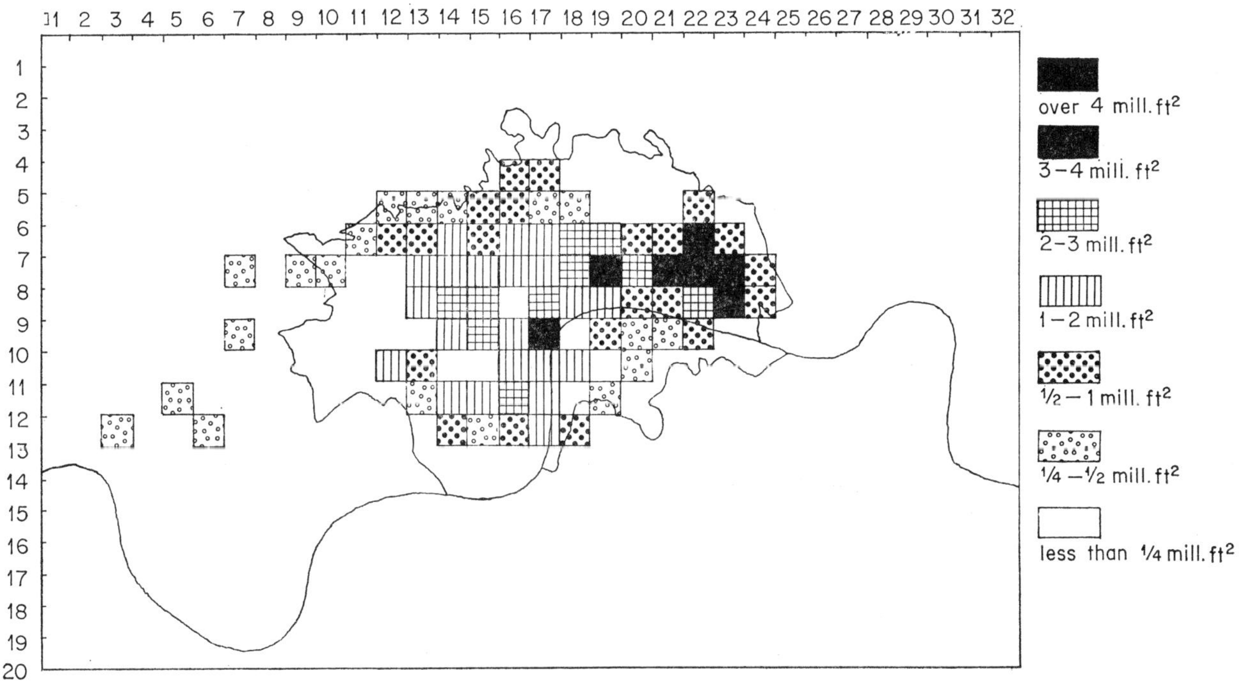

Fig. VII 6 Change in total office floor space 1957–62.

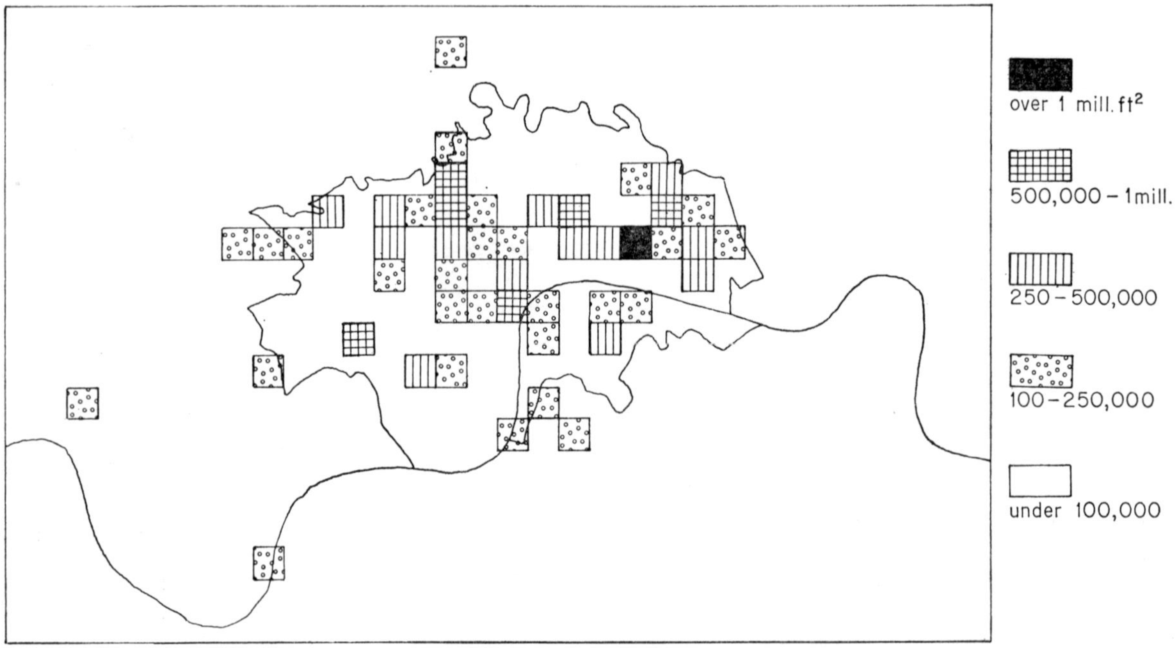

By far the greatest increase occurred in the St. Paul's quadrant (grid ref. 21.8). In this small area, a square of only 500 metres, office floorspace increased by 1·7 million sq. ft. Increases of just under a million square feet occurred in only two other quadrants—immediately north of the Bank Corner (22.7) and also in Knightsbridge (12.11) with the development of the Bowater House group of office blocks. The other quadrants with increases of over half a million square feet were also in the West End, with the exception of quadrant 19.7, on the north-west fringe of the City. (See Fig. VII 4 for reference map of central block of quadrants.) All these quadrants with particularly large net increases were isolated, except for the two quadrants including the area on the west side of Tottenham Court Road (15.6 and 15.7), in which taken together office floorspace showed a net increase of 1·1 million sq. ft. In these quadrants the analysis of planning permissions showed that more individual sites contributed to the fairly large increase which was not simply due to the completion of one or two very large blocks, as is the case for example with the Knightsbridge development. In quadrant 17.10 the net increase of over 700,000 sq. ft. is due to the completion of the new government offices between Whitehall and the Embankment.

Very few quadrants outside the central area proper (i.e., the Registrar General's definition used for the Census) showed net increase much over 100,000 sq. ft. The district west of Paddington Station (quadrant 8.8, 8.9, 8.10) was the only sector where the central area could be said to be expanding. There was no indication of an outward spread in any other direction, except perhaps on the South Bank, where quadrants 18.13 and 19.14 had larger than average net increases. But even in the central area proper, four of the fourteen South Bank quadrants showed a slight net decrease in office space. The total net increase in these 14 quadrants was only just over a million square feet in this period. The land use survey floorspace data should, however, be interpreted fairly broadly in terms of changes over such a short period, particularly in this case, where the use of a fairly fine grid can be misleading. One site in the process of redevelopment, for example, could result in a net decrease being recorded in that particular quadrant. Clearly the ideal would be to compare floorspace distributions before a period of intense activity and after it, but we are of course restricted to the years in which land use surveys were carried out.

Fig. VII 7 shows the amount of office floorspace approved in planning permissions issued between 1948 and 1965 for new buildings in the

Fig. VII 7 New building approved 1948–1965 (excluding extensions): office floor space in quadrants with 5 or more planning approvals for offices.

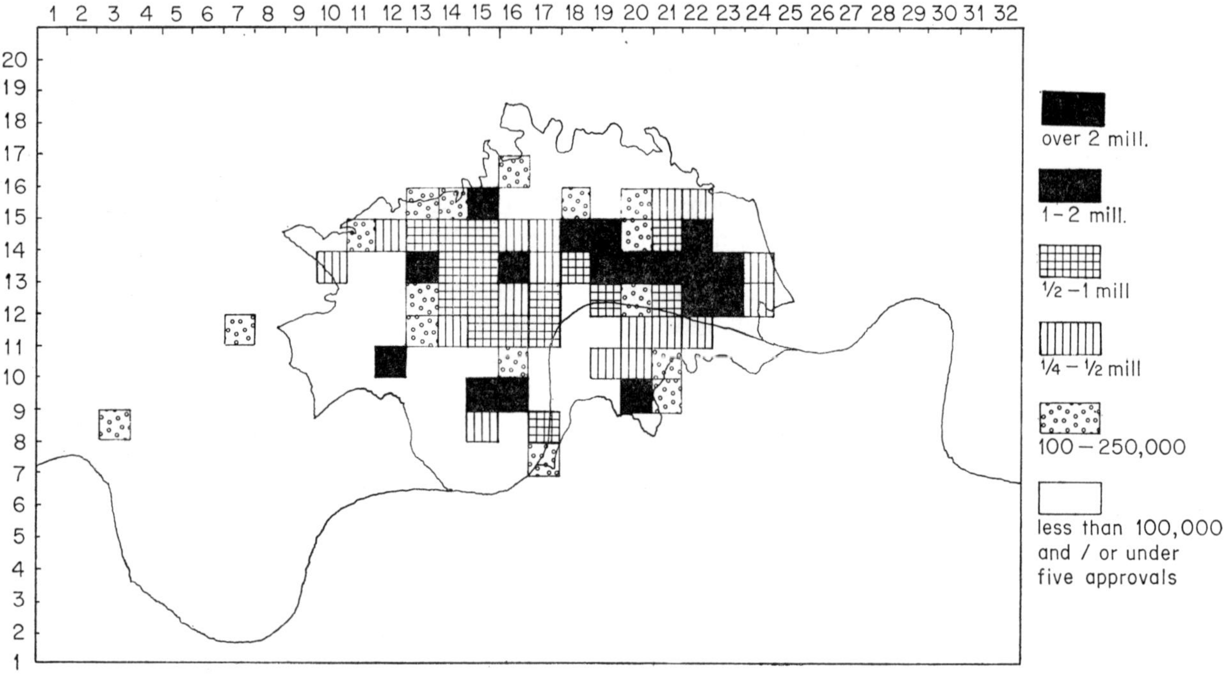

central block. This includes all planning permissions whether or not they have been implemented and, of course, the figures refer to the office space to be provided in a new building, making an allowance for office space previously existing on the site. The area of greatest activity has been, of course, in the City, because of the excessive war damage in that area (Fig. VII 2). Only two of the ten quadrants with over 2 million sq. ft. of approved office floorspace were outside the City—18.7 and 16.12—the Holborn and Victoria Street quadrants. The eight City quadrants with over 2 million sq. ft. were contiguous. In seven other quadrants, between 1 and 2 million sq. ft. of office space was approved in the post-war period. All of these were in the West End except the quadrant containing the new Shell building (18.10), on the South Bank. The map shows two clear concentrations of activity outside the City—one in the Victoria Street area, and a larger district stretching east from the Tottenham Court Road area into Holborn, the only part of the West End which had severe war damage.

The number of planning approvals for new office buildings varied a great deal from quadrant to quadrant, but in general the average size of new buildings approved in the areas of greater activity was about 70–80,000 sq. ft. Over the whole of the central block, however, the average new building was about 40,000 sq. ft.

The total amount of floorspace approved for new buildings in this central block of quadrants is thought to have been about 60 million sq. ft. between 1948 and 1966. Of this, about a million square feet was probably under construction and another 10 million sq. ft. (over 200 planning permissions) appeared to have been permitted but not yet built. This figure, however, is unreliable to the extent that some approvals for rebuilding may have been implemented without the appearance of a new building being detectable. (Those cases for which a completion date was suspect or not available were checked either by inspection or from street directories.)

The estimated amount of floorspace completed year by year in the central block of quadrants is shown in Table VII 3, with the number of approvals and the average floorspace per approval. The sharp rise in activity in the second half of the 1950's is again evident. Fig. VII 8 shows the proportion of office space which was approved by the end of 1955, in those quadrants with over $\frac{1}{4}$ million sq. ft. approved over the whole period. Unfortunately the dates of planning approvals which we have

Fig. VII 8 New office buildings approved 1948–1965 (excluding extensions): proportion of office floor space approved by end of 1965.
Note: *quadrants with less than ¼ million square feet of office space approved (1948–1965) are excluded.*

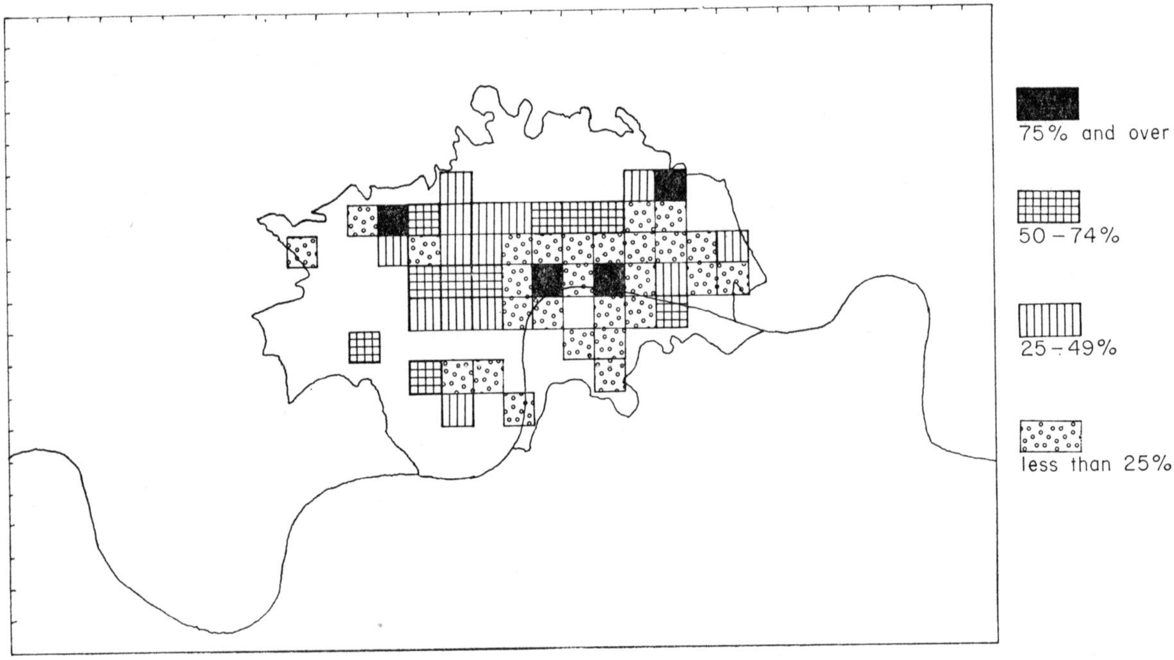

used do not always refer to the same point in a developer's decision process. The time-lag between this first approach to the L.C.C., usually in the form of an application for 'outline' planning permission, and the final detailed approval can vary immensely, according to how controversial his proposal is and, of course, according to the developer's own particular situation at the time. The dates we have used are in general the dates of the last detailed approval; without analysing each case in minute detail it was not possible to do otherwise. The latest application was used primarily because the proposed floorspace usually varies in a series of revised applications for the same site. Had the earliest permission of the series been used, adjustments to floorspace totals for subsequent years would have had to be made, thus injecting yet another element of uncertainty into the data. Even so, the figures are probably inaccurate in some cases where revised applications refer to floorspace which is additional to that approved in a previous application. Unfortunately, the L.C.C.'s records did not make this situation clear. This no doubt explains why there was a considerable discrepancy between our data and the annual totals produced by the L.C.C. for the two boroughs which we used for a test comparison.

Table VII 3 Estimates of completed office floor space, 1948–1966 central block quadrants.

Year	Estimated Amount of Office Space Completed (mills. sq. ft.)	Number of Buildings	Average Size Buildings (000's sq. ft.)
1949	0·1	5	26·3
1950	0·6	12	53·3
1951	0·6	14	45·6
1952	1·1	20	54·2
1953	0·9	19	46·8
1954	0·7	21	31·4
1955	1·9	47	41·6
1956	4·1	117	34·8
1957	4·2	105	40·2
1958	5·9	129	45·7
1959	4·6	142	32·2
1960	4·2	119	35·7
1961	3·0	100	30·1
1962	4·7	89	52·7
1963	3·2	106	30·6
1964	3·9	86	46·0
1965	2·2	66	34·0
1966	4·4	79	55·3
Total completed	50·3	1,276	39·6
Total approved	61·5	1,714	35·9

Change of Use in the Central Area

Very little data on change of use is available. The L.C.C. recorded for their office survey the total number of permissions issued anually for change of use to offices, and, from a small sample carried out in 1960, found that the average size of a change of use proposal was about 3,500/3,750 sq. ft. in the central area and 1,500/1,750 sq. ft. in the rest of the County of London. The L.C.C. estimated that, in the central area since 1948, permission had been issued for about 6·4 million sq. ft. of office floorspace through outright changes of use, and for about 2·7 million sq. ft. through still valid permissions given for a limited period only. Outside the central area, just under a million square feet of office floorspace had been permitted through outright changes of use since 1955, and another 657,000 sq. ft. through limited period permissions.

Although most sites with planning permission for new office building were inspected by the L.C.C. to determine when building was completed, no such survey was attempted for change of use permissions. It was therefore assumed that all had been taken up and all were still in being.

Fig. VII 9 shows the distribution of change of use approvals in the central block quadrants issued between 1948 and 1966. Very few of these were in the City and South Bank sectors of the central area, and by far the greatest concentration was in that part of the West End immediately north and south of Oxford Street. Only outright changes of use are shown.

The Rest of the G.L.C. Area

As explained at the beginning of this section, information on office planning permissions was not available from all 'pre-G.L.C.' planning authorities in the conurbation, and although Middlesex, Essex and Surrey had all carried out comprehensive surveys, the scope varied and information is therefore not entirely comparable. There is a lack of comparability in terms of the time period covered, the types of permission covered, and also the date at which sites subject to planning approvals were inspected to ascertain whether building had actually taken place. An additional difficulty was that because of insufficient information, not all permissions could be located to a quadrant.

Despite these difficulties, a fairly good impression of the general distribution of post-war suburban office development can be gained from the available information. Fig. VII 10 shows all known developments over 20,000 sq. ft. Those known to have been completed are distinguished from those approvals about which we have no further information beyond the permission stage. (This does not of course mean that the permissions have not been taken up.) Although the information is not comprehensive, concentration of suburban office

Fig. VII 9 Planning approval issued 1948–1965 for change of use to offices.

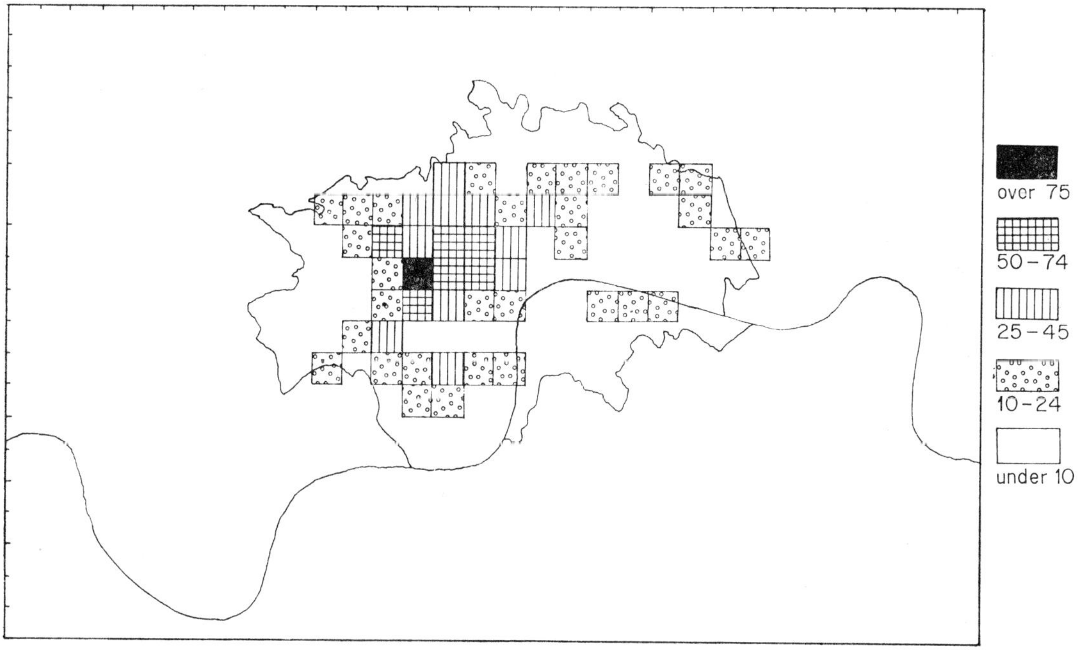

Fig. VII 10 G.L.C. Area —planning permissions for offices over 20,000 square feet.

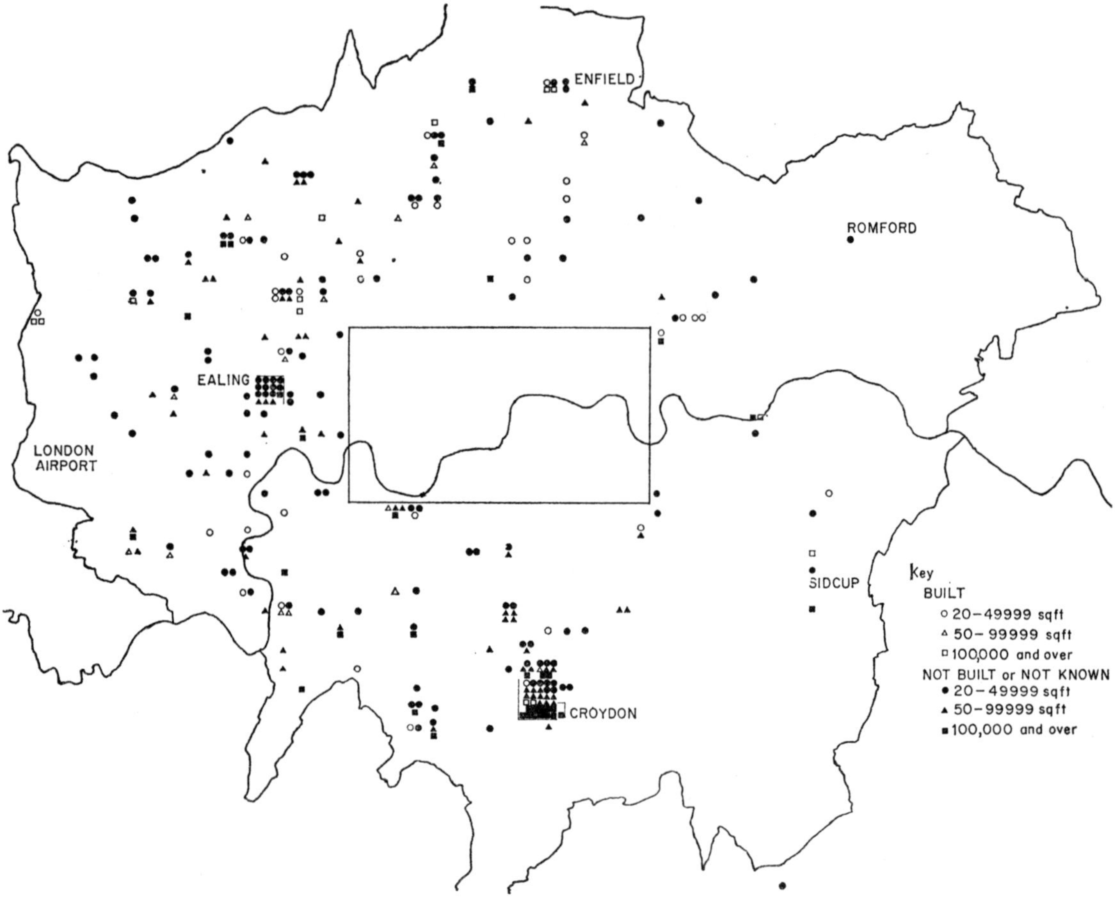

development to the west and south is fairly clear. It is also noticeable that a fairly small proportion of the new developments in the suburbs have been concentrated into local office centres, as was the original intention.

The total amount of office floor space approved (new buildings only) in the planning permissions for which information was available and which could be allocated to a particular quadrant was just over 25 million sq. ft. for this outer part of the G.L.C. area. The average floor space of these buildings, which were generally the larger ones, was about 35,000 sq. ft. But of the 300 quadrants containing permitted developments, a third had less than 20,000 sq. ft. of approved floor-space.

This total of 25 million sq. ft. with known planning permission is obviously considerably less than the actual total amount permitted. If all small schemes, extensions and ancillary offices were included, as well as developments in areas for which no information was available, the total would be a great deal more. Taking only the parts of the conurbation covered by planning authorities' surveys to which we have had access, a total of 30 million sq. ft. can be reached, if small and non-speculative developments are included. (See Table VII 4.)

Table VII 4 G.L.C. Area—office floor space approved.

Planning Authority	Period Covered	Total Office Floor Space Approved (mills. sq. ft.)
Croydon C.B.	1954/1966	5·9 (ancillary offices excluded)
Essex	1955/1964	1·6 (ancillary offices included)
Surrey	1957/1964	4·7 (ancillary offices included)
Middlesex	1955/1964	17·5 (ancillary offices included)
Total		29·7

The data for Middlesex is much more complete than for the other three authorities quoted above. The figure of 5·7 million sq. ft. in Croydon, for example, includes only the sixty-six largest planning permissions for speculative developments. No local offices or offices ancillary to other uses are included.

Conclusions

The main conclusion is that policy changes made to deal with the so-called 'office problem' have generally been either too late or so much in line with current trend that their effectiveness cannot be properly judged. Decentralisation, for example, is said to have been relatively successful as a policy because both the developers and their clients, the occupiers, were in any case quite ready to see the advantages of decentralised offices, and did not need encouragement from the government or planning authorities. Similarly, there is a fairly widely held view that the ban imposed in late 1964 shut the door on a horse that had already bolted. This is a little more debatable, but there is considerable evidence that office growth had in fact slowed down by the early '60's, or even completely stopped.

It seems that the 'office problem' itself is a doubtful concept, at least in the terms in which it has been generally discussed. It is not enough to condemn developers for having taken advantage of boom conditions in the '50's or to condemn the occupiers of the new developments for wanting a 'prestige' headquarters in Central London.

The main questions are whether a Central London location is as beneficial and essential to those firms which have it, or which seek it, as they claim. More basically, very little is known about the demand for offices in general, and the extent to which a firm's efficiency is a function of its office-based activities.

We feel strongly that the decentralisation of Central London offices to suburban locations deserves much more attention that it is currently being given. It has been virtually abandoned as a policy, solely because, although such schemes were often far more successful than anticipated (e.g., Croydon), they could not be seen to be having the desired effect, of reducing employment in Central London. They were also causing local traffic problems, scarcely a valid reason for rejecting the policy in principle. There can be little doubt that suburban office centres (rather than isolated, scattered developments), have many distinct advantages; they allow people to live nearer their work and to work in usually pleasanter surroundings, and they can also contribute to the local centre itself, which may lack the facilities which office development attracts. What seems obvious, however, is that such schemes need to be carefully located. There is clearly considerable dissatisfaction among employees who work in new office developments too far from public transport and shopping facilities.

The detailed examination of the distribution of post-war office development suggests very little tendency for the central area to spread outwards, except perhaps to the west. Although there has obviously been a considerable amount of suburban office development, this has in general been very scattered, except for the concentrations in Croydon and along the Uxbridge Road.

Chapter VIII
The Rising Number of Office Workers[1]

Although anything to do with offices—numbers, floorspace or employment—is notoriously difficult to quantify, particularly over any length of time, there is no difficulty about the validity of two major generalisations: than an increasing proportion of the country's total work is being done in offices, and that London has the lion's share of this kind of work. These observations do not, of course, take us very far towards answering more crucial questions, such as how far the trend to more office work will continue and at what rate, and whether London's share will go on growing—if, indeed, it *is* still growing.

These questions appear fairly straightforward. The fact is that because of severe difficulties with data, to assert anything beyond the two simple and undisputed facts mentioned above is dangerous, or at best so hedged about with qualifications and uncertainty as to reduce such assertions to hazardous guesses. One thing can be in no doubt after the experience of the last decade or so: had even half the effort expended in interpreting what has turned out to have been grossly unreliable data been expended instead in improving that data, we might by now have been able to answer some of the simple, basic questions about rates of growth and trends in distribution. And only when these can be answered will we be in a position to tackle the more intricate and important questions of policy.

Measuring London's Office Growth

Until very recently it was commonly accepted and rarely questioned that employment in Central London was increasing at the alarming

[1] We wish especially to thank the Location of Offices Bureau and the Greater London Council for their heip in providing much of the background material for this chapter, although the ideas expressed are purely those of the Joint Unit for Planning Research.

rate of about 15,000 extra office workers every year. Policy was based on projections of this trend, and the dramatic figure was constantly being quoted to back up complaints that too little was being done to avoid the unthinkable congestion that it conjured up in people's minds. It is presumably not too unlikely that, had the now revised growth rate estimate of less than 6,000 p.a. been available earlier, the ban on office development in November 1964 might never have been imposed.

The following statements illustrate need for reappraisal of the office problem that arose when the results of the 1961 Census were at last made available. Both the L.C.C. and the governments policies were until then based on the old figure. This was quoted fairly tentatively by the L.C.C. in 1960.

> The number of people employed in Central London seems to be increasing by about 15,000 each year . . . almost twice as great as the rate for the whole of England and Wales.
>
> L.C.C. Development Plan, First Review (1960)

In the government's South East Study, published in 1964, it was asserted more positively:

> In the congested heart of London—little more than the City and the West-End—15,000 more office jobs have been created every year.

Non-official comments were no less categorical, sometimes tending, in fact, to treat the figure as a minimum. This was true of the Town and Country Planning Association, in their report *The Paper Metropolis* (1962) anxious, as always, to make the most of any ammunition in their fight for dispersal from congested London:

> In London's central area, the number of jobs in the last decade has grown by *at least* 15,000 a year. This increase was almost entirely in office employment.

The figure was thrown into disrepute when the 1961 Census results were made available. The confusion was immediately admitted by the G.L.C. and the Standing Conference on Regional Planning in the South East (composed of the constituent planning authorities) and, of course, quickly appreciated by non-official commentators, many of whom had for long suspected the Ministry of Labour's employment data, on which the figure of 15,000 was based. In 1966, the G.L.C. produced a research paper on Central London employment and journey to work, in which the revised figure was quoted.

> Comparisons between 1951 and 1961 Census data indicate that the total increase in numbers employed . . . over the ten-year period is only of the order of 56,000 . . . considerably less than estimates of growth derived from other sources, principally Ministry of Labour employment figures.

At about the same time, the Standing Conference made the obvious comment that the revised figures undermined assumptions basic to regional planning policies.

'The analysis confirms the very considerable differences between the employment situation revealed by the Census and that hitherto deduced from Ministry of Labour figures. . . . Had the Census data been available when the South East Study was prepared, significantly different conclusions about the trends in the region and proposals to meet them might have been made.'

The whole confusion was described in detail in a paper by A. W. Evans in 1967, appropriately titled 'Myths about employment in Central London'. In this paper an even more disrupting view was advanced; not only had an examination of the available information revealed that the rate of growth had 'never been as high as was claimed', but there was evidence to suggest that since 1962 employment in Central London had actually *decreased.*

Far from causing the rejoicing one would have imagined, this suggestion seems to be having the opposite effect. It almost seems now that the evil of growth are perhaps to be preferred to the evils that no growth might occur: already, Ministry officials are stressing the need to locate any further office sub-centres well beyond the commuting area to Central London 'if the essential labour force of the centre is to be retained'. The wheel appears to have turned full circle. The decentralised suburban office, intended to take the pressure from Central London, to catch the commuter before he got to the centre, is now regarded as a threat to the efficient working of the centre by capturing the centre's 'essential labour force'. It is too early to say yet whether these views will be officially advanced by the Ministry, but it is likely that they will at least be put forward in the London Employment Study report soon to be produced by an inter-departmental group drawn from the relevant Ministries.

The 'drift to the south-east' is another long-held assumption that has been undermined by the 1961 Census. It is now doubtful even whether there has ever been such a thing; at the most, the Census has shown it to have been a 'very minor and diminishing facet of the country's and the region's population experience'.

As with the Central London employment situation, an accepted trend has been reversed; recent data suggests that the region is actually *losing* more people by migration than it is gaining in migrants from other parts of the country. And again, far from causing any rejoicing, this reversal of what was in any case a less significant trend than previously estimated is now unexpectedly provoking some alarm. In their first report, the South East Economic Planning Council warns that 'the movement of large numbers of workers from London could make the labour shortage there even more severe unless the situation is watched and the right action taken'.

So having apparently reached a situation in Central London and the south-east generally that has been earnestly desired by so many for so long, we are not, it seems, to be thankful that policies designed to achieve that situation have been successful (or that 'natural' trends have worked to the same end): rather we must adjust to new anxiety—that what have long been the goals in the planning of London—reducing its commuting labour force and reducing its magnetism for the population of other regions—could in fact threaten the healthy working of the capital.

The Data

Before discussing employment trends in more detail, it is necessary to draw attention to the main difficulties encountered in the interpretation of available employment data.

The Ministry of Labour's employment figures have already been referred to. Their unreliability had long been suspected, but probably the recent revelations exceed even the fears of those who had been most suspicious. Their main disadvantage is that being based on a count of insurance cards held by employers in that area, the count includes the cards of all workers employed by the firms, regardless of whether they work in the area or not. Clearly the presence of so many large companies' head offices affects the figures for Central London much more than for other areas. The returns can also vary from year to year for a variety of reasons unconnected with changes in employment, e.g., some firms simply omit to send in their returns, or perhaps send their cards to a different National Insurance office owing to a change in their organisation.

Although census employment data is not liable to these extraneous difficulties, there are other problems, mainly of definition, which make any inter-censal comparison dangerous. There was the added difficulty with the 1961 Census that employment data was collected only from a 10% sample of the population, and, although the General Register Office has produced a set of adjustment factors for sampling error and enumerator bias, there can be little confidence in figures for small areas or for small occupational groups.

The classifications of employment both by occupation and by industry (i.e., the kind of business the employer engages in) have been changed between the 1951 and 1961 census, making comparison difficult without laborious retabulations from the basic census forms. Added to this, occupation data is tabulated by place of residence, and not by place of work, while the industry tables show employment by place of work, and not residence. This means, for example, it was not possible to tell from published census material how many office workers were employed in London, because employment figures for workplace were classified according to the industrial groups, i.e., the kind of business of the employer. A typist working in the London office of a mining company appears therefore in the 'Mining and quarrying' group. As a typist she appears only in the figures for the area where she lives.

Three major retabulations have been carried out by the General Register Office, the Ministry of Labour and the G.L.C. to overcome some of these problems. For the country as a whole and the newly defined Economic Planning Regions (not the same as the Standard Regions in the 1959 Census) a 1951–1961 comparison has been made by regrouping the 1951 Industry groups to conform with the 24 categories of the Standard Industrial Classification (produced in 1958 and used in the 1961 Census). Changes in the classification of occupants presented greater problems, and these could be met only by reclassifying a sub-sample (1 in 20) of the 1961 Census forms (already only a 10% sample) into the 1951 occupation groupings in so far as this was possible. The smallness of the sample introduces wide margins of error where the numbers in any one cell of the occupation/industry matrix are not very large.

The third important retabulation was done for the G.L.C. only, showing occupations by place of work (1961).

Yet another source of difficulty is in defining office workers. There is no census occupation group for people who work in offices, and the figure can only be deduced by combining those occupation groups containing people who could reasonably be expected to work in an office rather than anywhere else.

The figures quoted here are based on a recent inter-departmentally agreed definition which, although not perfect, appears reasonable. The G.L.C. use a slightly different definition. It excludes two groups included by the G.R.O. (telegraph and radio operators, and also a miscellaneous assortment called 'professional workers not elsewhere classified') and it includes other groups which the G.R.O. does not include (e.g., salesmen, auctioneers, valuers, servicers, messengers, and managers in those industries where they are likely to work mainly on an industrial site rather than in a true office).

Certain terms which will be used in this chapter require some clarification. It has already been mentioned that the census does not distinguish office workers as such. Although two definitions of office workers have been devised (combining occupational groups which can be assumed to consist largely of office workers), these definitions both require special retabulations of census material. For most purposes therefore, a broader occupational grouping of employment is used—into three non-manual and three manual categories. Non-manual work, although it includes all office work, also includes a large number of other occupations, as shown below.

Non-Manual Occupations

Group 1: *Proprietors, managers, administrative and executive staff*
Including, for example, farmers, working proprietors of market gardens, garages, shops etc.

Group 2: *Clerical and allied occupations*
Including telephone and telegraph operators, commercial travellers, insurance agents.

Group 3: *Professional and technical occupations*
(i) higher: including, for example, doctors, dentists, judges, librarians.
(ii) lower: e.g. laboratory technicians, nurses, estate agents, journalists, social workers, actors and musicians.

Employment Trends 1951

The 1961 Census clearly confirmed that office work was the growth occupation of the post-war period. Between 1951 and 1961, there was a big general shift of employment from manual to non-manual occupations—that is, to administrative, technical and clerical work. Nor was the increase in non-manual work confirned to those industries which have traditionally provided most of the country's white collar jobs (those in the service sector); the association between particular kinds of work and particular industries had become much less marked by 1961.

The following important points emerge from a comparison of 1951 and 1961 Census data, and will be discussed in some detail in this chapter.

(i) Office employment grew by 1·2 million between 1951 and 1961, accounting for over 75% of the total national growth in employment.

(ii) By 1961 one in every three people employed did non-manual work (see definition in previous paragraph).

(iii) The growth of office employment accounted for 9 out of every 10 of the extra jobs in manufacturing industries, and for 6 out of every 10 of the extra jobs in the service sector. But well over half of the numerical increase in office workers was in the service industries.

(iv) In 1961, the South East, with less than a third of the country's total population, had a disproportionate share of the national total of office workers—nearly half.

(v) There was a marked increase since the war in the number of women in employment, and 78% of all extra clerical jobs were taken by women.

(vi) Over the economy as a whole, the fastest growing group was professional and technical occupations, which increased numerically and proportionately in almost all industries. The largest numerical increase was in clerical workers.

(vii) Six of the twenty-four main groups of industries accounted for nearly two-thirds of the total number of office workers in 1961:

S.I.C. Industry Group		No. of office Workers 1961
XX	Distributive Trades	450,000
XXIV	Public administration	445,000
XXII	Professional and scientific services	425,000
VI	Engineering and Electrical goods	424,000
XXI	Insurance, banking and finance	373,000
XIX	Transport and communications	342,000

In the U.K. as a whole, employment grew by 1·7 million ($7\frac{1}{2}$%) between 1951 and 1961, to a total of $24\frac{1}{2}$ million. All this increase was in the non-manual occupations (1–3 in Table VIII 1). There was, in fact, a slight fall in the number of manual workers.

The biggest gain, proportionally, was in group 3 (i), the higher professional and technical occupations, where jobs increased by 48%, compared with the 7½% increase in total employment. Numerically, however, the greatest rise was in group 2, the 'clerical and allied occupations', where there were 700,000 more jobs in 1961 than in 1951. Two out of every five of the extra jobs created in the decade were in this group.

Fig. VIII 1 Proportion of non-manual workers in each of 24 industry groups.

Just under half of the extra non-manual jobs were taken by women (808,000), mainly in clerical work. By 1961, 60% of all clerical workers in 1961 were women, compared with 55% in 1951.

The 8·4 million non-manual jobs accounted for just over a third of the total national labour force in 1961. Over 3 million of these jobs were in two of the 24 main industry groups (see Fig. VIII 1), 1·6 million in the professional and scientific services (XXII) and 1·5 million in the distributive trades (XX). In the manufacturing sector (III–XVI) as a whole the proportion of non-manual jobs had risen from 17% in 1951 to 23% by 1961. The highest proportion (over 30%) was found in the chemical and engineering industries.

As shown in Fig. VIII 2, most of the increase in non-manual work over the ten years up to 1961 was in the service sector. In several manufacturing industries, however, non-manual employment increased much more than the general growth in this kind of work over the whole economy. Whereas the national non-manual labour force increased by 27%, there were increases of over 70% in non-manual jobs in the construction industry (XVII), and the vehicle industry (VIII), and an increase of just under 70% in engineering and electrical industries (VI). Fig. VIII 2 also shows the widespread fall in the number of manual workers over the whole industrial structure. The distributive trades (XX) alone showed a significantly greater gain in manual than

Fig. VIII 2 Change in number of manual and non-manual workers in 24 industry groups 1951–1961.

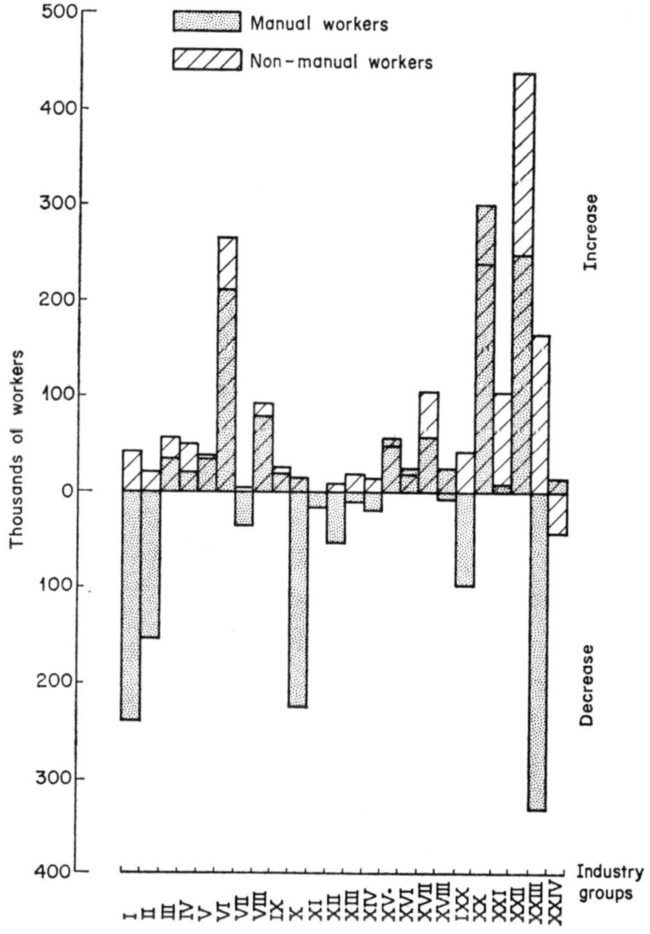

in non-manual employment. All the industrial groups with a fall in manual jobs were, however, providing a larger number of non-manual jobs in 1961 than in 1951.

The only group where non-manual employment decreased in the decade was public administration (XXIV). This fall was very slight and was, in fact, soon made up by a considerable increase in the early 1960's.

Office Workers

Office work was especially the growth occupation of the 1950's. Non-manual employment in general increased at a much faster rate than the country's total labour force—27% compared with 7%—but the number of office workers rose at an even higher rate, by about 40% over the decade. It has been estimated that there were about 1·1 million more people working in offices in 1961 than in 1951. By 1961, therefore, office workers accounted for 1 in every 5 people employed, a total of nearly 4 million people.

Table VIII 2 shows that although the service sector still provided the bulk of office employment in 1961 (62%), the three other sectors of employment showed greater proportional increase in office workers. In 1951 only 12% of the people employed in manufacturing industries were office workers, but by 1961 the proportion had risen to 17%.

The regional distribution of office workers is shown in Table VIII 3. Nearly half are in the South East, and in this region they account for nearly a quarter of the total work force, whereas the proportion in other regions is only 13–17%.

But although the national distribution of office work is clearly still dominated by the South East because of the tremendous concentration in Central London, the largest proportional increase over the inter-censal period did not occur there, but in the South West, East Anglia and the East Midlands. In these regions, the number of office workers rose by 47–48%, compared with 42% in the South East. Numerically, these increases formed only a small fraction of the total, but nevertheless they perhaps indicate that the dominance of London should not be regarded as a permanent feature of the distribution of office work.

Table VIII 1 Estimated numbers in civil employment by broad occupational groups, United Kingdom, 1951–1961.

Occupational Group	Estimated Numbers Employed				Estimated Change (000's) 1951–1961	
	1951	%	1961	%	Nos.	%
1. Proprietors, managers administrative and executive staff	2,271·8	(10)	2,674·3	(11)	402·5	17·7
2. Clerical and allied occupations	2,800·2	(12)	3,501·5	(14)	701·3	25·0
3. Professional and technical occupations						
(i) Higher	771·0	(3)	1,140·0	(5)	369·0	47·9
(ii) Lower	733·4	(3)	1,042·0	(4)	308·6	42·1
Groups 1–3 Non-manual	6,576·5	(29)	8,357·7	(34)	1,781·2	27·1
4. Manual: skilled	5,988·1	(26)	6,096·2	(25)	108·1	1·8
5. Manual: semi-skilled	6,254·6	(28)	6,198·3	(25)	−56·3	−0·9
6. Manual: unskilled	3,941·8	(17)	3,823·1	(16)	−118·7	−3·0
Groups 4–6 Manual	16,184·5	(71)	16,117·5	(66)	−67·0	−0·4
Total, All Groups (1–6)	22,761·0	(100)	24,475·2	(100)	1,714·2	7·5

Source: 1951 and 1961 Census material tabulated by the Ministry of Labour.

Table VIII 2 Industry by occupation: Economically active population in England and Wales. Changes 1951–1961.

Industry/Occupation Group	1951		1961		Change	
	No.	%	No.	%	No.	%
(1)	(2)		(3)		(4)	(5)
All industries and services (excluding armed forces)	19,396		20,815		1,419	7
Office workers	2,820	(15)	3,938	(19)	1,118	40
Others	16,576		16,877		301	2
Extractive						
Total	1,705		1,363		−342	120
Office workers	35	(2)	55	(4)	20	57
Others	1,670		1,308		−362	−22
Manufacturing						
Total	7,262		7,668		407	6
Office workers	907	(12)	1,274	(17)	367	40
Others	6,354		6,394		40	2
Constructive						
Total	1,237		1,426		189	15
Office workers	73	(6)	126	(9)	53	73
Others	1,164		1,300		136	12
Services						
Total	9,175		10,263		1,088	12
Office workers	1,800	(20)	2,465	(24)	665	37
Others	7,375		7,798		423	6

Table VIII 3
Occupational analysis: Economically active population England and Wales 1951 to 1961.

Economic Planning Region	All Occupations (excluding Armed Forces) 1951	1961	Change No.	Change %	Office Worker (000's) 1951	1961		Change No.	Change %
England and Wales	19,792	1,398	1,595	8	2,824	3,987		1,163	41
Northern	1,328	1,398	70	5	141	196	(14)	55	39
Yorkshire plus Humberside	2,958	2,156	98	5	221	305	(14)	84	38
North West	3,085	3,161	76	2	400	531	(17)	131	33
East Midlands	1,340	1,471	131	10	145	213	(14)	68	47
West Midlands	2,104	2,330	226	11	264	381	(16)	117	44
South West	1,377	1,463	126	9	166	245	(16)	79	48
East Anglia	566	610	44	8	60	89	(15)	29	48
South East	6,902	7,685	783	11	1,318	1,876	(24)	558	42
Wales	1,072	1,113	41	4	109	151	(13)	42	39

London's Office Workers

About half of the national growth in office employment occurred in the South East, and although the data for the London conurbation is less reliable, it seems that about 300,000/350,000 of the regional increase of 558,000 must have been in Greater London which provided about 1·4 million office jobs by 1961. Of these, it is thought that 763,000 are in Central London—nearly a fifth of the national total of 4 million. But even discounting Central London, the rest of the conurbation had a higher proportion of office workers than was found in the rest of the country—22% compared with 18%. This is due to the greater dominance of the service industries in this area, but it is likely to have been reinforced since the 1961 Census as a result of the development of suburban office centres such as Croydon.

Table VIII 4 shows the distribution of Greater London's office workers in 1961, both by work place and residence (G.L.C. definition of office workers). Table VIII 5 shows the proportions of office workers in the four main sectors of employment in London, compared with the region as a whole and the rest of the country.

Although over ¾ million people work in Central London's offices, it is not always appreciated that there are also more than half a million people doing non-office work in this small area, including the surprisingly high figure of 256,000 classified by the Census as operatives of one sort or another. Table VIII 6 shows Central London's labour force in six broad occupational groups. This table also shows the age and sex structure of Central London's 1·4 million workers. 37% of all workers were women, compared with about a third of the country as a whole. In clerical work, however, 58% were women. Less than 10% of Central London's administrative and professional office jobs were, however, held by women.

Table VIII 4 Office occupations by work place and residence, 1961 Greater London Council Area.

Area	Office Workers* 1961	
	Work place	Residence
Central London	751·7	118·1
Inner Ring	254·6	331·3
Outer Ring	410·4	768·6
Greater London Council Area	1,416·6	1,218·0

* As defined by the G.L.C.

Source: Reworking of Census data for G.L.C.

Table VIII 5 Office workers as % of total employment, 1961.

Area	Extractive Industries	Manufacturing Industries	Construction	Services	Total
	%	%	%	%	%
Conurbation Centre	100	45	38	57	54
Rest of G.L.C. Area	—	22	15	23	22
Total, G.L.C. Area	27	27	20	36	32
Rest of South East	3	21	12	20	19
Total, South East	1	25	16	30	27
Rest of England and Wales	5	17	11	21	17
Total, England and Wales	5	20	13	25	21

Table VIII 6 Occupations, age and sex of Central London workers, 1961.

Occupational Group		Age Group: % of Total				All Workers		
		15–24	25–44	45–65 (M) 45–60 (F)	65+ (M) 60+ (F)	%	No (000's)	
Administrative & Professional workers	M	11	45	40	4	100	204·1	223·9
	F	15	44	34	7	100	19·8	
Clerical workers	M	22	38	35	5	100	225·5	538·6
	F	43	33	20	4	100	313·1	
Operatives	M	17	29	29	5	100	206·7	256·5
	F	23	33	35	9	100	49·8	
Transport workers	M	12	44	42	2	100	67·0	70·7
	F	16	49	31	4	100	3·7	
Sales workers	M	13	39	42	6	100	81·6	135·2
	F	22	34	34	10	100	53·6	
Others	M	15	41	38	6	100	102·1	190·1
	F	19	32	34	15	100	88·0	
Total	M	16	41	38	6	100	886·8	1414·9
	F	19	32	34	15	100	528·1	

Sources: Special retabulation of Census data for G.L.C.

The age structure of male and female workers also shows marked differences. A third of all female workers were in the 15–24 age group, compared with only 15% of the male labour force.

Misconceptions about the growth rate of Central London employment due to misleading data have already been discussed. The rate of increase in total employment appears to have been in the order of 5,000–6,000 a year between 1951 and 1961, rather than 15,000 as suggested by Ministry of Labour figures. Although this much lower rate of increase indicated by the Census has been widely acknowledged to have undermined the validity of the Ministry of Labour's data, the real situation is still very much in doubt. Although the rate of increase of 5,000–6,000

Fig. VIII 3 G.L.C. Area —journey to work. Percentage of occupied residents working the six central London boroughs (1961 census).

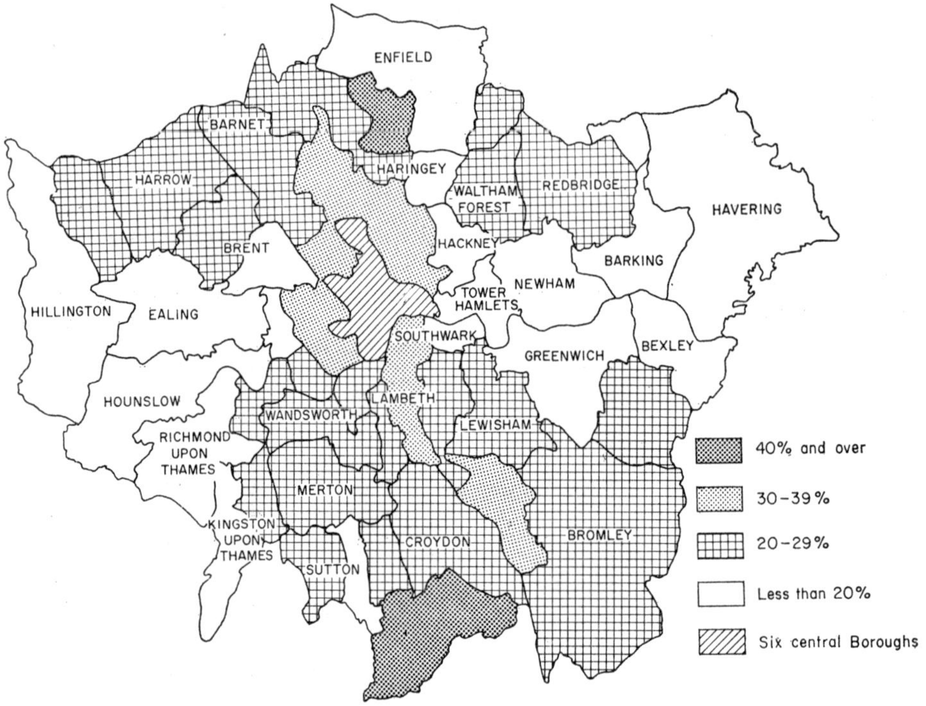

a year is now widely accepted, it has been pointed out that this refers to total employment, and that other evidence suggests that it may well represent only the net effect of a much larger increase in office workers largely offset by a fall in the number of non-office jobs in the central area.

Changes in the number of commuters into the Central London boroughs have been analysed, from census data, by the G.L.C. This study also revealed interesting changes in the distribution of London's commuters. Table VIII 7 summarises the results of the study. Of the 1·3 million people who worked in the six central boroughs (i.e. the pre-G.L.C. boroughs of Finsbury, Holborn, St. Marylebone, St. Pancras and the Cities of London and Westminster), only 12½% lived in these boroughs, a considerable reduction since 1951. The number who travelled to the centre from the rest of inner London (i.e. what used to be the L.C.C. area) increased slightly, but this was offset by a slight decrease in the number travelling in from the rest of the conurbation. In the other Metropolitan region, however, the number of commuters increased by more than 60%. There appear to be about 150,000 people, therefore, who now daily make a journey of between about 20 and 50 miles into Central London. Although the total number of very long-distance commuters (over 50 miles) is still under 20,000. This figure is 40% higher than it was in 1951. These data are shown in Fig. VIII 3.

Table VIII 7 Change in commuting into the six Central Boroughs 1951–1961, by place of residence.

Place of Residence	No. of People Employed in 6 Central Boroughs		% of Change in number of People Employed in 6 Central Boroughs
	1961	(%)	1951–1961 (mid-point in range)*
Finsbury, Holborn, St. Marylebone, St. Pancras, City and Westminster:			
(i) 6 Central boroughs	161,760	(12·5)	−8·3
(ii) Rest of old L.C.C. area	452,640	(34·9)	1·3
(iii) Rest of conurbation	491·430	(37·9)	−0·9
(ii)+(iii) conurbation excluding the 6 central boroughs	944,070	(72·8)	0
(iv) Outer metropolitan region	147,370	(11·4)	60·6
(v) Rest of S.E. economing planning region	17,040	(1·3)	40·4
(ii)−(v) S.E. planning region excluding 6 central boroughs	1,119,680†	(86·3)	6·3
(vi) Rest of England and Wales	16,050++		4·5
(i)−(vi) S.E. including 6 central boroughs	1,297,490†	(100)	4·5

* Absolute change calculated as range, because of bias and confinence limit of 95% for 1961 data.

† Totals include people not allocated to a specific area and therefore not appearing in items (i)−(v).

Source: G.L.C.

The G.L.C. concludes from this study, therefore, that 'a general spread outward is evident, which is more pronounced than would have occurred merely as a result of the net outward spread of population. Dependence on the centre for employment has tended to decrease in many of the inner areas and increase farther out from the centre.'

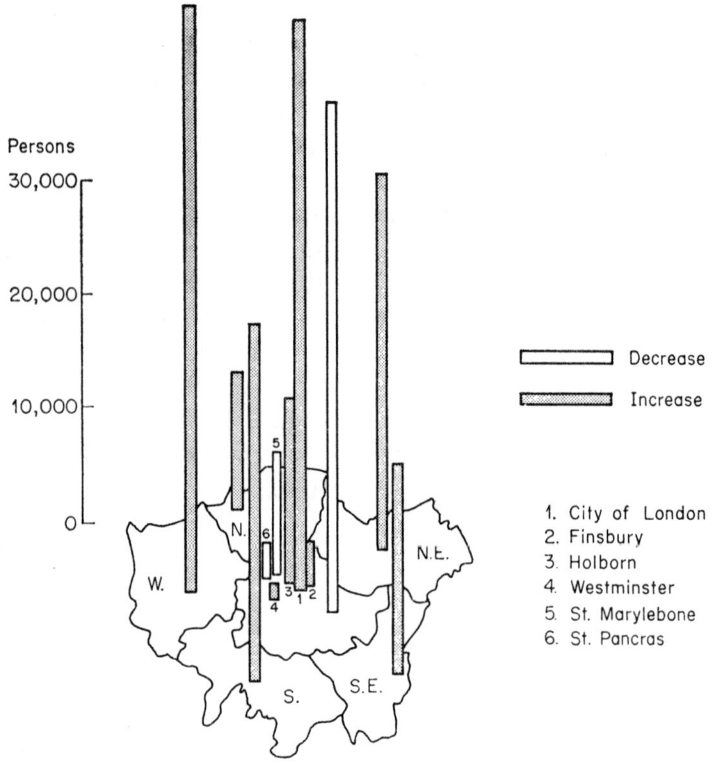

Fig. VIII 4 G.L.C. Area —employment changes 1951–1961 (sectors defined by S.E. Standing Conference).

Within these concentric rings, the changes were not evenly distributed, as is shown in Fig. VIII 4. More people travelled in from the south and east than ten years previously, and fewer came from the north and west. This is thought to be the result of the substantial growth of industry along the London Airport—Watford axis, which has considerably reduced this area's dependence on Central London. At the same time, the south and east have increased their dependence on the centre for employment, probably because of their obvious 'commuter attractions' of electrified rail services and their convenient accessibility to the coastal resorts.

The study also identified substantial 'commuter growth points' at, for example, Bishop's Stortford, Reigate, Dartford and Gravesend and Sevenoaks. In several of these towns, dependence on Central London for employment almost doubled in the ten years. It is pointed out that these are all 'well-established local centres on main rail routes, and are stopping points for relatively fast train services linking coastal and main South Eastern provincial centres with London. This combination of conditions appears to have been most favourable for commuter growth.'

The small increase in the number of really long-distance commuters was also concentrated to the south and east—on the Sussex coast between Brighton and Worthing, and along the North Kent coast from Whitstable to Broadstairs. The electrification of the North Kent coast railway, completed in 1959, must have been the main factor in drawing this area into the commuter belt.

Changes since the 1961 Census

At the time of writing the results of the 1966 Census are not yet fully processed, nor is it known yet the extent to which they can be relied on as reasonably accurate, even after the bias factors have been applied. First reports suggest, however, that although the population of Greater London seems to be decreasing at a rather faster rate than over the 1951–1961 period, there has been little change in total employment and it seems extremely unlikely that there has been any employment increase since 1961. On the other hand, there may be some significance in the fact that male employment seems to have been falling, balanced by an increase in female employment. As most of London's female labour force is employed in offices, this trend perhaps confirms the suggestion mentioned earlier that the fairly modest 1951–1961 employment growth rate in Central London concealed a considerable increase in office employment.

The 1966 Census also shows that although the flow of commuters into Greater London continued to increase, the rate was much slower—perhaps down to 6,000–7,000 a year compared with an average of double this number between 1951 and 1961. There appears to have been, however, no increase, or perhaps even a decrease, in the number of people commuting into Central London. The forecast increase of 200,000 more commuters travelling into the central area by 1981 may therefore have to be revised.

Two other sources of information confirm this indication that Central

London's employment growth has already dwindled to nothing. Precisely when this reversal in the trend occurred, if indeed it has occurred, is uncertain, nor is it clear what has caused the run-down, and it is certainly not at all safe to put much faith into any one of the three sets of data which point to such a run-down. Nevertheless, the fact that three sets of data, gathered from completely different sources, all suggest the same thing cannot be ignored. The defects of the Census data have already been mentioned, as have those of the Ministry of Labour's employment figures, the second of the three sets of data which suggests the reversal in the trend. The third source of information is passenger traffic data collected by London Transport, which has three major drawbacks. The count of passenger arrivals by main line and underground transport exaggerates the total because of the unknown number of people (L.T.E. assume 25%) who change from main line to underground to complete their journey and who are therefore counted twice. The count is, on the other hand, underestimated to the extent that people arrived before and after the 7 to 10 a.m. peak hours during which the count is made, and exaggerated by the unknown number arriving during the peak hours but for purposes other than to go to work in Central London (e.g., shoppers, visitors etc.). Another difficulty is that the L.T.E. data (until after 1961) apply to the 1951 Census definition of the central area. (The 1961 Census used a larger central area, extended to include parts of the south bank.)

Despite the important defects in the available data, it is significant that Ministry of Labour figures and L.T.E. data show that a more rapid rate of growth from about 1959 to 1962 or 1963 was followed by a decrease, confirming the Census findings that Central London's work force had stabilised or even started to fall by 1966.

There is as yet no agreement on why this has happened. We have already mentioned the view that office work might still be increasing masked by a reduction in the number of people doing non-office jobs. Evans (1967) suggests three reasons, none of which it is yet possible to prove or disprove: that the decrease in Central London may be a reflection of the 'declining fortunes of some industries in the rest of the country', or of decentralisation resulting from the rising costs of central locations and L.O.B. propaganda, or it may be that restrictions on central area office development are 'finally having an effect'.

Until the 1966 Census information is fully analysed it is impossible to do more than speculate on these trends. The Census should show, however, whether there has been any decrease in office employment, as distinct from the overall reduction in Central London's labour force. This, on the available evidence, seems unlikely. Between November 1964 and the spring of 1967 it has been calculated that about 14 to 15 million sq. ft. of new office space had been brought into use. This figure represents the difference between two estimates of potential office space made at the above dates by the Greater London planning authorities at the request of the Ministry of Housing and Local Government. The total amount of office space which was completed but still vacant, still under construction, or subject to a valid planning consent but not started was put at about 26 million sq. ft. in late 1964, and at about 12 million sq. ft. in the early part of 1967, two and a half years later.

The rate at which new office space is created cannot be translated reliably or even roughly into terms of extra office workers. This is because it is not known how much of the new space replaced demolished buildings, nor what proportion of the new space was 'usable' rather than for ancillary uses such as canteens etc. Furthermore, the occupation density of office space varies a great deal, making it dangerous to apply an average multiplier. The above trend in the creation of new office space is however broadly confirmed by Inland Revenue data showing net changes in rateable office floorspace. The net increase in the G.L.C. area between 1964 and 1966 was about 8½ million sq. ft. of which 3·2 million was in the central area, 1·3 million in the inner ring and 3·9 million in the outer suburbs.

The Future

There seems no evidence that the growth of office employment, in the country as a whole, will slacken in the foreseeable future. Although it was in the past suggested that automation in offices would reduce the office labour force, this is showing no signs of happening yet. A report produced by the Ministry of Labour's Manpower Research Unit in 1965 concluded that although automatic data processing obviously replaces clerical labour in the particular job it is being used for, this effect is lost in the general increase of employment following on the expansion of business which A.D.P. makes possible. In addition, of course, it must be remembered that A.D.P. creates jobs for its own technical operations. It tends to mean, in general, that more work can be done by a given labour force rather than that the same amount can be done by a reduced labour force. Experience in the U.S.A. suggests, moreover, that the use of computers tends to increase the demand for higher grade office staff. Presumably the tendency is towards a higher proportion of skilled office workers and a decrease in the number of unskilled, as in the manual labour force.

The working-age population resident in Greater London is expected to fall by over 9% (nearly half a million people) by 1981. This is shown in the latest projections by the Registrar General, which include the expected effects of migration, and is in contrast to a national increase of about 6% in the working-age population as a whole. The South East Economic Planning Council (1967) anticipates, therefore, that 'as the numbers of working-age had already fallen by 125,000 between 1964 and 1966, and in view of probable labour supply problems elsewhere in the region, labour shortages seen likely to be intensified'. Employment in the central area is relatively stable, the report concludes, but is increasing in the outer areas of Greater London. With the possibility of a large fall in the population of working age, there could be 'serious difficulties in the provision of essential services and facilities in the London area'.

Chapter IX
Model Building in the Social Sciences and Some Alternative Approaches to the Office Model

We have considered many aspects of the growth and evolution of office activities and accommodation in London since the war. As we said at the beginning, our aim was to turn at least part of our attention to the construction of mathematical models which will help us to understand those phenomena more clearly. The time has come to take up these problems. In this chapter we begin by describing the general problems of model building in the social sciences, and then discuss different approaches to a model of office construction. Some of these models have not been tested, although we do present a programme for carrying this particular set of models through to a final stage. However, we also present one model—a Monte Carlo simulation—which has been built and tested. These different approaches not only enable us to compare methods, but also show the wide variety of techniques which are available to the model builder.

Model building in the social sciences has received a great impetus in recent years, due partly to an increased interest in planning.

Every plan has a set of goals, and indeed goal setting can be said to be a semantic corollary for planning. In social planning the specification of goals is a community decision. The goals themselves are of course subject to change, just as the set of community values upon which the goals are based may change with time. Community values lead to the specification of goals and to establishing constraints. Zoning regulations, which occur in most town planning legislation, are an example of such constraints. Once goals have been established, the object of planning is to prescribe a course of action which leads to their attainment. Very often some alternative courses of action are considered, and their results are then evaluated in relation to the goals. In order to choose between courses of action, some principle of optimisation or, failing that, satisfaction may be adopted. When an *optimising* principle is used, all possible outcomes and actions must be considered, and the course of action chosen is the one which will maximise or minimise some function of the possible outcomes. In a complex decision problem enumeration of all outcomes and actions may be difficult, time consuming and expensive. In order to sidestep this drawback, the decision maker may restrict himself to those courses of action which, on an intuitive basis, seem worthy of further investigation. The basis for this intuitive procedure will be a level of *satisfaction*. Raiffa and Schlaifer (1961) call this process *satisficing*.

In these circumstances planning would be of a kind that aims to adjust or manipulate existing mechanisms in order to reach specified goals. It is reasonable to expect that the better understanding we have of the mechanisms involved the better our planning will become.

It is the purpose of model building to provide just such an understanding. Suppose that we isolate a certain process for study. We may want to construct a model of the process. This could be done by constructing a hypothesis and testing predictions based on this hypothesis, using observations of the process as it actually occurs. The next stage would be to repeat the procedure, using a new hypothesis assuming the relationship between previous predictions and observations. The procedure of testing hypothesis-based predictions can never *prove* a hypothesis is true. Even if the predictions are verified, then *either* the hypothesis is true, *or* some other (perhaps unthought of) hypothesis is true. If our predictions are not verified, the hypothesis may be taken as disproved or doubtful.

Such an approach is common in the natural sciences. The impact of scientific method upon the social sciences has been quite noticeable, especially since 1945.

First of all, we have seen the adaptation and application of the *concepts* of natural science to phenomena observed by social science. Examples of such adaptations are the use of gravity models, and the concept of potential, as suggested by Carrothers (1956). Gravity models have been widely used in transportation studies to distribute trip ends, and in retail market analysis to distribute sales. The basic idea used is an inverse power law, derived from the inverse square law found in physics.

The concept of potential, also found in physics, has been used by Stewart (1963) to analyse population distribution.

The second manifestation of the natural sciences—social sciences interaction, has been the adoption of a large number of *techniques* initially used in the natural sciences. Among the more common methods are regression analysis; component analysis, as used in the definition of urban sub-areas by Gittus (1964); and Markov processes, demonstrated by Prais (1955) and Goodman (1961). Regression analysis is usually used in static models, to demonstrate statistical relationships, and hence to infer causal relationships. Component analysis and factor analysis, described by Kendall (1961), are used to clarify basic units, using observed attributes. Markov processes are a major tool in the explanation of dynamic processes. Some techniques used in the social sciences have been adopted from fields outside the natural sciences. For example linear programming has come from operations research. Stevens (1961) and Lowry (1964) have shown the wide variety of applications of linear programming which are possible in the social sciences.

The use of methods borrowed from other scientific disciplines does not at present appear to offer a complete solution to the problems of urban studies. There are a number of reasons for this. Many, if not all, of the problems that arise in the social sciences are rather complex, both conceptually and in the amounts of data that have to be handled.

To some extent this difficulty can be alleviated by the use of the computer, but there are other difficulties, which may not be so easily overcome. For example, in the natural sciences progress is usually made by using observations on phenomena that are complete, but in the social sciences the reverse is more likely to be true. The phenomena observed are unlikely to be complete and the problem of complicated time lags has to be overcome. This latter problem occurs occasionally in the natural sciences (in oceanography with the study of wave generation, and in meteorology in weather forecasting) and can be described as the analysis of spatial time series. With this kind of problem, the use of such tools as regression analysis for forecasting by extrapolation is dangerous, particularly where causal as distinct from statistical explanation is weak. An alternative approach, with a more behavioural bias, would be some sort of game-theory based model or a gaming simulation model, both of which could give some insight into causal mechanisms. Despite these drawbacks a large variety of models has been developed. These can be classified in many ways, depending upon the purpose of

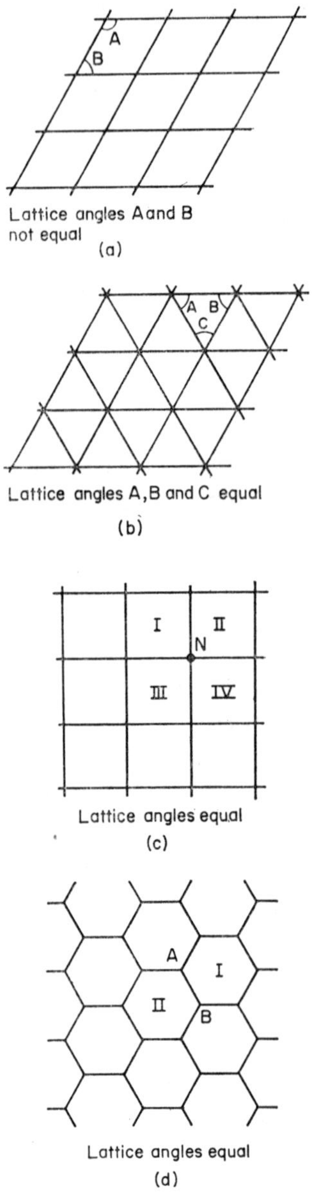

Fig. IX 1 Alternative grid lattices for data arrangement.

the model, the scale of work, and the method by which outputs are derived. Descriptions of various classifications can be found in Loewenstein (1966) and Lowry (1965).

Certain general points apply to most types of model. A model will often be looking at the pattern of variation of some variables such as population, economic activity, land use, retail sales and so on. Whatever is being observed, there is usually a basic unit on which the observations are made, such as a household, a plot of land, an enumeration district, a borough, a town, a region, a week or a decade. It is sometimes possible to amalgamate basic units to form larger ones; for example, enumeration-districts can be amalgamated to form boroughs. The choice of unit will depend upon the scale of output required. If it is a spatial distribution which is to be analysed, basic units are usually formed either by using a grid system or by using a system of zones.

A grid system divides the study area into equal regular figures by means of a lattice, as shown in Fig. IX 1. If, on grounds of symmetry, we stipulate that lattice angles be equal, three and only three possibilities arise, equilateral triangles, squares, or regular hexagons. A square grid is usual, presumably because most maps are of this form. Hexagonal grids have the unique property that flows from one unit to another are completely across faces and not across nodes.

Thus the flow from I to II in Fig. IX 1 (d) is across AB, whereas in Fig. IX 1 (c) the flow from II to III is across the node N. In a square grid, it may be possible to regard the flow from II to III as being from II to I and then I to III or II to IV to III, but this may lead to complications in dynamic models. For example, if population was being investigated and the data showed a flow in unit time from II to III in Fig. IX 1 (d), the method mentioned above would lead to difficulties, because one has to decide whether, or how much of, the flow from II to III travels via I or IV, and also decide upon the times taken for these journeys. For more complicated flows, that is, between non-neighbouring grid units, the hexagonal unit appears best, although there is the difficulty of deciding upon the route taken. One way of treating this particular problem might be to give probabilities to the transitions between neighbouring units and then, for more complicated flows, sum over all possible flow paths. A disadvantage of the hexagonal grid is that, unless some sort of transformation is made, it is not possible to aggregate hexagonal units to make larger hexagonal units.

A common alternative to a grid is a system of zones; examples are enumeration districts, traffic zones, boroughs, regions and nations. A system of zones normally has the following major properties. First, the shapes of the zones will not be similar or regular. Second, each zone will have a characteristic which serves to define it; to put it another way, there is a rule by which zones can be defined. Thus for enumeration districts the defining rule is that there should be (roughly) a fixed number of households within the zone, which are also situated so as to be manageable for the zone enumerator. Traffic zones, as in the London Traffic Survey (1964), are defined by a maximum traversal travel time, maximum population and homogeneity or compatability in land uses. Boroughs and nations are defined by boundaries and administrative barriers of some sort. Clearly it is possible in many cases for aggregation to take place; for example, enumeration districts can be aggregated into traffic zones. The problem of flow between zones is much the same as that for grids. In this respect the position of zones appears to be roughly between a square and hexagonal grid.

If the model is to be used for prediction, care should be taken to see that, during the planning period, the basis for zone-selection is not invalidated. If this happened the basis of prediction might be upset. Also, if zones rather than a grid are used, change-over time is difficult to measure. A system of zones might be better suited for a static model. For both a grid system and a system of zones, computer capacity and sampling properties also serve to determine the number of zones or grid units and therefore, for a given area, the size of zones or grid units.

Time can be discussed in a similar manner, although it is normal if not universal practice for observations depending on time to be made at regular intervals. The choice of intervals, apart from consideration of feasibility, depends on what is desired. A further discussion on this topic can be found in Kendall & Stuart (1966).

A final problem of some importance lies in the testing and comparison of models. Basically this amounts to testing the hypotheses upon which the model is built. For statistical models, such as regression analysis, the usual statistical tests of significance will apply, and these will give an indication of how well the model's output fits reality. For those models where there is no underlying statistical distribution upon which to base a significance test, the problem is more difficult. So far the only solution seems to be to use non-parametric tests of the kind suggested by Siegel (1956). Similar considerations apply to comparing two or more models to determine which is the better, though in this case we should also compare the costs of collecting the data and of operating the model.

Towards a Model of the Construction of Office Space

Having considered the general problems of model building in the social sciences, we can move on to the more specific questions involved in a model of changes in office space over time. Office space can be measured either as a continuous variable or in terms of office space classes, which can be obtained by dividing the office space continuum into intervals.

Suppose the process is being observed at equally spaced points of time. For the *t* th time interval, which may also be called time *t*, the following variables can be defined for each cell.

X_t = Office space newly constructed during the *t* th interval
Y_t = Office space removed during the *t* th interval
Z_t = Increase in office space due to change of use in the *t* th interval

Clearly $X_t \geqslant 0$, $Y_t \geqslant 0$, $Z_t \geqslant 0$.
The net change in office space C_t in the *t* th time interval is given by

$$C_t = X_t - Y_t + Z_t \qquad \text{(i)}$$

Clearly C_t can be negative, zero or positive.

If the initial amount of office space C_o is also known, then at the end of any interval the total amount of office space in the cell at time T, M_T, is given by

$$M_T = \sum_{t=o}^{T} C_t \qquad \text{(ii)}$$

The above discussion deals with one land use, namely office space. This can be generalised to several, H say, land uses. The following set of H equations can now be written for each cell.

$$C_{h,t} = X_{h,t} - \sum_{\substack{m=i \\ m \neq h}}^{H} Y_{h,m,t} + \sum_{\substack{m=i \\ m \neq h}}^{H} Z_{h,m,t} \quad \ldots \quad (h = 1,2 \ldots \text{H}) \qquad \text{(i)}'$$

$C_{h,t}$ = net change in land use *h* in the *t* th interval.
$X_{h,t}$ = new construction of land use *h* in the *t* th interval.
$Y_{h,m,t}$ = loss of land use *h* to land use *m* in the *t* th interval.
$Z_{h,m,t}$ = gain of land use *h* from land use *m* in the *t* th interval.
Clearly $X_{h,t} \geqslant 0$, $Y_{h,m,t} \geqslant 0$, $Z_{h,m,t} \geqslant 0$
and $C_{h,t}$ may be negative, zero or positive.

There are two sets of constraints which may be applied to the variables of (i)′. The first set, which might be called consistency constraints, can be expressed verbally by saying that in each cell the sum of the losses due to change of land use *m* is equal to the sum of the gains due to change to land use *m*. This can be expressed by the equation

$$\sum_{\substack{h=l \\ h\neq m}}^{H} Y_{h,m,t} = \sum_{\substack{k=l \\ k\neq m}}^{H} Z_{m,k,t} \quad .\;.\;.\;. \quad (m=1,2 \;.\;.\;.\;.\; H) \quad .\;.\;.\;.\;.\;.\;.\;.\;.\;.\;.\;.\;.\;.\;. \quad \text{(iii)}$$

Since the gains of one land use must be the losses of another the equations of (iii) are automatically inviolate and the $Y_{h,m,t}$, $Z_{h,m,t}$ are, therefore, not independent.

The second set of constraints may be called social constraints. Examples of these are zoning regulations, availability of labour to provide office workers or the capacity of the construction industry in relation to the projected change of use. In contrast to consistency constraints, social constraints can be violated. Thus, if there are not enough office workers for the offices in existence, there will be vacant office space and this in turn may affect the formation of new office space. Social constraints can be subdivided into control constraints, which are defined by public control and/or legislation, and feasibility constraints, two examples of which would be the capacity of the construction industry to produce the forecast office space and the capacity of the nation to provide office workers for the satisfactory use of the forecast office space.

The resolution of the general problem may be divided into two parts. First we must determine functions for $X_{h,t}$, $Y_{h,m,t}$ and $Z_{h,m,t}$, and second, the set of social constraints must be derived. If we determine these functions from observations of previous occurrences, there may be difficulty in isolating the effects of social constraints which were then acting. Under these circumstances some comparative experiments may be useful, but with so many other possible factors it would be difficult to isolate social constraints.

Two possible model building approaches are (a) deterministic and (b) stochastic.

A simple deterministic approach might run as follows. Take time, *t*, as the only independent variable. This can be justified on the grounds that all other variables change with time. The total amount of office space in a quadrant at time *t*, M(*t*) may be given by equations like these.

or

$$M(t) = a/(1 + be^{-kt}): \quad \text{(iv)}$$

$$M(t) = e^{\alpha - \beta/t}: \quad \text{(v)}$$

The curves for (iv) and (v) are drawn in Figs. IX 2 (a) and IX 2 (b). Both equations for M(t) have the property that M(t) possesses a finite limiting value.

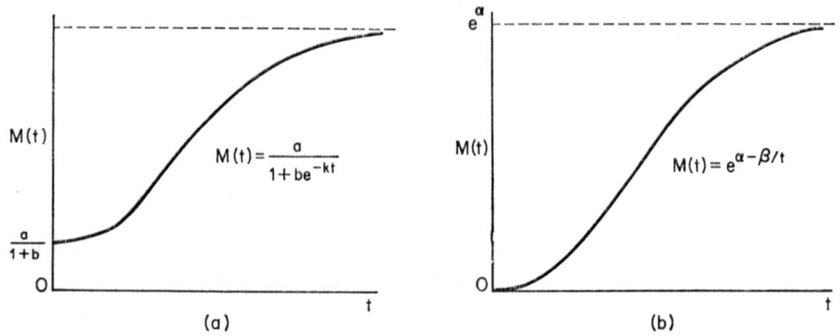

Fig. IX 2 Possible curves of office growth, based upon simple deterministic models.

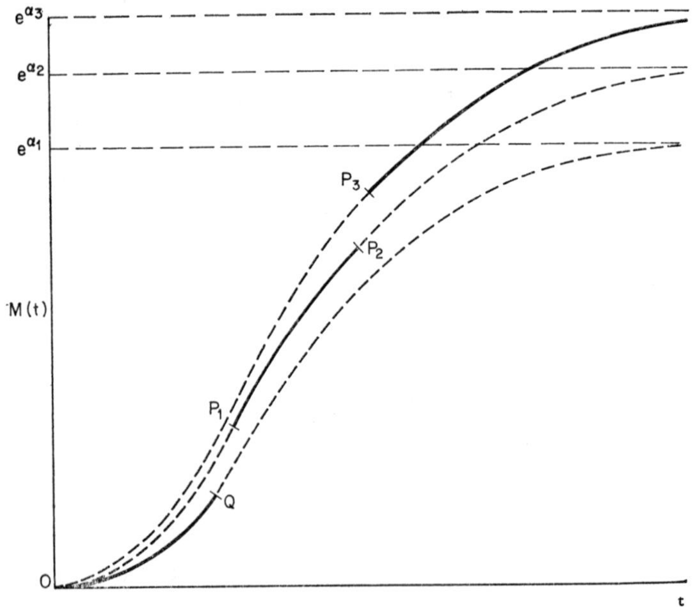

Fig. IX 3 Effect on office space, M(t) *of changes in social constraints, etc.*

A finite limiting value is postulated because we feel intuitively that there is a limit to the amount of floor space that can be built on a given site area. This would be the true upper limit, but the social constraints can be regarded as refining this to a more practical limiting value. Whenever there is a change in the limiting value, there is a change not in the family of curves but in the particular curve for M(t). Fig. IX 3 shows what might happen when the process is represented by a curve of the family $M(t) = e^{\alpha - \beta/t}$. The parameter can be determined by the fact that the limiting value of $M(t)$ is e^{α}, and this comes from the set of social constraints. As a first step β could be assumed constant for all curves of the family and could therefore be calculated by regression from the portion OQ, provided of course there are sufficient points in this section.

The idealism and/or uncertainty in this deterministic model has led us to the development of a stochastic approach. The results from such an approach, rather than giving the completely specified event characteristic of a deterministic approach, give a *range of outcomes*, each member of which will have a probability of occurrence. The method of determining the range of outcomes is based on probabilities of occurrence of events. This is not because the events themselves are necessarily uncertain but given the information obtained, and perhaps even with the maximum information available, outcomes cannot be predicted with certainty. This may not be such a drawback as it first appears.

This approach can be applied to the study of office development. A developer wishing to build an office block on a piece of land will need to know more than the bare probability of the venture being a success. He investigates all the variables that influence the outcome to see whether they are favourable. Favourability or otherwise is determined by some sort of model, or set of rules, which will probably be an estimate based on experience and intuition. When the overall picture of office development is being studied, this kind of information is unlikely to be universally available. It is also possible that the accuracy of the property developer's predictions may not be very high. For our own model we assume that, given certain probabilities, different distributions of office space can be obtained. A rough analogy can be drawn between this and the results of tossing a coin, if we take land (or site) as the coin, various states of office floorspace quantities as corresponding to the states of the coin (i.e., heads or tails), and the factors affecting office development (some if not all of which are considered by the developer) as the forces acting on the coin.

Let us consider the generation of new office space. At time t this is given by X_t. We write $P\{A|B\}$ = probability that the event A occurs given that the event B has occurred.

For quadrant k there are N states of area of newly constructed office space in the t th interval. These states can be numbered 1,2 . . . . i,j . . . . N. Then ${}_kP_{ij}$ is defined by:

$_kP_{ij} = P\{_kS_{t+1} = j \mid {_kS_t} = i\}$ . . . . (vi)

where $_kS_t$ is the state (from the point of view of newly constructed office space) of quadrant k at time t. Each quadrant k now has associated with it an $N \times N$ matrix of transition probabilities $\{_kP_{ij}\}$

Similar transition probabilities can be defined for Y_t and Z_t. From (vi) we see that the transition probability $_kP_{ij}$ depends only on the initial and the final state. There is no dependence on those urban variables which intuition, at least, indicates do affect office development. From now on our approach is to see how closely reality can be reproduced, using calculated values for the $_kP_{ij}$, based on the simplest possible hypotheses. If the simplest hypothesis does not give a satisfactory fit with observed events, we test a more complex hypothesis.

Our initial hypothesis has three parts.

H_1:—$_kP_{ij}$ is independent of k; that is, all quadrants have the same set of transition probabilities.

H_2:—The behaviour in state S_{t+1} is only dependent on behaviour in state S_t.

H_3:—$_kP_{ij}$ does not depend on what occurs or has occurred in neighbouring quadrants; that is, behaviour within a quadrant is statistically independent of behaviour in neighbouring quadrants.

H_1 *is unlikely to be true for an area like the London conurbation.* It is more likely that there are classes of quadrants, such that the quadrants is any one class have the same set of transition probabilities. For a model which determines new office space it may be possible to put the quadrants into classes, using change of use figures (the change being to offices). This assumes there is a statistical relationship between this change of use and the occurrence of new office space.

The problem raised by H_2, *of time lag effects, can be tackled in two ways.* Firstly, $_kP_{ij}$ could be assumed to be some function of time. Alternatively, behaviour earlier than the previous year can be accounted for by the following method. Suppose we wish to take into account the behaviour of the previous two years. A new state S_t^* is defined by the vector

$S_t^* = (S_{t-1}, S_t)$ . . . . (vii)

Clearly, $S_{t+1}^* = (S_t, S_{t+1})$

Since there are N possible states for S_t, S_t^* has $N \times N = N^2$ possible states. These states can be labelled in some way 1, 2, . . . , N^2. Now $_kP_{ij}^*$ is defined by $_kP_{ij}^* = P\{$Quadrant k is in new state j at time $t+1$. It is in new state *i* at time *t*}, where *i* and *j* are new states defined as in (vii). This will give an $N^2 \times N^2$ matrix of transition probabilities, which means a considerable increase in size. However, it will automatically have several zero elements, each of which corresponds to an impossible transition. Thus, if at time *t*, $S^*_t = (S_{t-1}, S_t) = (1,2)$ say, then since $S^*_{t+1}, = (S_t, S_{t+1})$ for any S^*_{t+1} whose first element is not the state 2, the transition probability is zero, since the transition itself is impossible. This may make manipulation of the transition matrix easier. For example, consider a process with three states (1, 2, 3) with transition matrix P, given by:

P =	1	2	3
1	X	X	X
2	X	X	X
3	X	X	X

where X denotes a non-zero transition probability. Transition occurs from row to column; that is, the element in the second row and third column is the probability of transition from state 2 to state 3. For this example, the transition matrix for S^*_t will be P^*, where

P* =	(1,1)	(1,2)	(1,3)	(2,1)	(2,2)	(2,3)	(3,1)	(3,2)	(3,3)
(1,1)	X	X	X	0	0	0	0	0	0
(1,2)	0	0	0	X	X	X	0	0	0
(1,3)	0	0	0	0	0	0	X	X	X
(2,1)	X	X	X	0	0	0	0	0	0
(2,2)	0	0	0	X	X	X	0	0	0
(2,3)	0	0	0	0	0	0	X	X	X
(3,1)	X	X	X	0	0	0	0	0	0
(3,2)	0	0	0	X	X	X	0	0	0
(3,3)	0	0	0	0	0	0	X	X	X

Intuition tells us that H_3 *will be untrue.* The effect of events in neighbouring quadrants could be tackled in the following way. Consider as part of the grid the block of nine cells shown below:

1	2	3
4	5	6
7	8	9

For quadrant 5, let i denote its actual newly constructed office space state. Let r be the value of some function of the new office space figures for the other eight quadrants; for example, r could be the class into which the sum of newly constructed office space in the quadrant falls. A new state S'_t is defined by

$S'_t = (i,r)$

$S'_t + _1 = (j,s)$ say . . . . (viii)

For each quadrant k transition probabilities ${}_kP_{ijrs}$ are defined by:

${}_kP_{ijrs} = P\{S_{t+1} = (j,s) \mid S_t = (i,r)\}$ . . . . (ix)

Clearly the remarks on H_1 and H_2 could be applied to refine (ix).

The parameters ${}_kP_{ij}$ can be estimated by finding the relative frequencies of events from empirical data. A difficulty arises over the definition and abstraction of empirical constraints, but it may be possible, using the ${}_kP_{ij}$, to obtain a good reproduction of office development without the constraints, if the assumption that these constraints are already built into the estimated probabilities is true. A further problem arises when the constraints change. As a first attempt in developing the model we might disregard the constraints, except perhaps for zoning, and see what results are obtained.

Because of lack of resources we were not able to test the model against real life. However, this part of the work could be carried out fairly easily, using certain simulation procedures.

The following flow charts give a general indication of the procedure by which hypotheses about the ${}_kP_{ij}$, such as H_1, H_2, H_3, might be tested.

These flow charts are for new office construction, but the procedure could be generalised.

Assume the data for new office construction has been classified into size groups and the relative frequencies of these groups is known. We also assume that each quadrant has a number k.

Our main objective is to find the simplest hypothesis (in terms of like transition probabilities, ${}_kP_{ij}$) which gives an adequate explanation or reproduction of the data.

Flow Chart for the Simulation of the behaviour of quadrant k

Observe ${}_kS_t$ $t=0, 1, \ldots . (n-1)$ [${}_kS_o$ is taken from data, ${}_kS_t$ ($t>0$) is simulated].

↓

Simulate ${}_kS_{t+1}$. This is done using a pseudo-random process, such that $P\{{}_kS_{t+1} \mid {}_kS_t\} = {}_k\hat{P}_{ij}$, where ${}_k\hat{P}_{ij}$ is an estimate of ${}_kP_{ij}$ made from the data.

↓

If it is desired to make a comparison of an intervening simulated and observed situation, then the appropriate sum can be computed and stored.

↓

If $t<n-1$ increase t by one and return to start. If $t=n-1$ [i.e.: ${}_kS_n$ has just been simulated], compute $\sum_{t=o}^{n} {}_kS_t$ which gives the *total* (simulated) new office space.

Note: If the behaviour of quadrant k is independent of other quadrants, the simulation for the quadrants over the n time periods can be done sequentially, that is, in series (or first the behaviour of quadrant 1 is simulated then quadrant 2, etc.). If, however, the behaviour of quadrant k is dependent on other quadrants, this dependence will be part of a hypothesis H_1, and then the behaviour of the quadrants must be simulated in paralle. This last point may make a difference to the sequence (2)→(3) in the overall flow chart.

Overall Flow Chart

Select Hypothesis, H_i.
Initially, $i=1$ (1)

↓

Simulate behaviour of quadrant 1 assuming H_i is true, for n time intervals. (2)

↓

Repeat for quadrant k
$k=2, 3, \ldots\ldots$ (3)

↓

Plot and map $\sum_{t=o}^{t=n} {}_kS_t$ for all
$k=1, 2, \ldots\ldots$ (4)

↓

Repeat a sufficient number of times so that a frequency distribution is obtained for the final (and if desired intervening) set of states. (5)

↓

Compare the simulated result with observed result and assess goodness of fit. (6)

↓

If fit is bad, modify H_i to get H_{i+1} and return to (1). If fit is good accept H_i. (7)

Note: The comparison can be made at the end of the simulation period and also at intervening stages. This latter may, however, affect subsequent tests for goodness of fit.

Our model is not quite complete because we have not followed the system through to a stable state, if one exists. However it should be possible to follow the flow of floorspace through states which are defined in terms of age and type of use including demolition. It might provide a way, even if we were able only to guess at some of the missing parameters, to test some interesting hypotheses. For example, to the extent that planning controls and policies are effective, transition probabilities ought to differ among groups of areas defined by public policies. Thus the probabilities limiting office uses and demolition should be higher in an area in which the authority generally permits new office construction than in areas where this is not permitted, *if and only if* there is a real demand for office space where the restrictive policy is in effect.

Unfortunately our resources did not permit us to test such ideas, but the act of constructing the model itself led us to believe that this kind of approach avoids some of the pitfalls of more behavioural type modelling, and that it has considerable potential as a powerful tool in urban analysis.

Nevertheless our quasi-Markov approach does not offer a very full explanation of the phenomena which it considers. Explanation enters into the testing of hypotheses through Markovian analysis and to some extent in assigning transition probabilities, but we felt that an alternative was needed.

A Simulation Model

We adopted a more traditional approach to our second model, the Monte Carlo simulation. At the current stage of urban model building, simulation continues to offer a number of advantages. As in all model building, it imposes rigorous description upon the modeller, and it possesses some flexibility for later modification and addition. Simulation does not provide the kind of precision which is available in more formal mathematical treatment, but it has made considerable contributions to urban studies in the past and there were good reasons for us to adopt such an approach in our own work.

Simulation is basically an experimental approach. Efforts are made to reproduce the system and events of the real world. As in all models, the representation is simplified, with only the major components in-

Fig. IX 4 Office stock —1957.

	1	2	3	4	5	6	7	8	9	10	11	12	13	14	15	16	17	18	19	20	21	22	23	24	25	26	27	28	29	30	31	32
1						29	4	9	105	15	6	15	4	18	4	13	23	5	9	61		1	3	25	3	137	3	3	1	1		
2						13	4	1	1	23	5	5	7	9	23	1	6	9	14	102	5	1		2	1	24	7	1		1	1	
3						2	25	5	4	13			70	143	40		1	5	18	31	4	3	8	4	5	21		1		1	3	
4					4		2	12	13	27	3			20	177	2	145	6	131	33		2	5	7	11	72	19		3	1	3	2
5	2			3	5	1		9	7	6	75			175	89	517	724	186	107	127	151	471	219	11	5	11	7		7	24	90	16
6				19	5	20	46	7	25	13	97	314	348	287	186	929	380	413	107	235	85	414	95	22	1		13	5	2	2	3	
7			1	27		1	12	79	37	49	106	887	474	1600	391	1041	1380	2517	2008	684	295	2298	664	208	16	36	25	4				
8			1	1	17	13	250	56	301	84	59	420	1144	1919	1048	1412	1513	2547	2909	1625	2509	5897	4850	460	71	47	9	28	7	48	5	3
9				5	8	4	11	46	92	23	9	194	941	2546	2184	1309	2155	1525	1245	864	599	2797	2894	470	105	13	3	2	16	16	12	24
10	7	9	16	5	34	23	633						499	1621	2117	1705	2549	62	610	172	267	559	115		3	47	3	4	1	1		
11	22	3	26	165	1		38	197	22	101	95	211	629	259	178	1514	1993	1217	125	45	58	48	38	47	21	12	4					
12	10	14	22	4	322	16	61	104	91	63	92	180	344	1025	1484	2880	1158	9	99	152	48		7	39	8	9	1				1	
13	10	7	207	204	50	460	11	56	64	235	43	66	74	469	419	515	1271	286	17	37	49	5	16	17	3	5	7	5				
14	1	66	11		6	7	7	9	53	7	148	15	24	119	12	56	66	1	25	11	37	3	1	5			1		1			
15			2	19	8	9	10		31	25	19	7			3	11	48	18	14		18	6				13	2	3		3	5	1
16			21		38	2	159	23	6	8	3					1		20	74	5	3	2	3			9	2	1	5	9	12	22
17				2	4	27	29	1	1	7	3	13		10	7	1	5	31	5		12	37	50	9	65	9	13	11	35	20	46	16
18					8	5	7	4		5	39	1	28	2	6	23	9	6	24	5	23	12	2	2	34		1			2	11	
19				3	6			2		1	9	93	3	23	47	8	6	18	45	2			10	1	9	1			3	3		
20			4	62	26		16	3	1	16	64	9		27	47	23	5	86	42	3			1	7	17				3	2		

cluded. Simulations are stochastic rather than deterministic in character so that the chance elements present in real processes are specifically structured.

This is not to suggest that the outcome of such a model is uncertain, for continuous recycling will usually give a distribution of outcomes clustered around some mean value. Let us consider the evaluation of an irregularly shaped area, A. If A is enclosed within a square of unit side and a point taken at random, then the probability that it lies within A is simply A. For a large number of points taken at random, the proportion lying within A is an estimate of A. The technique remains valid when generalised to higher dimensions, the advantage being that a result may be obtained with any number of points, n. A series of runs generates a distribution of outcomes. Methods are available for reducing the variance of this distribution for a specified number of runs.

The Model Design

For a rectangular area of 160 square kilometers covering the whole of the Central London region, we knew the total office stock for 1957 and 1962 existing within each cell. There were 640 cells in the region. The information was derived from the G.L.C. Land Use Surveys.

Our second batch of data comprised a complete list of all planning applications for offices from 1948 to 1965. These were divided into three main types—new buildings, extensions and changes of use. In nearly every case we knew both the cell concerned and the year of approval of the application. We also knew, for new buildings and extension, the size of the unit, in thousands of square feet. However, only about 20% of the change of use applications were as complete.

These data had one major limition. This was due to the method employed by the G.L.C. in measuring floorspace, which differed in the two exercises. A series of tests by the G.L.C. showed that if a third was subtracted from the land use figures, a reasonable approximation to the office survey values was obtained. It is these reduced land use values for 1957 and 1962 which appear in Figs. IX 4 and IX 5, whilst the yearly numbers of planning approvals for the three types of input are given in Fig. IX 6.

Fig. IX 5 Office stock —1962.

	1	2	3	4	5	6	7	8	9	10	11	12	13	14	15	16	17	18	19	20	21	22	23	24	25	26	27	28	29	30	31	32
1						30	4	7	94	23	2	13	4	23	8	12	23	5	8	67		2	9	23	2	151	5	3	1	2		
2						15	5	1	3	25	7	7	7	9	124	2	11	7	15	101	6	2		2	1	12	8	1			3	
3						2	33	5	4	13			87	222	52		1	7	17	45	5	5	5	4	3	23	7	2	1	1	3	
4					4		2	15	14	28	3			20	214	4	234	71	142	42	3	1	4	7	9	74	5	3	1	1	2	2
5	3	1		3	5	2	1	8	7	6	75			113	288	570	769	187	111	117	204	178	201	12	9	49			5	25	84	14
6				13	8	28	39	7	5	29	152	293	399	237	776	888	370	384	187	210	221	845	132	21	15	1	16	6	13	1	3	
7			1	25		2	14	80	19	51	448	943	886	1759	921	1155	1406	2804	2083	815	542	3255	814	169	16	32	25	4		2		
8				6	21	11	250	200	409	313	53	491	1615	1962	1304	1557	1748	2572	3321	2078	4215	6108	5251	696	85	40	9	23	16	58	4	2
9				4	9	3	23	53	86	22	21	241	1124	2610	2420	1341	2454	1539	1211	909	678	2842	3329	594	141	13	3	10	16	14	11	24
10	7	12	15	3	34	19	390						449	1637	2301	1919	3250	238	601	337	491	551	132	29	3	49	3	6	1	6		
11	22	3	62	199	8		31	175	29	101	112	1128	642	249	183	1555	1790	1384	127	351	73	69	86	81	27	10	4					
12	7	13	25	3	320	10	61	105	208	82	115	201	320	1312	1292	2759	1227	7	263	139	60	5	6	39	7	4	4				1	
13	12	44	371	156	54	460	14	37	90	217	64	125	75	512	466	550	1258	511	16	17	67	5	15	17	5	9	6	7				
14	3	66	34		9	7	7	9	59	7	151	26	23	123	18	101	180	1	183	11	43	5	1	3	1	3	·		1			4
15			2	22	7	7	16	1	33	31	18				3	2	36	20	15		23	10	1	2		20	1	3		3	11	
16			21		38	3	164	17	7	7	13			1	1			19	65	4	6	2	5	1			4	1	9	7	16	47
17				1	4	29	29	1	1	7	3	14		13	7	2	5	34	7		11	35	50	11	70	8	39	11	34	21	40	17
18					8	7	7	3	109	6	7	2	27	2	7	23	7	7	27	10	1	8	2		56		1			5	9	
19				5	27			3	1		9	113	7	30	42	10	7	20	114	3				1	13		3		3	3		
20			5	72	37	7	50	2	3	16	84	15		16	40	24	5	99	49	3			5	7	14				4	2		

Fig. IX 6 Time series of numbers of approvals.

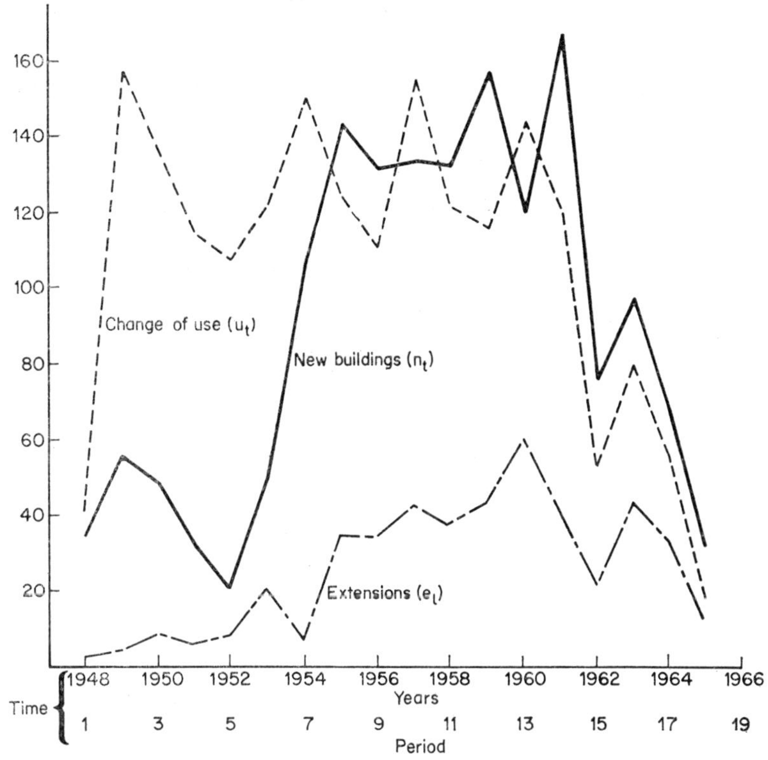

A number of severe limitations were imposed upon the model by the data. These are as follows.

1. Different possible forms of offices required by users were ignored.

2. Office units differed only in size.

3. Decision makers, both users and developers, were not explicitly specified.

4. General economic considerations were neglected.

5. Locations were stated only in terms of cells.

6. All other land uses were ignored.

The aim of our model can be stated quite simply. Given the position in 1957, generate the situation in each cell for 1962 and compare with that actually occurring. The time period t of the simulation was chosen as one year, and the recursive procedures of the model consisted of the following main steps.

1. Given the total number of approvals for each of the three types of input for the current period t, estimate the respective values for time $(t+1)$.

2. Derive lists of actual units from the size distributions of the three types.

3. Allocate each unit in turn to some cell in the region, and update the value of each cell's stock.

4. Repeat steps 1 to 3 for period $(t+2)$.

5. Continue until the estimated position for 1962 has been generated.

6. Recycle until a distribution of outcomes for 1962 has been constructed.

7. Compare the most likely outcome with the actual position.

In order to discuss the steps in detail, we introduced the following notation, capitals referring to amounts of office stock and small letters to numbers.

$t =$ Amount of office stock existing over whole region in period t.

$O_{i,j,t} =$ Amount of office stock existing in cell ij in period t.

$n_t =$ Number of approvals for new buildings for whole region in period t.

$e_t =$ Number of approvals for extensions for whole region in period t.

$u_t =$ Number of approvals for changes of use for whole region in period t.

$N_{i,j,t}(p) = p^{th}$ new building completed in cell ij in period t.

$E_{i,j,t}(q) = q^{th}$ extension completed in cell ij in period t.

$U_{i,j,t}(r) = r^{th}$ change of use completed in cell ij in period t.

$N_t(x) = x^{th}$ new building given approval over whole region in period t.

$E_t(y) = y^{th}$ extension given approval over whole region in period t.

$U_t(z) = z^{th}$ change of use given approval over whole region in period t.

and

$D_{i,j,t}(s) =$ Amount of office stock demolished in cell ij in period t to permit insertion of $N_{i,j,t+c,N(s)}(s)$, and/or $E_{i,j,t+cE(s)}(s)$.

Plate 5
Typical development at the height of London's office boom: Thorn House, St. Martins Lane.

Plate 6

The twentieth-century city rises above factory chimneys: New York skyline.

It is self evident that for any cell ij:

$$O_{i,j,t} = O_{i,j,t-1} + \Sigma N_{i,j,t}(p) + \Sigma E_{i,j,t}(q) + \Sigma U_{i,j,t}(r) - \Sigma D_{i,j,t}(s) \quad \ldots\ldots \text{(x)}$$

whilst for the whole region:

$$O_t = \Sigma O_{i,j,t}$$
$$= O_{t-1} + \Sigma\Sigma N_{i,j,t}(p) + \Sigma\Sigma E_{i,j,t}(q) + \Sigma\Sigma U_{i,j,t}(r) - \Sigma\Sigma D_{i,j,t}(s) \quad \ldots\ldots \text{(xi)}$$

The double sigmas in equation (xi) indicate summation not only over all p,q,r, and s, but also over all cells ij.

The basic relationship displays both the method of attack and some of our assumptions. By starting at period t (1957) the cell positions for period $t+5$ (1962) may be generated. Equally the definition of $D_{i,j,t}$ explicitly states that only offices are to be considered. Any demolition of old office stock to make room for uses other than offices is heroically neglected.

The small amount of transient office stock due to other types of input, such as temporary leasing of stock for office use and short-term new buildings, is ignored. Our early analysis indicated that such factors contributed less than a few per cent. to the overall picture. The first step in our simulation was the recursive estimation of future numbers of approvals for the three types of input. This will be discussed in some detail for new buildings. The solutions for extensions and changes of use are completely similar.

The technique employed in estimating the most likely value for the number of approvals in any period n_t was one commonly utilised in operations research, and is referred to as exponential smoothing. It evaluates the mean value of the distribution to which the value of the variable belong. More explicitly, given time series, with $\bar{n}_t$ being the value of the variables for period t, then the smoothed or average value of the variable n_t is given by:

$$\bar{n}_t = \alpha n_t + (1-\alpha)\bar{n}_{t-1} \quad \ldots\ldots \text{(xii)}$$

where, α is a constant between zero and unity and $\bar{n}_t$ may be used as the estimate of the value of the variable for the $(t+1)^{th}$ period. However, if a trend either increasing or decreasing exists in the series, this simple average will lag the actual value. It is possible to compensate for any linear trend by adding $\alpha\bar{g}_t$ to the original estimate, n_t. Here $\bar{g}_t$ is a smoothed estimate of the gradient of the trend, and is derived by a relationship analogous to equation (xii). The variable in this case is the changes in the average $\bar{n}_t$ through time. Hence the new estimate, n'_{t+1}, for the period $t+1$ is given by:

$$n'_{t+1} = \bar{n}_t + \alpha(\alpha g_t + (1-\alpha)\bar{g}_{t-1}) \quad \text{(xiii)}$$

where

$$g_t = \bar{n}_t - \bar{n}_{t-1} \quad \text{(xiv)}$$

and n_t is evaluated from equation (xii).

In order to estimate the value of the variable for the kth period in the future, the relationship must be modified to:

$$n'_{t+k} = \bar{n}_t + \left(\frac{k+1-\alpha}{\alpha}\right)(\alpha g_t + (1-\alpha)\bar{g}_{t-1}) \quad \text{(xv)}$$

Employing this method, we derived values of the number of approvals for each of the three types of input for any period in the future. These were the global estimates for the region, and the method seemed a reasonable way of cutting into the causal chain of decisions generating future offices. A detailed examination of migrations into and out of the region, of the growth of existing firms, and of the structure and decision making of developers could obviously improve upon this simple procedure.

The second major step concerned the derivation of lists of actual size units for each approval. This was easily done by drawing at random from the respective size distributions. Examples of the form these took, from early pilot data of Croydon, are displayed for new buildings and changes of use in Fig. IX 7 (c) and (d).

The major element of the model concerned step 3, which concerned the spatial allocation of each unit of stock and the periodic updating, using equation (x), of each cell's position. For clarity, let us track a unit of new building through the system.

Having started as one of the estimated number of approvals, n_t, it will have become, via step 2, a unit $N_t(x)$ with a specific size, ready to be assigned to some particular cell in the region. To accomplish this, we assumed that every cell could be given successively through time an index of attraction, $I_{i,j,t}$, which specified the relative probability that it would attract any unit.

We calculated the index in three ways. First, we evaluated the amount of completed stock in each cell as a proportion to that existing over the whole region. Second, we estimated a measure of a form of accessibility to the twelve main railway termini. Third, a combination of the first two was utilised.

Fig. IX 7 Typical distribution curves.

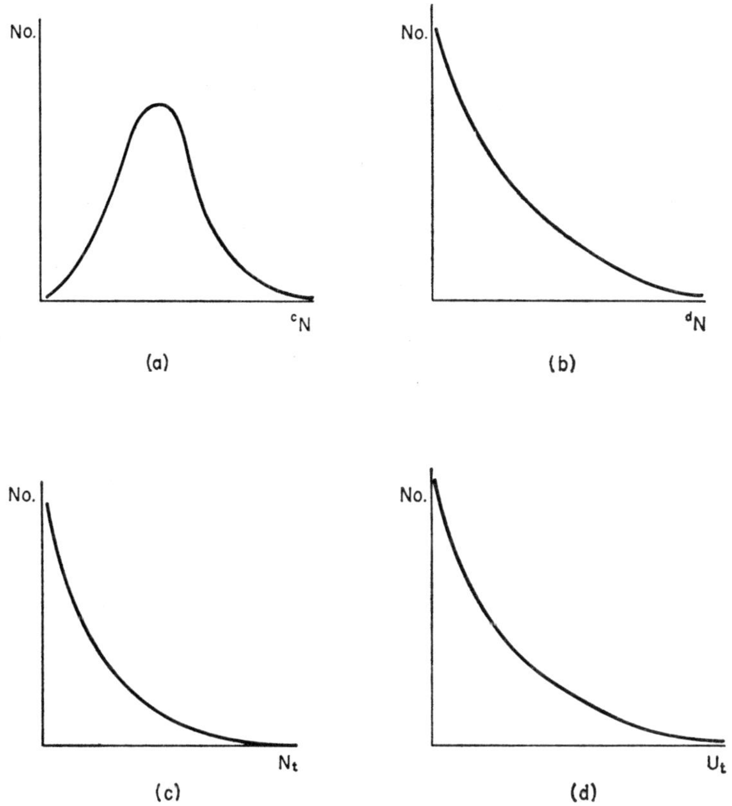

The method of calculation of the first $^1I_{i,j,t}$ is self explanatory. The second matrix $^2I_{i,j}$ is a little more complicated. For each cell the reciprocals of the distances $1_{i,j,u,v}$ to each of the main railway termini were calculated, where the stations were located in cells *u,v* and are indicated by square markers on Fig. IX 3. The sum of these reciprocals gave the indices for each cell, as specified by:

$$^2I_{i,j} = \sum_{uv} (1_{i,j,u,v})^{-1} \qquad \text{(xvi)}$$

The third index $^3I_{i,j,t}$ was merely the arithmetic mean of the other two. The second index is invariant over the period considered, whereas the other two change with any increase or decrease in office stock. In such cases we had to determine the year whose indices must be inspected for spatial allocation of any unit. This was based upon the following argument.

Although we did not specify a population of developers in concrete terms, we assumed that each unit $N_t(x)$ had an input process, corresponding to a probable real world pattern. Any developer who chose a cell for any unit would have based his decision upon the situation occurring at that point in time. Discussions with the local authority and initial attempt to acquire the land would occur, preceding the granting of the planning application. This time was designated as $d_N(x)$, and was a function of the size of the unit and the willingness of the authority to accept such development.

Once planning permission had been granted, a construction phase, $c_N(x)$ would follow for the unit, and our preliminary Croydon analysis suggested distribution of the form given in Fig. IX 7 (b) and (a), respectively. The difficult time period $d_N(x)$ was in this case evaluated from the time intervals between outline permissions and detailed approvals. It was possible that if a developer wished to inject a unit, he would immediately apply for an outline approval to test the reaction of the local authority. After obtaining detailed approval he could then start construction. The calculations of $I_{i,j,t}$ were based upon the presence of completed buildings, and hence only after time $c_N(x)$ would the unit $N_t(x)$ begin to influence further development. These two time intervals $d_N(x)$ and $c_N(x)$ for any unit were both derived by drawing at random from the two distributions. The actual cell chosen we also determined by this random approach. In order to complete the process implied by equation (*x*), it was necessary to evaluate the amount of old offices demolished. It was obvious that this stage applied only to new buildings and extensions, changes of use merely increasing each cell's stock. We estimated the amount demolished in any cell in period *t*, $D_{i,j,t}$, by utilising the G.L.C. data given in Table IX 1. This indicated that an increasing percentage of new stock was merely replacement of old structures. A dramatic increase occurred after the mid-1950's, the period prior to this being largely devoted to rectifying the damage of the war years.

We estimated the most likely value of the replacement percentage in period *t*, P_t, and reduced any cell's total stock by that proportion of any new unit given approval in the cell. We assumed that as soon as approval had been given, demolition occurred within the same period, and thus any cell's total stock could decrease for a limited time interval.

A nett increase would of course materialise after a few periods or so, when the new unit had been completed. Again considerable improvement to the model could be initiated at this point, not merely to evaluate demolitions of office stock to enable other uses to be injected, but also by considering the office stock itself. If the age profile of the currently existing stock were known, it could be continuously updated within the model, and the amount demolished made some function of the amount in existence for longer than a certain number of years.

In the model as it now stands, future estimates of P_t were calculated by an exponential smoothing equation.

The remaining steps of the model are largely self explanatory. They will be discussed when the actual computer simulation and the results are described and analysed.

The Simulation Model

Prior to any development of the model, a number of initial analyses had to be carried out. These involved the specification of the distributions displayed in Fig. IX 7. Our information on the sizes of units of both new buildings and extensions was virtually complete, whilst 20% of changes of use were known. Using this information, we constructed the histograms displayed in Figs. IX 8, IX 9 and IX 10. In each case, the size of each group is 2,000 sq. ft. Thus in the case of new buildings, 301 units had sizes between zero and 1,999 ft., 164 between 2,000 and 3,999 sq. ft. and so on.

Table IX 1 Growth of replacement percentage 1956–1963.

Year	New Buildings and Extensions Amount Approved	Replacement Percentage	Nett Increase	Increase 1957–1962	Increase Mid-1957 to Mid-1962
1956	3,771·4				
1957	6,434·3	5·3	6,093·3		
1958	4,493·8	21·4	3532·1		
1959	5,771·7	24·7	4,346·1		
				21,988	18,328
1960	4,852·6	26·2	3,681·2		
1961	6,137·6	49·5	3,099·5		
1962	2,699·5	54·2	815·8		

figures in 000's of sq. ft.

It would have been possible to utilise random numbers to construct a simulated distribution of points. For example, in the case of new buildings, 1,654 known units had been inspected for size to derive the distribution. Hence, if a random number between zero and 1,654 was drawn and lay between zero and 302, the probable size of the unit, N_t (x), to which it referred, would have been taken as 1,000 sq. ft., or 1 size unit. A series of random numbers could either have generated the

Fig. IX 8 Size distribution for new buildings.

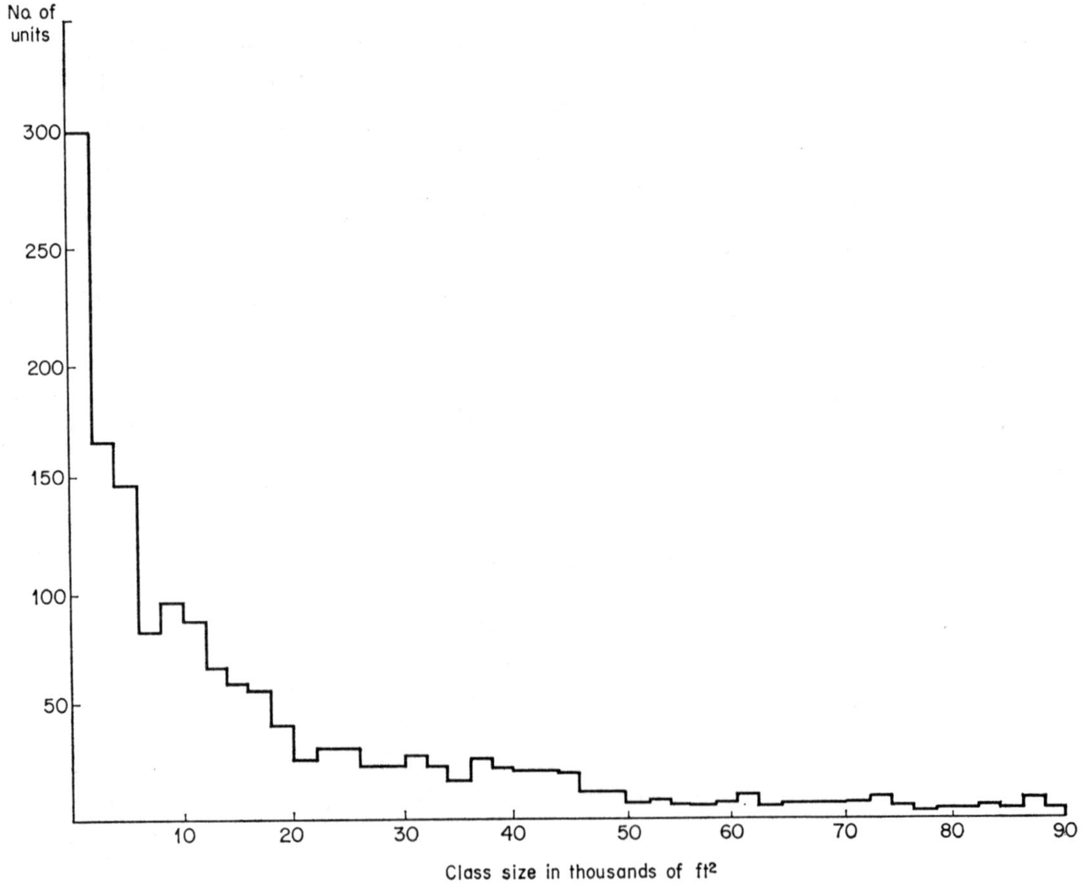

Fig. IX 9 Size distribution for extensions.

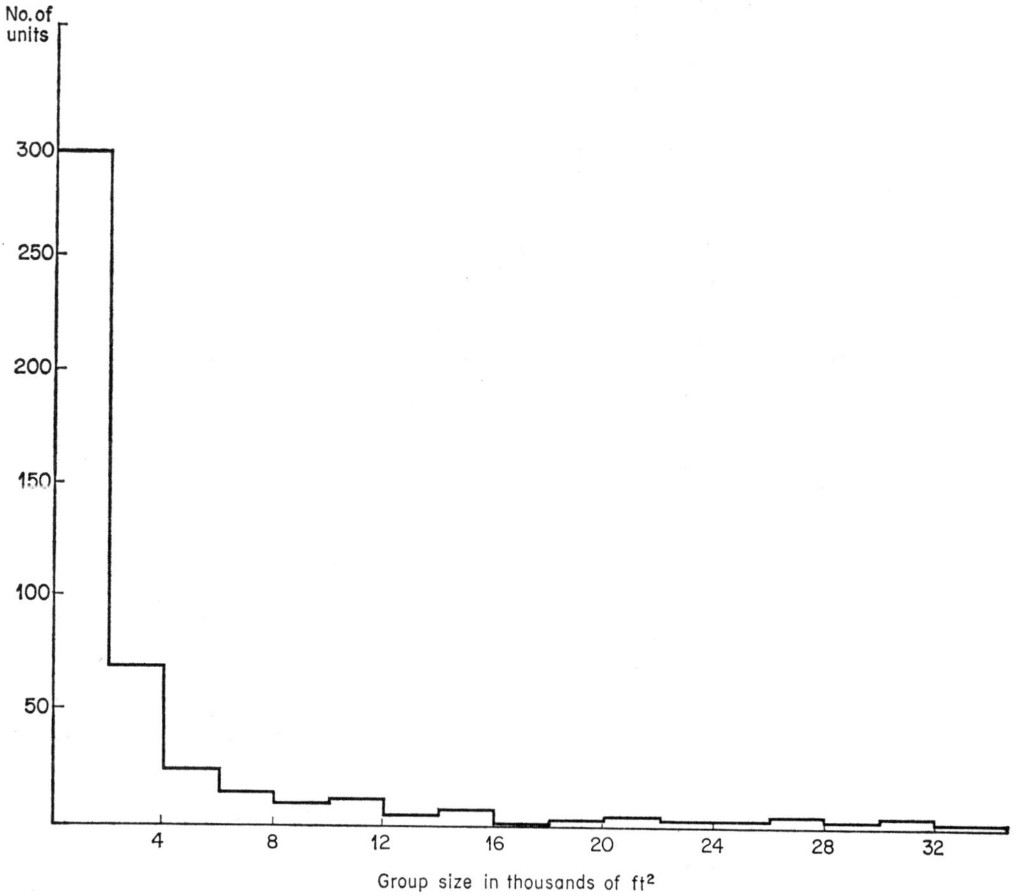

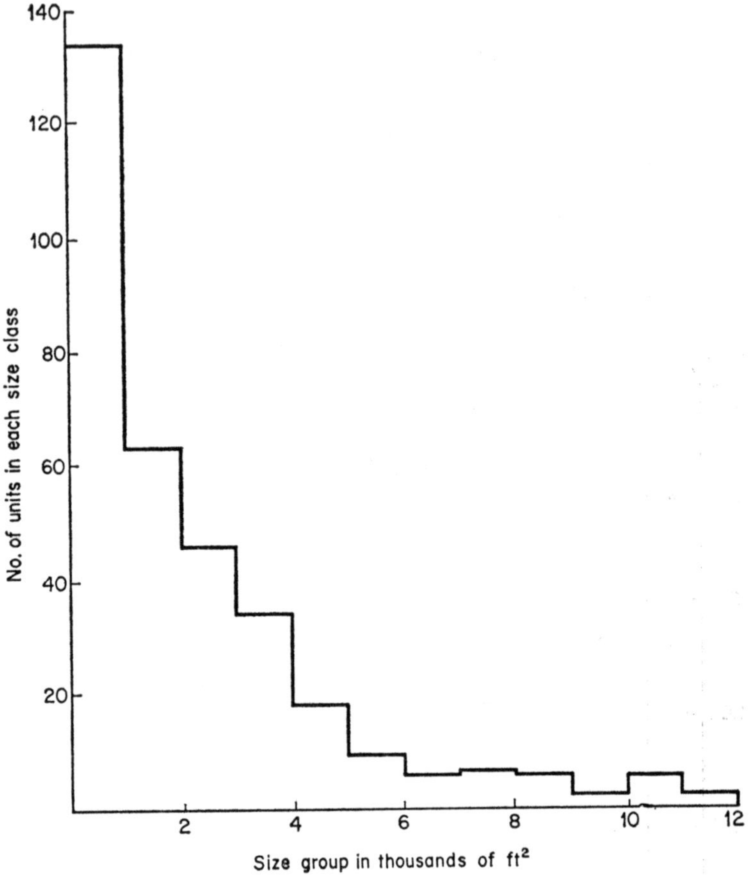

Fig. IX 10 Size distribution for change of use.

distribution or been employed in the computer simulation to assign a size to any approval $n_t(x)$.

However, this would have been wasteful of computer time. We therefore attempted to derive relationships between the number of units Y(*f*) and the size class *f*.

The procedure can be illustrated for the case of changes of use as indicated in Fig. IX 11. Here the logarithm of the number of units in each class in U(*f*) is plotted against the class number *f*. It is evident that a good approximation to linearity was achieved, which suggested a negative exponential relationship of the form:

$$U(f) = 272\, e^{-0.37f}$$

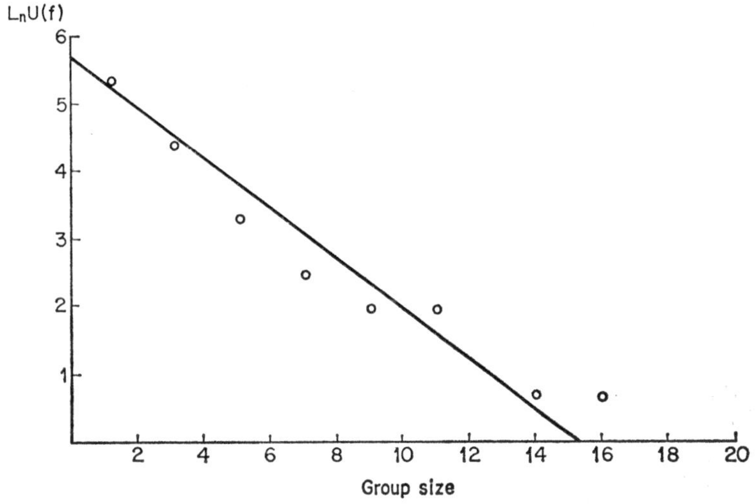

Fig. IX 11 Graph of change of use distribution analysis.

Employing this equation, we constructed the simulated histogram of Fig. IX 14; similar analyses gave Figs. IX 12 and IX 13, using the relationships

$N(f) = 124e^{-0.24f}$

and

$E(f) = 111e^{-0.24f}$.

In the latter two cases, however, the low end of the distribution was not completely specified by the relationships. To counteract the discrepancy, we used the random technique discussed above to generate the lower portion of the diagrams, the equations being utilised only for points above class 9 and 5 respectively.

We determined the construction period $c_N(x)$ for any new unit by inspection of Fig. IX 15. It may be seen that a small number of units had an apparent negative 'construction time'. This is due to some applicants going ahead with construction before detailed approval had been obtained. In the case of the building of an expensive commodity such as an office building this is a rather rare phenomenon, and we therefore considered only non-negative construction times.

It can be demonstrated that the graph fits two normal curves, firstly considering the points from two years and more, and secondly from one year and less. However, as there were only a limited number of years,

Fig. IX 12 Simulated size distribution for new buildings.

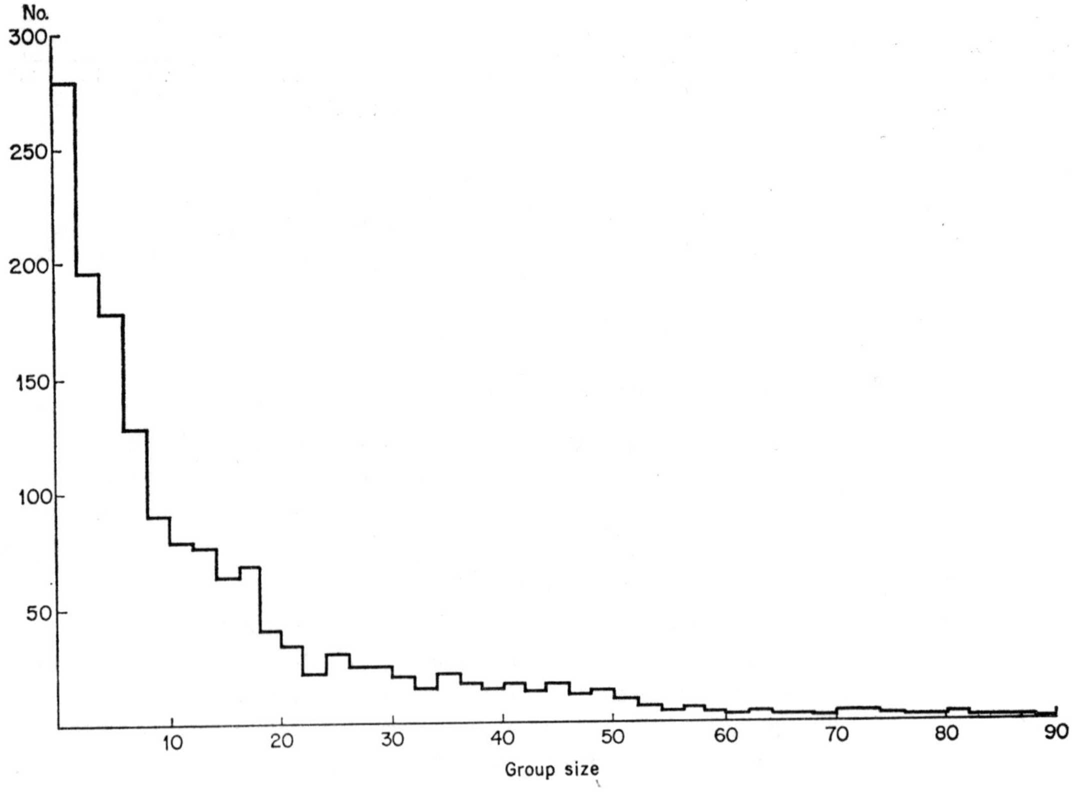

Fig. IX 13 Simulated size distribution for extensions.

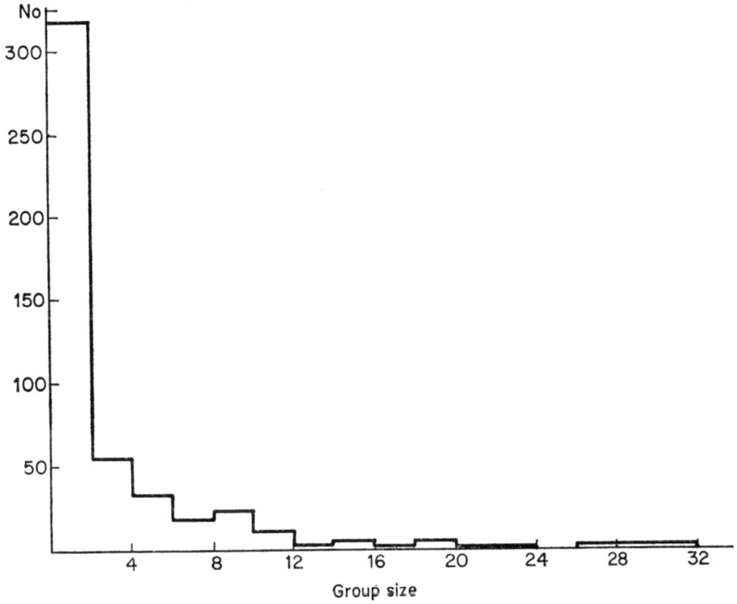

the calculations were done on a proportional basis and no curve was fitted. Any unit was taken to have 3–4% chance of being completed in the same year as the approval, an 18% chance in the following year, and so on. The derivation of distribution for $d_N(x)$ and $d_E(x)$ presented some difficulties. As we had already mentioned, this was a hypothetical time interval between a developer deciding that a site was ripe for development and obtaining detailed approval for a building. It is not quite the same interval as between outline and detailed approvals as given in fig. IX 7 for the initial Croydon data. The idea was that $d_N(x)$ was to decide the year whose indices must be inspected, or, in other words, the environment occurring when the developer chose the site.

The derivation was as follows. As the indices were known initially only for 1957 and 1962, we decided to choose fifty and then thirty-five cells at random. We then made a record of the total amount of new stock inserted in each of these cells for each year from 1957 onwards, and the totals were correlated with the indices for 1957. The results are displayed in Fig. IX 16, from which it is obvious that no systematic peaking occurs. This suggests that the 1957 position was not responsible for the events

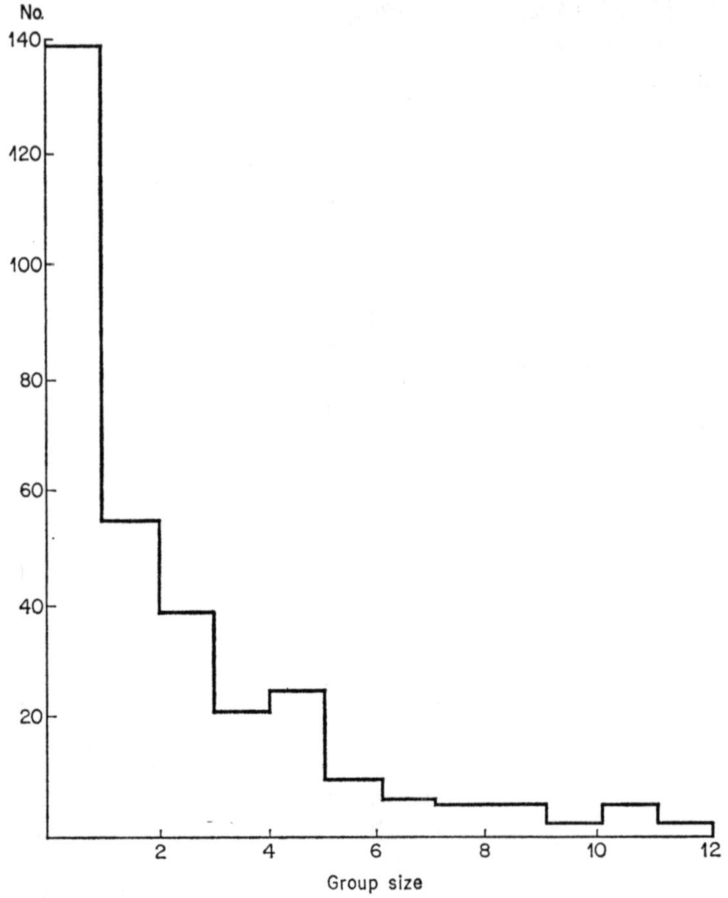

Fig. IX 14 Simulated size distribution for change of use.

of any one later year, and, in view of the evenness of the response, it was decided to attempt the first trials without reference to times $d_N(x)$ and $d_E(x)$. Self evidently, a more detailed analysis of the time lags involved is required in this model.

The Simulation Model

The three dimensional matrix $O_{i,j,t}$ was stored within the computer, with i and j specifying the row and column of any cell, whilst t, the time, was permitted to vary from one to twenty. Two separate arrays were read in, $057_{i,j}$ and $062_{i,j}$, stating the office stock in each cell for

Fig. IX 15 Distribution of construction times.

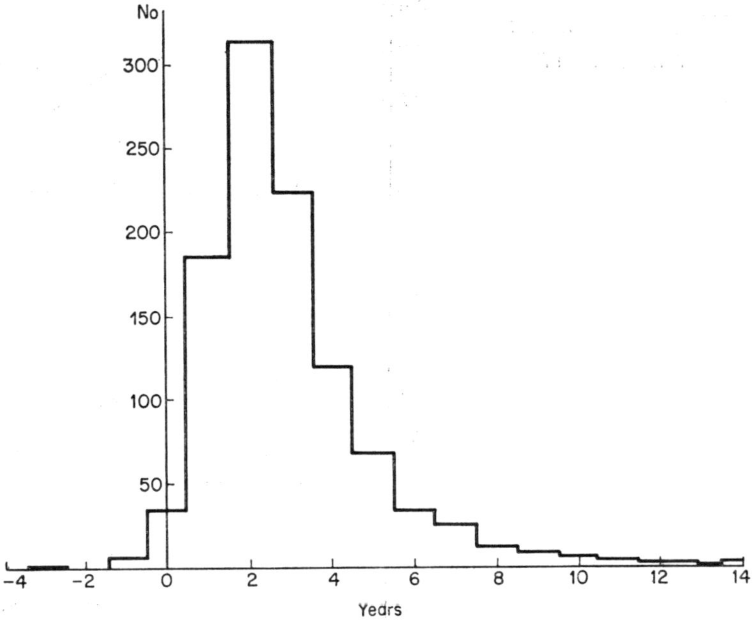

the two land use survey years, together with the actual number of approvals, n_t, e_t, u_t, for all periods and the demolition percentages, P_t.

We decided not to estimate these latter variables in the early runs of the model, but concentrated upon the spatial distribution side of the problem. Moreover, to reinforce this aspect, the actual units given approval in each period, $N_t(x)$, and $E_t(y)$, were read straight from cards. However, the sizes of $U_t(z)$ were unknown and so it was necessary here to refer to the subroutine generating $U_t(z)$.

The first computer routine scrutinised every $N_t(x)$ and $E_t(x)$ for each period from one to ten. To each was assigned a probability, given by the c_N distribution, of being completed during some period after 1957. If this happened, the unit had to be inserted within some cell in the region. The cell was chosen by reference to the set of indices being utilised for the run, ${}^1I_{i,j,t}$ say. This particular array was recalculated each period after 1956, by determining the relative amount of stock in each cell. For procedural purposes these proportions were accumulated and factored to allow their sum to reach ten thousand. A random number between zero and this sum then specified the chosen cell. Naturally, employing the array ${}^1I_{i,j,10}$ for all years prior to 1957 meant that the

Fig. IX 16 Correlation of index and total cell input.

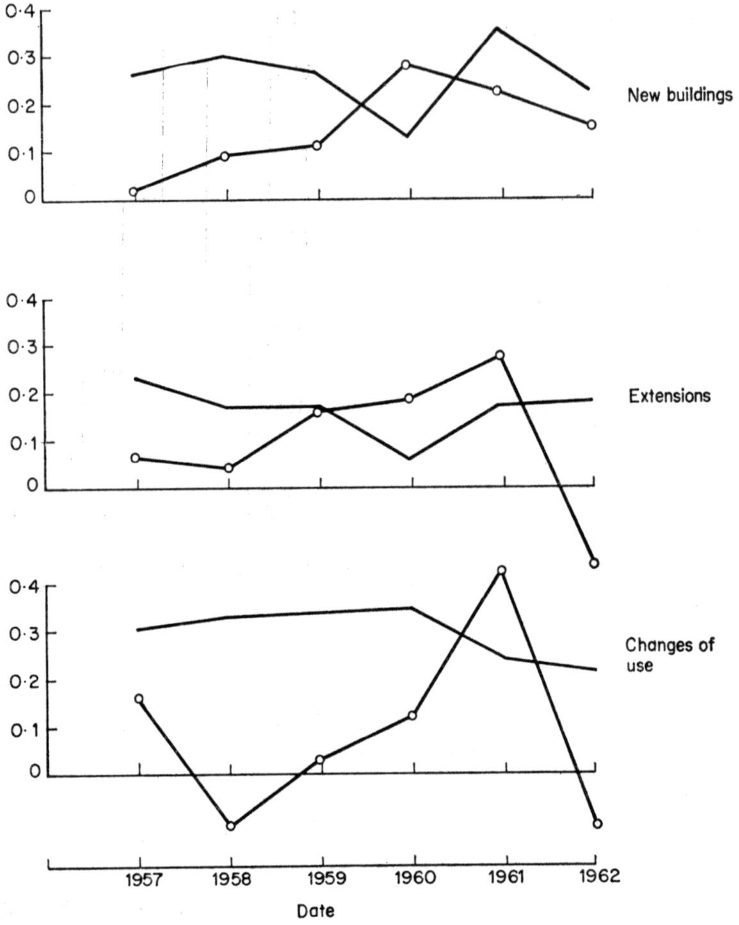

earlier the unit the greater the inaccuracy in its positioning. However, this matrix had to be employed, as 1957 was the first year for which overall data was available. Moreover the situation was not as bad as might be expected. The indices changed slowly, and for the earliest years the probability of a uhit being completed after a period 10 became exceedingly remote.

If any unit had such a long construction time we increased the particular cell's stock by the unit's size, the period $t+C_N(x)$. Those units due for completion during or before 1957 were of course ignored, as they would have been included in the total stock position recorded for period 10.

From period 11 onwards, both changes of use and demolitions had to be included within each period's procedures. This was mandatory so as to derive the current total stock position within each cell as specified by equation (x). Both of these events, should they occur within any cell, were assumed to have been completed by the period for which approval occurred.

The first procedure for each period after 10 was the recalculation of ${}^1I_{i,j,t}$ as dictated by the total stock position at the end of the previous period. The second involved the addition of the stock in all cells, as given in the previous period, to any units due for completion from previous years' approvals.

The recursive system was repeated until we evolved the overall position at the end of period 15. This array was stored as a unique record, and the system retracked to period 1 by zeroising $O_{i,j,t}$ and ${}^1I_{i,j,t}$. Recycling generated a second record for 1962, and forty such trackings produced a distribution of outcomes for the test year. The means of the distributions were determined as the final stock positions for period 10.

Fig. IX 17 is an example of the distribution of outcomes for a specimen cell. A good approximation to a normal curve was achieved, which supported the method of evaluating the arithmetic mean of the outcomes as the final pattern. One of these simulated final positions is given in diagram IX 18, where in this case the index utilised was ${}^3I_{i,j,t}$.

Fig. IX 17 Distribution of outcomes for specimen cell.

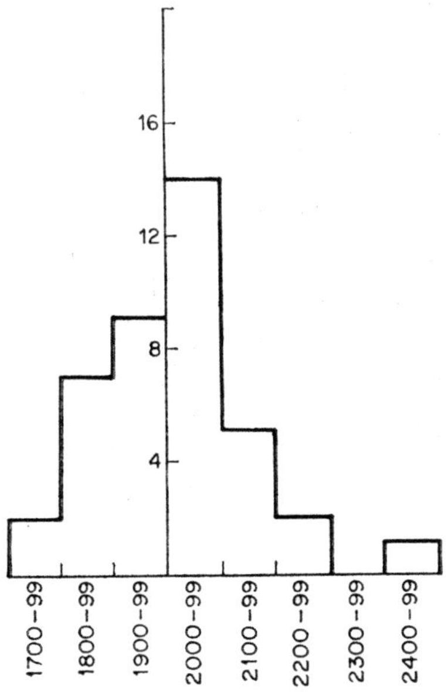

Fig. IX 18 Simulated position 1962.

	1	2	3	4	5	6	7	8	9	10	11	12	13	14	15	16	17	18	19	20	21	22	23	24	25	26	27	28	29	30	31	32
1						30	12	9	128	18	6	13	5	43	14	13	81	5	32	86		22	13	24	3	135	3	3	1	1		
2						13	4	1	7	42	5	14	7	25	96	1	97	9	91	247	3	40	35	2	1	24	7	1		1	1	
3						2	22	1	32	13			73	146	41		25	5	41	31	5	25	27	4	2	21		1		1	3	
4					4		2	12	24	29	2			31	197	2	281	8	140	44		10	8	10	11	81	28		3	1	7	2
5	2			3	5	1		10	43	6	77			221	68	619	775	241	126	145	169	563	301	11	6	18	7		7	24	54	27
6				21	5	20	70	4	44	13	103	365	443	351	225	1096	533	522	181	266	90	528	129	24	1		15	5	2	2	3	
7			1	32		1	12	52	56	49	139	974	531	1704	508	1104	1581	2747	2175	767	298	2739	758	203	16	41	44	4				
8			1	14	15	19	414	55	370	83	68	433	1310	2204	1153	1599	1741	2832	3440	1923	2704	6715	5536	486	85	99	9	31	8	55	5	15
9				5	8	4	10	40	86	28	9	234	1065	2841	2416	1438	2486	1664	1378	966	722	3204	3191	527	118	14	3	2		16	12	34
10	10	8	16	5	35	28	741						605	1780	2463	1998	2896	59	620	188	335	617	133		2	56	3	4	1	1		
11	24	3	26	222	1		38	228	27	115	98	245	706	339	206	1648	2154	1291	178	47	58	22	36	51	22	12	4					
12	16	16	23	4	315	18	74	99	97	68	85	157	381	1198	1789	3188	1289	9	120	187	52		7	33	8	7	1				1	
13	10	7	201	193	48	471	11	60	65	299	83	70	76	554	478	534	1435	291	23	38	50	5	30	17	3	5	4	5				
14	1	60	11		6	7	7	9	48	7	170	25	32	155	12	95	87	1	24	11	37	3	1	6			1		1			
15			2	22	8	9	10		31	32	20	7			3	10	29	31	14		21	6				13	2	3		3	5	1
16			21		40	2	177	24	6	8	3					1		19	79	5	3	2	2			9	2	1	5	9	12	22
17				2	4	30	30	1	1	7	3	13		10	7	1	5	42	5		12	37	112	9	68	9	14	13	35	20	55	16
18					8	5	7	4		5	41	1	29	2	6	23	9	6	24	5	25	12	2	2	45		1			6	11	
19				3	4			2		1	9	99	3	23	56	10	8	18	39	2			10	1	9	1			3	5		
20			4	66	26		16	3	1	32	73	8		27	47	23	5	87	41	4			1	7	17				3	2		

Table IX 2 gives a more detailed history of the specimen cell of Fig. IX 17. Here the actual units were recorded and the assumption was made that all $N_{10,16,t}(x)$ and $E_{10,16,t}(y)$ took two years to complete. Demolition of old stock was determined as in the model by multiplying the incoming unit by P_t. Starting in period 10 the estimated yearly totals were determined, and it can be seen that $O_{i,j,t}$ rose and fell, with both the simulation model output and the above simple procedure over-estimating the actual 1962 stock.

Table IX 2 Growth of specimen cell 10,16.

Period Year	6 1953	7 1954	8 1955	9 1956	10 1957	11 1958	12 1959	13 1960	14 1961	15 1962	16 1963	17 1964
New buildings					120		100	18	55	55		
$N_{10,16,t}(p)$					72		13					
Extensions			11	2						2		
$E_{10,16,t}(q)$												
Demolitions					6		3	5	27	30		
$D_{10,16,t}(s)$					3		25			1		
Changes of use						1		31				
$U_{10,16,t}(r)$						1						
Actual Total stock					1,705					1,919		
Expected total stock					1,705	1,705	1,869	1,895	1,981	1,968		
Simulation model output										1,998		

As a further exercise, Figs. IX 5 and IX 18 were restated as Figs. IX 23 and IX 24 with large cell stocks $O_{g,h,t}$ constructed from groups of four small cells according to the relationship:

$$O_{g,h,t} = O_{i,j,t} + O_{i+1,j,t} + O_{i,j+1,t} + O_{i,+1,j+1,t} \quad \text{(xvii)}$$

In the first instance we produced this restatement to permit comparisons, when the model was completely reworked in terms of larger cells. Time forbade the latter, however, and the large cell positions are shown for interest.

Analysis of Results

Evaluation of spatial simulation models has been discussed by several authors including Hagerstrand (forthcoming) and Morrill (1965.) Aspects of analysis that have received attention are the statistical testing of some spatial properties of the real world and a simulated pattern.

This type of analysis calls into play non-parametric statistics such as the Kolmogorov-Smirnov and Chi-square tests. In our own work we generated a distribution of outcomes to specifically reproduce a real world pattern. Our interest was in the degree of correspondence within each cell between the 1962 land use information and the simulation position. Three types of attractive index were constructed from the unique pattern of development actually occurring, and we made no attempt to utilise some generalised 'mean information field'. A fourth type of index, $rI_{i,j}$, was used as a control. This gave every cell an equal probability of attracting any unit and so effectively ensured a random assignment over the region.

An assessment of the relative strength of these indices was provided by evaluating the percentage of simulated cell stock $O_{i,j,15}$ to the actual amount in each cell. With accumulation in terms of numbers of cells falling within ranges of 10%, Figs. IX 19 to IX 22 were evolved. Similar

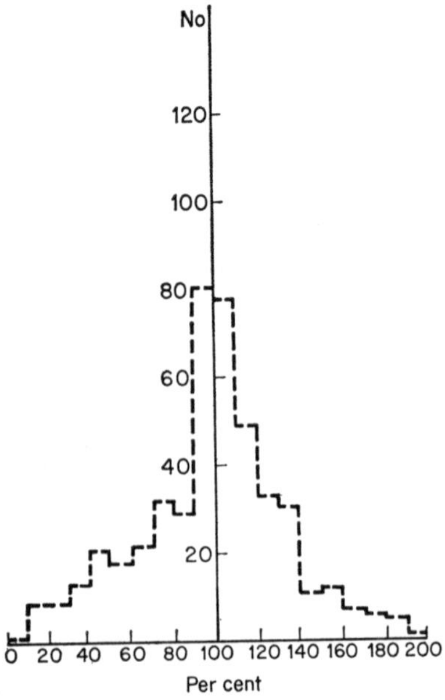

Fig. IX 19 Distribution of cell percentages using $^1I_{i,j,t}$.

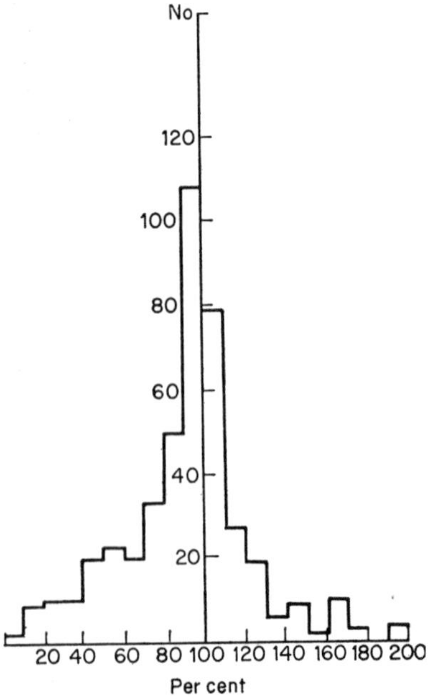

Fig. IX 20 Distribution of cell percentages using $^2I_{i,j}$.

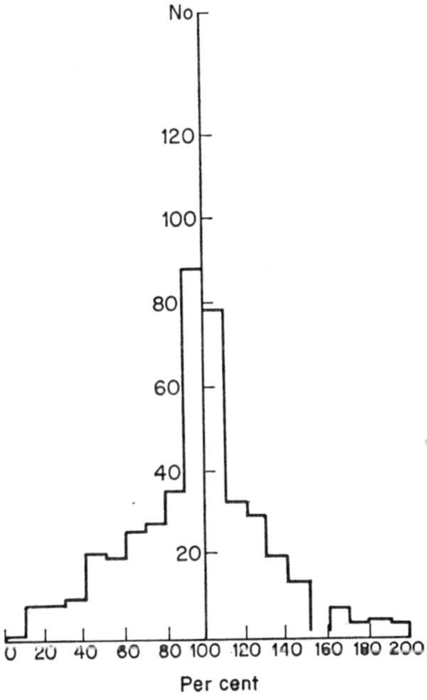

Fig. IX 21 Distribution of cell percentages using ${}^3I_{i,j,t}$.

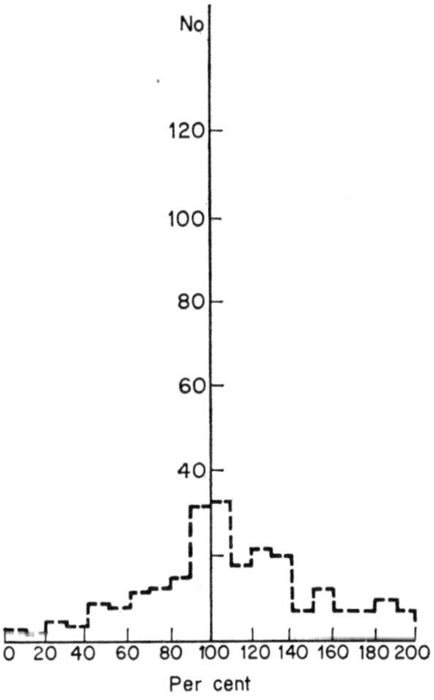

Fig. IX 22 Distribution of cell percentages using ${}^rI_{i,j}$.

results for large cells were constructed from Figs. IX 23 and IX 24, and are given in Figs. IX 25 to IX 28. These results are restated in Table IX 3, where the percentage of cells falling within plus or minus a stated range of percentages from actuality are records. It may be seen that ${}^1I_{i,j,t}$, ${}^2I_{i,j,t}$, and ${}^3I_{i,j,t}$ give very similar results, with the second marginally better than the other two.

A considerable degree of sensitivity testing could be applied to the model, even in its current somewhat limited form. For example, the

Table IX 3 Summary of Cell Distributions.

Index	Small Cells Percentage of Cells Within ±30% of Actuality	Small Cells Percentage of Cells Within ±50% of Actuality	Large Cells Percentage of Cells Within ±30% of Actuality	Large Cells Percentage of Cells Within ±50% of Actuality
${}^1I_{i,j,t}$	46	70	63	78
${}^2I_{i,j}$	49	69	63	76
${}^3I_{i,j,t}$	46	69	58	78
${}^rI_{i,j}$	25	28	28	38

Fig. IX 23 Large cell office stock 1962.

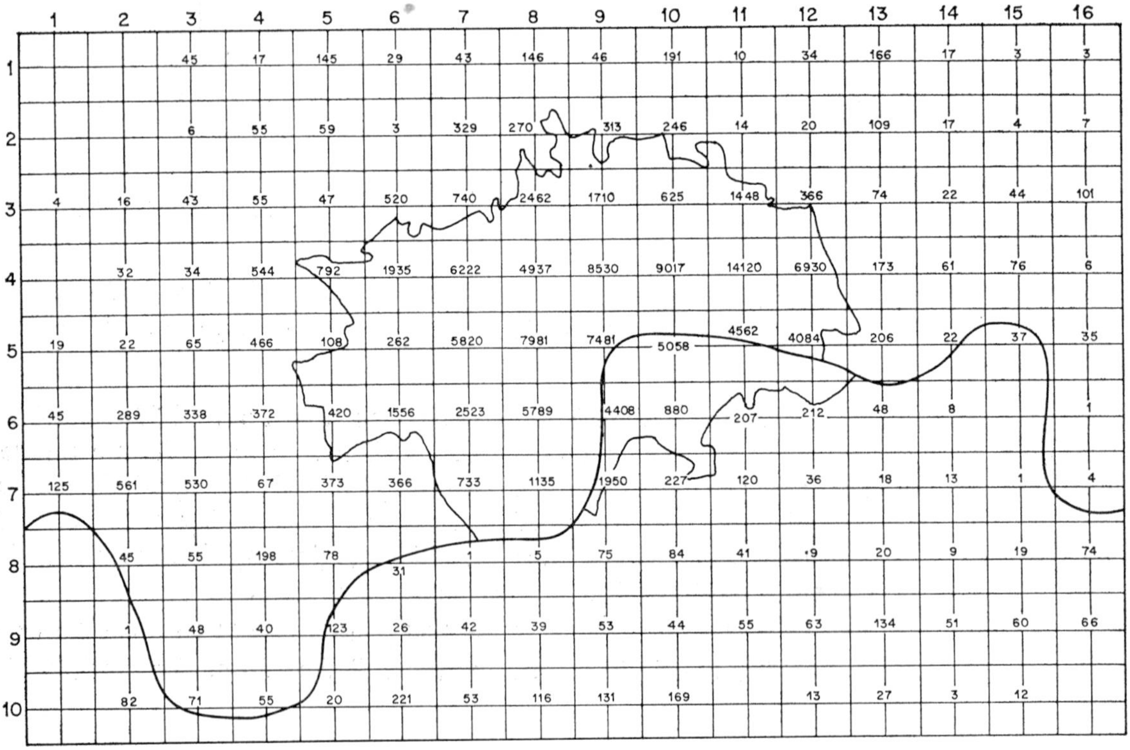

Fig. IX 24 Simulated large cell position 1962.

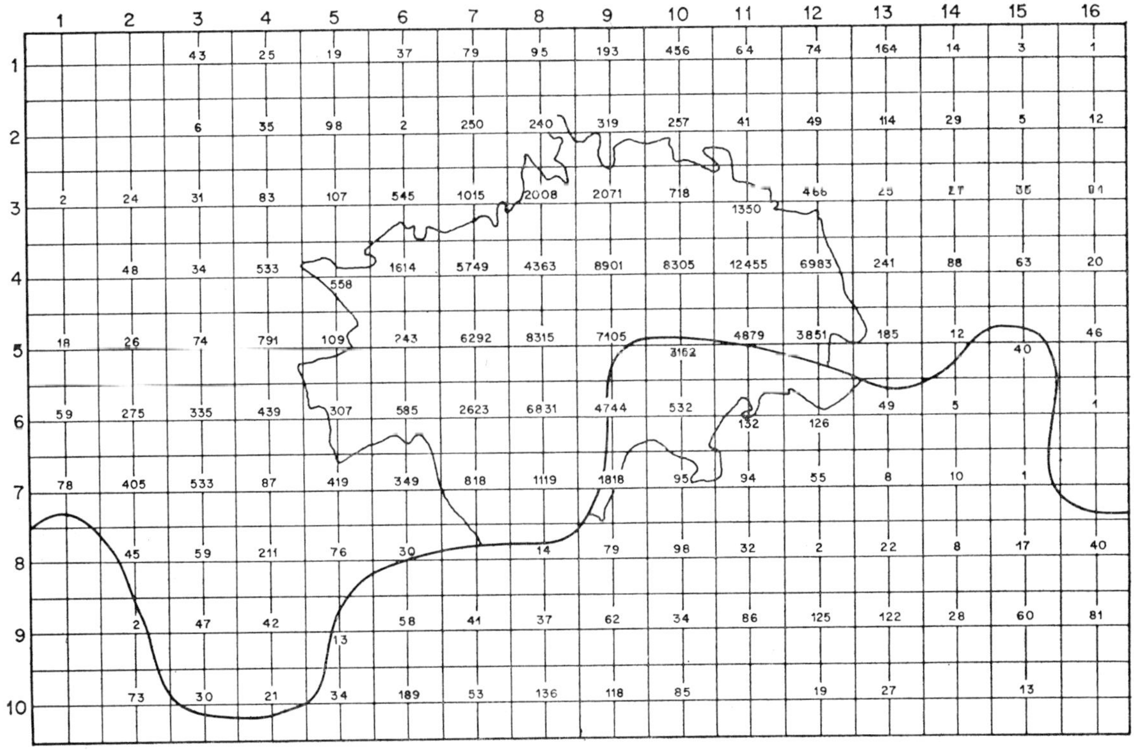

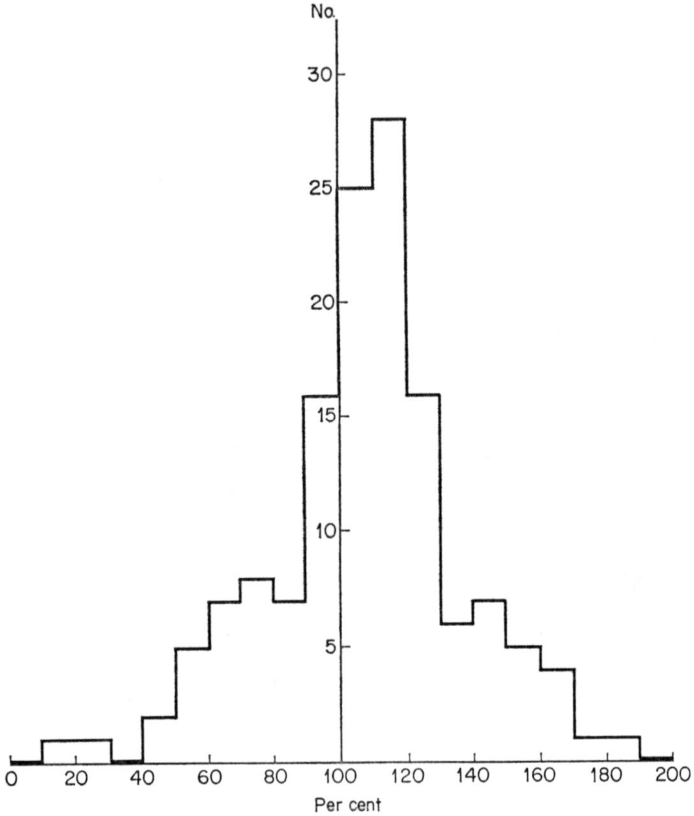

Fig. IX 25 Distribution of large cell percentages using $^{1}I_{i,j,t}$.

best type of index could be successfully determined by such experimentation. Later on other land uses could be added, perhaps in a hierachical form, to cater for competition. By such flexible additions the present conceptual base could be turned into a powerful planning tool.

Discussion of Point Patterns

Inadaquacies of classical location theories have been recognised for some time. These results from the assumptions of 'economic man' operating with perfect knowledge without behavioural and social constraints. As any attempt to include these permits a number of solutions to the location problem, the suggestions have been made that they should be treated as random disturbances upon the ideal pattern.

Fig. IX 26 Distribution of large cell percentages using $^2I_{i,j}$.

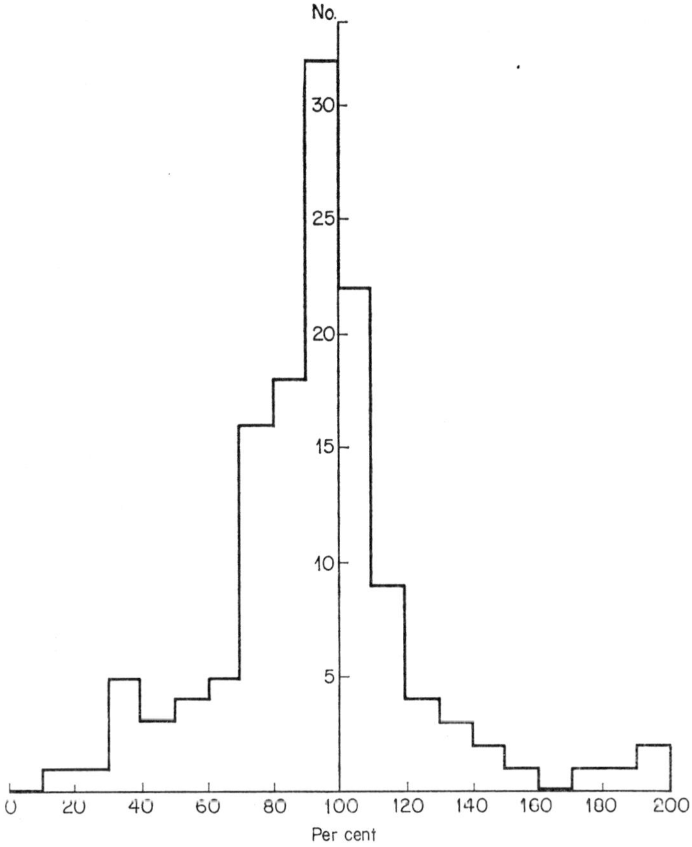

As Harvey (1965) states, the question becomes one of identifying when the real situation deviates from the ideal by more than some random component, where this random component summarises the imperfections inherent in the decision-making process. Several workers including Harvey (1965) and Rogers (1965), have discussed the spatial location of events or activities by fitting a number of theoretical distributions to empirical data. The techniques have been largely borrowed from ecology (Grieg-Smith (1964)), and involve dividing the study area into cells and recording the number of events in each.

We focused upon two theoretical distributions, and it may be useful to recall their main features.

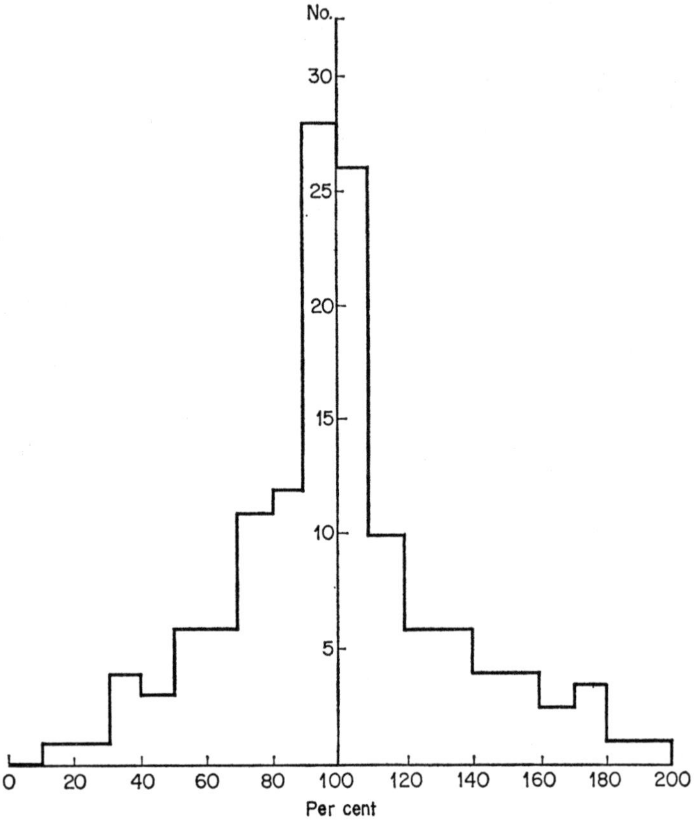

Fig. IX 27 Distribution of large cell percentages using $^3I_{i,\,j,\,t}$.

The Poisson Distribution

If the distribution of events is random over the area, then the probability $p(x)$ of finding x events in any cell placed at random in the area is given by the Poisson function:

$$p(x) = \frac{o^{-\mu}\mu^{x}}{x\,!} \qquad x=0,1,2 \ldots \ldots \ldots \ldots \ldots \qquad \text{(xviii)}$$

where μ is the mean of the distribution.

One difficulty is that a successful fit of a Poisson distribution does not necessarily prove randomness, as such a distribution can often be obtained from a non-random pattern by choosing an appropriate cell size. The reverse, however, does not apply, since the distribution will

Fig. IX 28 Distribution of large cell percentages using $^{r}I_i$, .

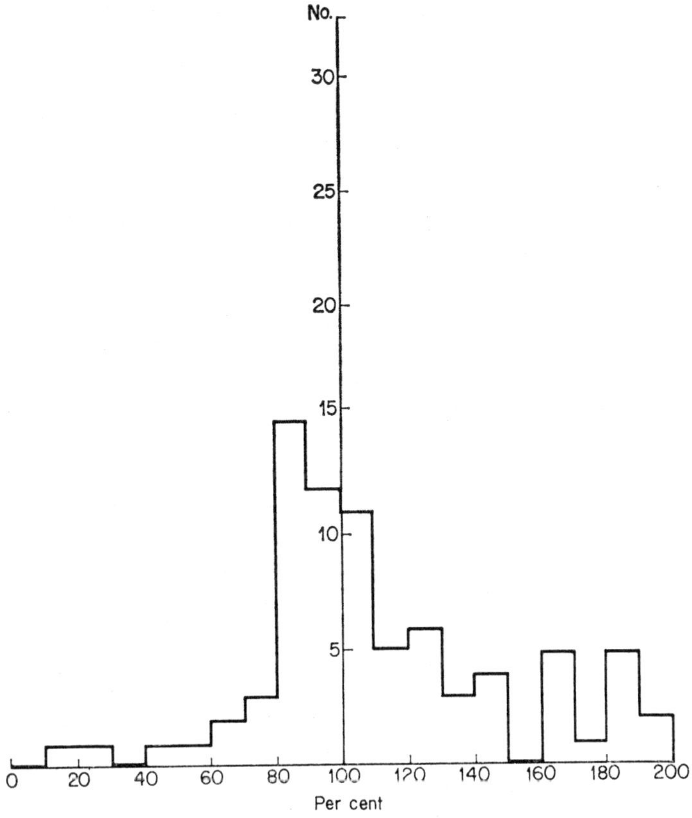

always be generated by a random pattern. If the events are not randomly distributed, however, some degree of clustering must result and several theoretical distributions have been proposed.

Negative Binomial Distribution

This distribution may in similar fashion be discussed in terms of a contagious spread of events or activities. The model assumes that there occurs a random assignment of initial events which then 'trigger' clusters of events around them, these clusters growing logarithmically over time. Should this occur, then the probability of finding a cell with x events is given by the negative binomial distribution:

$$p(x) = \frac{x+k-1}{k-1} p^k q^x \qquad x=0,1,2, \ldots \qquad \text{(xix)}$$

The mean of this distribution μ is given by:

$$\mu = \frac{kq}{p}$$

where the most likely estimates of μ is the sample mean, m, given by the relationship:

$$m = \frac{1}{N} \sum_{x=0}^{z} x n_x \quad \text{(xx)}$$

Here N is the total number of observations and z is the maximum of x. The other parameter, k, the exponent, may be derived (Anscombe (1949)) from the expressions:

$$p(x_o) = \frac{(1+m)^{-k}}{k} \quad \text{(xxi)}$$

where $p(x_o)$ is the probability of finding a cell which has zero events. The sample estimate of this is $\frac{n_o}{N}$ and hence $\log \frac{N}{n_o} = k \log (1 + \frac{m}{k})$ which may be solved by the iterative process of Newton-Raphson.

In our own work we attempted to compare the number of approvals for new buildings in the real world with a unique simulated pattern. Table IX 4 gives the number of cells with a specified number of approvals for each year from 1957 to 1962 and for all these years. The latter situation is also recorded in Table IX 5 together with the analogous picture for large cells. Also recorded are the results for one simulated pattern and the theoretical points of the negative binomical distribution.

Table IX 4 Number of small cells with stated number of approvals.

Number Within Cells	1957	1958	1959	1960	1961	1962	1957–1962
0	562	577	540	554	526	584	414
1	47	47	67	64	80	44	108
2	14	9	21	15	22	7	48
3	7	10	9	4	7	2	20
4	5	4	2	2	3	2	6
5	4	1	1	0	2	1	8
6	1	2		1			6
7							5
8							5
9							3
10							3
11							3
12							2
13							2
14							0
15							1
16							2

Table IX 5 Number of cells with stated number of approvals.

Number Within Cells	Small Cells Actual	Small Cells Simulated	Large Cells Actual	Large Cells Simulated
0	414	464	46	76
1	108	63	29	29
2	48	25	24	6
3	20	18	18	8
4	6	8	6	3
5	8	10	6	2
6	6	7	3	2
7	5	4	4	5
8	5	5	1	0
9	3	5	1	1
10	3	3	1	3
11	3	4	1	1
12	2	3	0	0
13	2	4	3	3
14	0	1		
15	1	1		
16	2	4		

The comparison is made precise in Figs. IX 29 and IX 30. These show quite explicitly that the spatial distribution of approvals actually occurring compared well with the simulated pattern. We infer from this

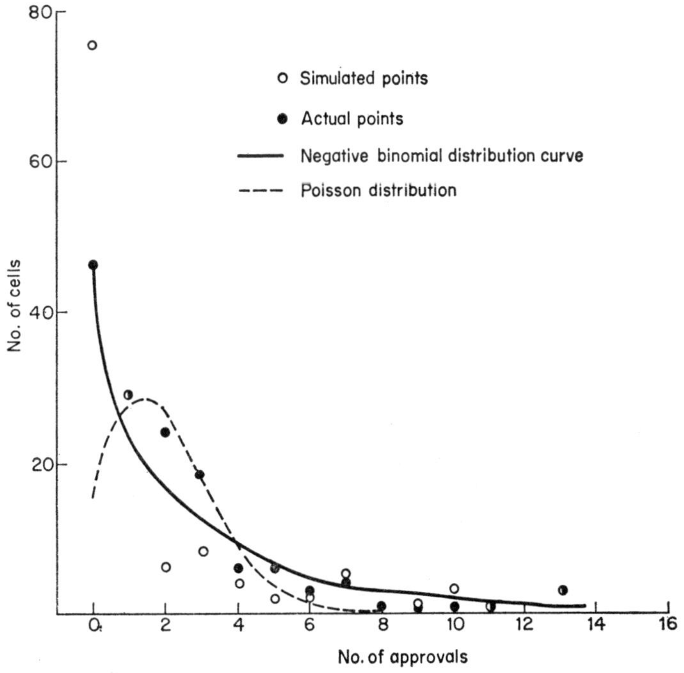

Fig. IX 29 Number of approvals within small cells.

Fig. IX 30 Number of approvals within large cells.

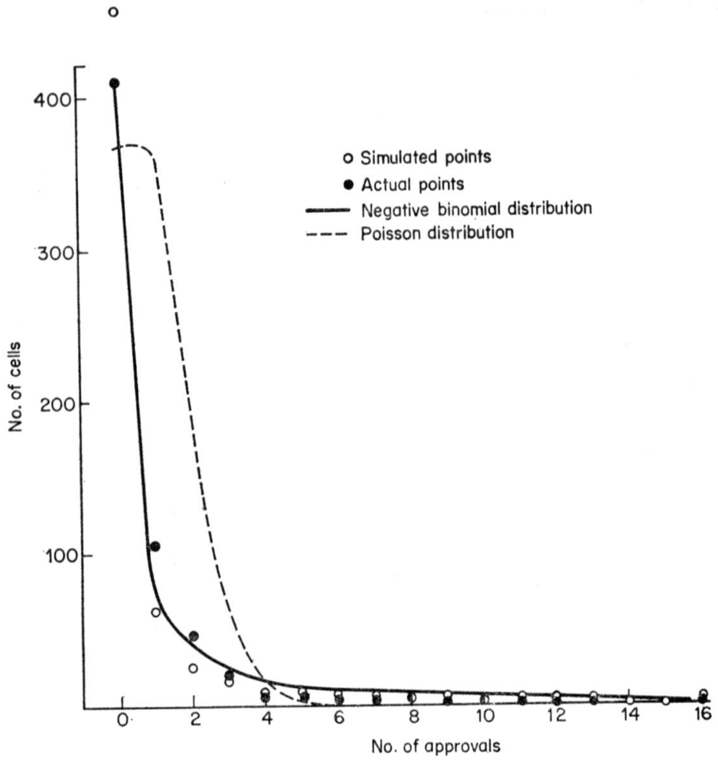

that the spread of office permissions is not a random process. There appears to be some mechanism at work which makes the phenomena behave in a manner akin to that described by the negative binomial distribution.

A Concluding Footnote

As a final comment, it has occurred to us that it might be possible to link our two models by some linear programme which allocated users to space so as to minimise rent or some function of distance. The disaggregation necessary to get a reasonable fit would be of some theoretical interest, because it would reflect different kinds of locational preference functions that ought to be associated with different kinds of firms.

Chapter X
Conclusions

We have reached the end of our book, but this does not mean that the whole story has been told. Although we have managed to present the pattern of office evolution and growth in a number of different ways, there remain many approaches which we have not tried. What is more, the processes we have been looking at are changing all the time, and our work must always remain slightly out of date.

But, accepting these limitations, we must try to bring together at least some of our main themes and arguments, to show how they connect and to suggest some possible courses of action for the future.

Our approach has been to consider a particular problem from a number of different points of view—to hold the phenomenon of office growth up to a light which changes direction from chapter to chapter. Each section of our book has therefore sketched in some conclusions seen from a particular viewpoint.

Some of the most interesting aspects arise from the interplay of the different approaches, and it is important to point out these connections, even if the task is rather difficult.

Perhaps the best way is to devise a series of headings, which cut across the spectrum of disciplines and subjects with which we have been dealing. We shall then be able to show how each part of our work has raised issues of theory, method, policy and so on, and how these issues are interrelated. These headings will be rather arbitrary, for many issues overlap from method into theory and from empirical findings into matters of policy. With this reservation in mind let us move on.

First, problems of *method* arose during the study, and if we were to start all over again we might organise our work on different lines.

Discussion of such problems may be useful to other research workers. Second, we have reached conclusions of a *theoretical* nature. Our studies raised several such issues, especially about the use of mathematical analysis, and the theoretical aspects of these must be explored. Third, we carried out a great deal of *empirical* investigation about the growth of offices and office employment in London. The patterns revealed by such empirical work may be of interest and use to planners and policy makers. Fourth, we have dealt with matters of *policy*, and have tried to assess the effects of different policies upon the pattern of offices. We hope our conclusions about such matters will help in developing new policies in the future. Fifth, our work has lead us to consider certain aspects of *future research*, and we have made some suggestions for the kind of studies which seem to flow naturally from our work. We now consider each of these issues in turn, adding some observations about urban studies in general at the very end.

Method

A particular feature of our work has been the attempt to combine mathematical models of urban growth and change with more empirical and descriptive studies. How far has this been a success? At first glance, there appears to be little connection between the two approaches. The results of our empirical studies do not link directly with what our models have shown. But, if we look a little deeper, we can begin to see that there are certain quite strong links between the two approaches. What is more, these connections work in both directions.

It is, of course, easier to see the connections from our empirical work to the models which we have developed. Clearly the hypotheses on which the models are based could not have been developed without empirical studies. For example, notions concerning the behaviour of property developers, which are incorporated in our stochastic model, could not have been evolved without empirical observations of the development process itself. Again, our simulation of office growth and spatial distribution incorporates specific ideas about the way new office space and changes of use are brought into the pattern of existing land uses. None of these ideas could have been developed without some appreciation of empirical evidence.

Finally, our models could not be tested without an adequate supply of empirical data from the real world. The progress of our work has been from very general empirical observations to the formulation of hypotheses and models and back again to empirical evidence in order to test and modify the hypotheses and models.

It is more difficult to identify the connections in the opposite direction, from models to empirical studies. Such connections arise from the rigour of the model-building process. The need to express ideas in mathematical terms imposes special demands for clarity and rigour. This requirement helps to refine our empirical studies in a rather special way. In our own case, testing mathematical models gave rise to new thoughts about the nature of empirical evidence, especially concerning the development process and accessibility in the metropolitan area, and the whole process of observation, model building and testing began over again at a more sophisticated level. Clearly the two approaches are really part of a single process, but of course we obtain different results from each of them.

Our models provide tests for the hypotheses which we have developed, which are themselves based upon empirical evidence. The models also create ideas for new hypotheses, and these in turn lead to a renewed quest for further empirical evidence. Empirical studies thus help to generate hypotheses and at the same time accumulate information which may be of immediate use to planners and policy makers. In a sense, models lead to deeper understanding in the long run, while empirical studies are useful as a spring-board for immediate action. In our work, we have tried to bring these two approaches closer together, so that our study may be a stimulus to both thought and action.

We have also suggested a number of different approaches to the model-building effort itself. The use of mathematical models in urban studies is still in the early stages of development, and we felt it was appropriate to suggest more than one type of model. Our original object was to compare the outputs of each model, and to see which provided the better explanation of the real world. Because of limitations of resources, we failed to do this, and we believe this is a serious weakness in the study. We have, however, tried to show how this comparison could be done and we believe that our objective was a useful one.

Data presents a major difficulty to any social science research. In both model building and empirical work, the availability of data often conditions what can be achieved, and even what questions can be asked! In the nature of things, data cannot be available in a unique form for each particular study. It is usually gathered for the purposes of national regional or local planning, and we must expect either to adjust the data or adjust our research programmes accordingly. But it should be possible for most data to be placed upon some standard basis. The demands of urban research and national planning are increasing rapidly, and the accumulation of data by different authorities and research programmes is mounting day by day. Discussion is going on concerning various kinds of co-ordinated data systems, and the recent development of grid co-ordinate systems for organising geographical data is only one aspect of a larger problem. For example, the difficulty of analysing employment data over time, because of changes in classification from one census to the next, means that many important facets of national life and work may be obscured. We know enough about the requirements of urban research and policy to be able to design quite an effective system. What we now need are the resources to bring it into being.

Theoretical

Several issues of method emerged in connection with the theoretical aspect of our work. Some of these concern our efforts towards mathematical model building. Perhaps the most basic issue has to do with the level of explanation offered by such models. It is clear that any model can only be as good as the hypotheses upon which it is based, and the level of explanation which the model provides will also depend to a very large extent upon the framing of these hypotheses. For example, a model may demonstrate that 'like attracts like' or the 'attraction increases with accessibility' but in order to explain why this is so, we need to develop more behavioural models. This problem occurs again and again in model building, especially when analogies are borrowed from other areas of scientific activity. For example, a gravity model tells us *that* trips to a given point fall off as a function of distance, but does not tell us *why* such effects should arise or what causes them.

And there are difficulties attached to achieving better explanations. These concern the way we go about our task. On one hand we could begin with a rather abstract model, and then probe deeper and deeper through a series of sub-models. Each sub-model would deal with more detailed behaviour patterns, and thus provide better explanations of large-scale changes. On the other hand, we might *begin* by modelling behaviour patterns in some detail, and then aggregate these sub-models into a more general model framework. Of course, we would still need the framework for such an aggregate approach. The problem is that behaviour may change with aggregation, and this is difficult to model adequately. But overhanging all these approaches is the question of what we *mean* by explanation. We could never hope to explain everything, nor can we say that, if our model reproduces the real world or part of the real world, it is correct or true. All we know is that it has not been disproved. Clearly, there may be many factors which we have not taken into account and which have somehow cancelled themselves out, so that our model takes no account of them. Nevertheless, it may be just these factors which are important for a true explanation of the phenomena with which our model deals. As we move from the natural sciences towards the social sciences, so the lack of experimental conditions works against adequate explanation. In some ways, the automatic computer can help, especially in simulating and setting up alternative test conditions for running models. But we must remember that we are dealing with changing phenomena, and that what may appear to be a good explanation this year may not be at all true in five years' time. Since the information we use is usually historical, this raises many difficulties, especially when the problem of prediction is raised. We should be very sure of our ground, our data, our hypotheses and our models before we claim to predict the future outcome of present policies with any accuracy.

A further theoretical difficulty arises when we test our models. Even if a model did explain certain phenomena, we would still need to ask how good an explanation this is. In simulation it is possible to apply fairly standard statistical tests to compare the outcome of model simulation and the real world, so that we can judge whether the model offers 50%, 70% or 90% explanation, but of course, we may still not know *why* the model achieved this level of explanation. With other kinds of models, testing becomes very difficult. Non-parametric tests are practically the only tools available to us. Our own work contains examples of the use of such tests.

In spite of all these difficulties, it is possible to reach some theoretical conclusions. The pattern of offices and development of office space over the years does seem to follow certain rules of clustering and attraction. The interaction of construction time, planning permission procedures and the actual moment when a piece of new office space comes on to the market can be predicted, at least for short periods. We have demonstrated that planning approvals for new office buildings are not random events, but follow a pattern, so that initial events or permissions trigger clusters of other events, and these clusters then grow regularly over time. Of course, we have dealt with only short-term changes, and it would be interesting to relate our 'micro' changes to the longer cycles of the building industry and the national economy. We know, from the work of Professor Parry-Lewis and others, that building cycles are linked with other facets of national growth, and it should be possible to evolve an econometric model which would incorporate the sort of patterns which we have outlined with such longer changes.

At an even broader level our study has shown that the office function is closely tied to changes in society, and that its present ascendancy in the centres of our cities is the outcome of a particular phase of urban life, in which communications are highly important but the technology of communication is still developing. If our analysis is correct, and assuming that present trends continue and certain technological advances occur during the next few decades, we may find that a larger number of office jobs disappear from the centre of the city, leaving only an elite core behind. Eventually, with further technological advance, even this elite may leave the city centre. Home decision making may be the rule, and office work may become a cottage industry. Such changes are not likely for some time and lie outside the source of our models, but they are possible, and it may be possible to use the techniques of scientific forecasting to write alternative scenarios for the long-range future of the office function.

Empirical

The post-war growth of office employment in London falls into three fairly distinct phases. First of all, the period from 1947 to about 1955 was characterised by a fairly steady annual increase in the number of workers. During this period, post-war reconstruction of Central London and the beginnings of new office development combined to replace and add to the number of jobs in the area. That the rate of increase was not greater is due partly to the controls governing the development of new office space and partly to the austerity conditons which held until 1953 or 1954.

The second phase, which lasted from about 1955 to 1962, saw a much more rapid rise in office employment in the central area. This was the period of 'office boom', and of rapidly increasing affluence. The number of jobs in service industries grew at a faster rate than manufacturing, and increasing congestion resulting from the influx of office workers to the centre of London gave rise to great concern and pressure on the government to impose stronger measures to control office building.

The third phase, which has lasted from 1962 at least until the figures revealed by the 1966 Census, shows a slowing down of the rate of growth of office jobs in the centre and the beginnings of a trend towards dispersal of office employment into the surrounding region. For the first time, this period showed a faster growth of employment in regions outside the south-east. This change and slowing down may be due to the total ban on the construction of new office space in the south-east, combined with propaganda for dispersal through the Location of Offices Bureau. It may also be part of a much deeper underlying trend, caused by the increase in mobility which enables cities to spread at an ever-increasing rate.

These phases of office growth in the centre of London have been compressed into a relatively short time-span—twenty years or so. Do they represent anything more than local fluctuations in a long-term secular pattern? Should we now begin to worry about a possible dearth of office workers in the central area of London? It is too early to make firm judgements on such issues, but given the immense and continuing attraction of London in terms of prestige and the number of government businesses and quasi-government institutions which are concentrated there, it seems unlikely that we should worry too much about the survival of London's central area. Although the City may spread, it seems that its attraction, especially for the young and unmarried will continue to provide all that is necessary to maintain its position as the capital of the nation and centre of the Commonwealth.

Our case studies have thrown up some very simple patterns. The most striking concerns the lack of knowledge of the general processes of office development, and the naivety of even quite a large and sophisticated organisations when confronted with the need to acquire office space. Unless an organisation is in some way connected with the process of development, its hunt for accommodation is a very hit and miss affair. Strategies are planned which bear little relation to the facts of life. Although the problem of accommodation is a constant worry to most organisations of any size, few of them seem to have acquired any special policy or skills with which to cope. It must be obvious to any manager or executive that the amount of office space needed by an organisation fluctuates over quite short periods of time. Yet in the cases we examined, most decisions seem to have been taken from the view that the ideal space or location would be available when it was needed.

There is need for better strategy in firms requiring office space. It seems strange that while advance planning plays a large part in general industrial and commercial development, so little forward planning is done in the case of such a large item as office accommodation. Finally, the locational behaviour of these cases was highly oriented towards the centre of London. Whatever decisions might have been taken about decentralisation, they were taken in the shadow of the central area which retains its pull on management at all levels.

Our empirical findings concerning developers cannot be regarded as complete. The people who responded to our questions were not a statistical sample. However, these fifty development firms did provide us with some interesting information. The developers comprised a very mixed bag. A few were very large and controlled a great many subsidiaries and provided a large proportion of the office space in London. There were in addition a much larger number of smaller firms who showed no signs of increase in size or output. A large proportion of development firms had come into being during and after the office boom of the 1950's, and it seems clear that they stepped in to fill a gap which was not apparent to most planners and policy makers. The developers operate in a very straightforward way, relying largely on borrowed finance. They were able for a short time to take advantage of loosely framed policies and the problems and naivety of local authorities in order to make very large sums of money. At the same time they provided a large quantity of office space which was sorely needed for the growth of an important facet of national life. The boom is now over. It will be interesting to see how many of the fifty development companies we questioned are surviving in ten years' time. Once again the central area of London retains its hold, most companies are clustered there, and most development takes place there. Whatever the reasons, the centre of London is *de facto* the place for developers.

Our study of the growth of office space in London since the war confirms the suspicion that policies have either been too late or simply gone along with current trends. An outstanding illustration of this theme is given by decentralisation, where official policy seems to have reinforced a trend which was already clear to both the developers and occupiers of office space.

There seems to have been very little tendency for the central area of London to spread outwards. There has been some small expansion to the west, together with a considerable amount of rather scattered suburban development. But the massive increase in office floorspace in London during the post-war years has been contained within the pre-existing central area—which of course includes the West End. Thus the office floorspace density of the central area has increased greatly, and its position as a national focus of the office function has been reinforced.

Our study of the occupants of new office space in London revealed a very high degree of mobility among firms. It seems that most office organisations cope with growth by means of short stays and frequent moves, and the longer a firm stays in a building, the more crowded the accommodation becomes.

Some surprising conclusions were presented on the issues of locational preferences and the role of prestige in choosing a location. We discovered no strong feelings among the firms we questioned on either of these two issues. There appear to be some differences between large and small firms so far as their locational preferences are concerned, but on the whole location choice did not seem to be a strong factor governing the occupation of office accommodation. The notion of prestige has assumed an important place in other surveys of office location, and indeed our own case studies, presented in Chapter III, indicated that locational factors played a very real part in the choice of office accommodation; but our survey did not back up these notions. These differences may have been due in part to the way we asked certain questions, but, since there has been a good deal of 'conventional wisdom' about the importance of prestige and locational considerations in previous discussions of office growth and development, we suggest that some further exploration of these rather fundamental topics would be worth while.

Policy

Throughout the post-war era, a most elaborate system of policies and legislation has been built up to direct and control the growth of London. At the same time the spectacular growth of offices has been an outstanding feature of the City. What lessons can we learn from these two developments? Perhaps the most striking feature is that policies seem always to lag behind events. The growth of offices was ignored by planners and policy-makers during the early post-war years, partly because statistics did not reveal the office function properly and partly perhaps, because their minds were still focussed elsewhere—on the industrial growth which had characterised British cities for the past one hundred and fifty years. Later on, as general control policies were relaxed, the office boom erupted, revealing a massive market for office space.

Planners and policy-makers have tried to treat the office problem on its own, and have not realised that it is just a part of much wider and deeper changes in society. Of course, if we see the role of policy making simply as a means to correct undesirable tendencies as they become apparent, we shall be forced to treat each one in isolation. For the problems of urbanisation do indeed present themselves as a series of isolated issues—twilight areas, congestion, surburban sprawl and so on, and we build up a series of measures to deal with each one in turn as it arises. In such circumstances policy must always be trying to catch up with the problems. Unless we can construct a coherent *overview* of the process of urbanisation in Britain, we shall remain trapped in this situation; without an overall framework our policies will remain piecemeal.

The need for such a framework in connection with office development is quite clear. Suppose we assume that our present evolution towards a society which is oriented to tertiary and quaternary activities continues. We might then feel that we should *encourage* the growth of offices in Central London. After all, the office function is partly a mechanism for the exchange of ideas, upon which the prosperity of the country may depend. To sum up; we have suggested that there may be more than one 'office problem' and that these may be mixed up with a larger pattern of change from a manufacturing society to one concerned with transactions. If we are to come to terms with these changes we may find that the office is *an* essential and perhaps *the most* essential key to national development. If we are to manage our affairs properly, we must combine strategies for the growth of offices with the wider policies of urbanisation as a whole.

On a more detailed level, we suggest that not enough consideration has been given to suburban locations as office centres. The experiment of planning offices at suburban locations was abandoned too quickly, and often, it seems, for the wrong reasons. A number of advantages of suburban office locations have not been fully explored. Our present policy, which places a ban on the construction of new offices in the

South East, may need revision. The probable effect of removing the ban would be to reduce pressure on existing space, and office blocks in bad locations which are at present beginning to find tenants would remain empty. It may be that not much new office space would be constructed. For one thing, there is not much vacant land remaining, and where existing property must be acquired for redevelopment, both owners and authorities are wiser now than in the heyday of the office boom.

But it will be useless to make any detailed changes in office policy without corresponding adjustments to other aspects of urbanisation. This conclusion, that policies must be co-ordinated within a general overview of desirable patterns of urbanisation, may not be new; but in the case of offices it may be vital to our future national well-being.

Future Research

Most research raises more questions than it can hope to answer. We have studied one facet of urban growth in one city over a rather short space of time. Clearly there are many things which we were not able to accomplish but which we would like to see done. It is possible to extend this study in many different ways, and from time to time we have suggested certain directions for future work. Let us review some of these possibilities.

First of all, it would be possible to study other facets of urban growth in the same way, by using different disciplines to look at the pattern of activities and accommodation in a given city over a similar span of time. Thus, we could build up bit by bit, an understanding of the total pattern of change in a city. Second, we could undertake similar studies of office growth in other cities in Britain, the role of the capital and the provinces would be of special interest here. Third, we could make cross-cultural studies of the rise of offices in different countries. It would, for example, be fascinating to compare the growth of offices in Paris and New York with that of London. Such studies might well reveal something of the operation of laws and controls within different economic and cultural systems. Fourth, we should like to see the pattern of government offices and office employment treated in the same way that we have examined commercial offices. This is at present a serious gap in our knowledge of the office function, and one that should be repaired as soon as possible.

But in addition to these rather direct extensions of our work, there are a number of new themes which we might pursue. Perhaps the most important of these concerns the linkages which bind together the various institutions which make up the City. We have seen again and again, how important are these links to firms occupying offices in London. The need to be near colleagues, clients and so on has often been a major determinant of the pattern of locations in the City. Yet, despite its importance, this network seems little understood. It is obviously of first importance to uncover the structure of this network, and to show how flows of information and patterns of contact affect the shape of the City. For example, we suspect that many institutions may be held in a kind of symbiosis in the City, and that if we removed one of them all the rest would have to follow. But we do not yet know enough to be able to predict the effect of removing or replacing such institutions. Clearly a study of these networks of urban activities would be of immense value to planners and policy-makers.

Finally there are a whole range of *techniques* which could be applied to the topics which we have dealt with. For example, we might adapt the techniques of activity analysis and time budgets to the central area of the City. Such analyses have hitherto been confined to residential neighbourhoods, but there is a rich field for such studies in other locations, and the central area seems especially promising. Again, we might attempt to construct some kind of econometric model of the supply and demand of office space. We have already suggested that there are short-term patterns in the way office space is injected into the City, and that it should be possible to link these short-term patterns to longer cycles of national building activity. Such a model could easily form part of the system of urban model building which will undoubtedly be a major endeavour during the next decade or so. Finally, we might apply the techniques of scientific forecasting to the office phenomenon in order to anticipate changes which are likely to occur and to plan for them. The use of forecasting studies is gaining ground in Europe and in the United States, and, since office functions are likely to assume an increasingly important role in future society, it seems appropriate to incorporate them into this new branch of study.

These are just a few possibilities for research which have been suggested by our studies; there are many more. Clearly, we shall not be able to pursue them all, but it may be that other research workers will find them of some use. If so, much of our effort will have been justified.

Generally

The growth of offices and office employment is not a passing phase. We happened to choose a time and place when office growth was obvious, but the underlying processes which lead to this pattern are at work everywhere in the post-industrial societies of the world. New York has had office booms in the post-war years, and the mushrooming of offices is a feature of many other cities throughout the world. The new plans for Paris show office towers rising over the city, and in Moscow great office buildings dominate much of the scene.

The changes in society which give rise to the growth of offices seem universal and continuing. There are no signs at present of demand for office work falling off, although there are perhaps some indications that the location of office jobs is changing. It is possible that we are at the beginning of a new stage in the evolution of the office function, when it will become sub-divided into different sets of activities, some of which will need to remain clustered closely together, while other parts may be dispersed or diffused according to the residential patterns of office workers. Such a pattern may be emerging already in some cities of the United States, such as Houston, Texas. Los Angeles is often quoted as an example, but it may be that Los Angeles represents a different development where *whole* units of office activity, both routine and elites, are dispersed across the face of the city. The future pattern of office activities depends upon changes in the technology of communications and upon changes in the pattern of work and leisure in post-industrial societies. For the time being it seems likely that London will continue to exert its pull. The signs, such as they are, indicate that the central clustering of office activities will remain the most important single element in the country, so far as tertiary and quaternary activities are concerned. The sheer number of offices and office jobs which already exist in Central London assures it of a dominant position for several decades to come. What is more, the *image* of London still attracts 'ideas men' and 'ideas industries'—those who will assume an ever-increasing importance in post-industrial society. These people come to the metropolis for special reasons of access to others of their kind; they are not put off by the high cost of living, and often welcome the overcrowding of a large capital city.

For London *is* a capital city, as well as being one of the world's great ports, and the financial, business and political heart of the country. There is no equivalent in the United States and very few anywhere else in the world. New York is no capital city and Los Angeles misses huge sectors of those ideas activities which are contained closely together in the few square miles of Central London. It may be that in the long run such a peculiar dominance is unbalanced and will wither away, but in the short term it is unlikely to be swept aside.

Further ahead there may be some big changes in store. Since the heart of the office function is in the exchange of messages, two things seem possible. First, routine messages and instructions can be automated. There seems no problem in principle to putting most routine office functions on computers. Thus, the routine parts of offices may become more footloose. The computer unit may be located almost anywhere, provided it is connected at one end to decision makers and at the other to manufacturing plant, transport terminal and so on.

Routine office functions may move out into suburbia, where the labour force is handy. But as automation takes over this part of the office, the need for labour will diminish, leading again to a freedom of location. The problems created by such a reduction will need attention. It may be this human factor which slows down the process from centralised routine clerical activities to dispersed automatic data processing.

Decision makers need to communicate in the course of their work, under two sets of circumstances. The first is on matters of emergency, when a quick joint decision is called for to regulate the working of routine functions of production, marketing and so on. The second is in matters of consultation, when broad strategy and speculation about the future are being planned. In the first case, individual communication via television may enable the elites to carry out most of their work from home. In the second case, the need for conference centres could replace central business districts. And as the affairs of the world become ever more inter-linked, the location of these meeting places may change. If Britain entered the Common Market, some adjustment of the status of London and Brussels would take place. This pattern is bound to be repeated on a world-wide scale. The importance of some cities will decline while others will move up the scale. The development of South America or Japan, may lead world attention away from Western Europe. In the long run, Africa and South East Asia may become primary nodes in the world network of transactions. Such global changes may be complemented by the growth of new city centres at airports, hoverports or other communications' interchanges.

Such a picture is one possible future and there are many others. After all, it may be that the formality needed to arrange long distance encounters prevents the proper exchange of ideas. But whatever our speculation about the mode of work and life, it seems very probable that the office function will remain a major element in society for many decades to come, even if it is modified by technology, demography and social development. The office function has grown up in the centres of great cities, and its future form is tied to their development. The future of great cities is a fascinating prospect, but it is a subject for another time and another book.

References

Ackoff, R. L. (ed.) (1962). *Progress in Operations Research.* Wiley, New York.

Anscombe, F. J. (1949). 'The Statistical Analysis of Insect Counts Based on the Negative Binomial Distribution.' *Biometrics*, 5.

Archer and McGuire (1965). 'Firm Size and the Probabilities of Growth.' *Western Economic Journal*, Vol. III, No. 3, pp. 233–246.

Beesley, M., and Foster, C. D. (1963). 'Estimating the Social Benefits of Construction on Underground Railways in London.' *Journal of the Royal Statistical Society*, Series B, Vol. CXXVI, Part 1.

Berry and Pred (1961). *Central Place Studies.* Regional Science Research Institute, University of Pennsylvania.

Brown, R. G. (1963). *Smoothing, Forecasting and Prediction.* Prentice Hall, New York.

Carr-Saunders, A. (1963). *World Population*, Clarendon Press, Oxford.

Carrothers, G. A. P. (1956). 'A Historical Review of the Gravity and Potential Concepts of Human Interaction.' *Journal of the American Institute of Planners*, XXII, pp. 94–102.

City Offices Company (1966). Annual Report.

Cowan, P., and Sears, A. (1966). 'Growth Change, Adaptability and Location.' Report of a Study Carried out for the Ministry of Public Buildings and Works (unpublished).

Cullingworth, J. B. (1964). *Town and Country Planning in England and Wales.* Allen and Unwin, London.

Department of Economic Affairs (1965). 'Office Decentralisation.' Mimeograph.

Derry and Williams (1960). *A Short History of Technology*. Cambridge.

Deutsch, K. (1962). 'On Social Communication and the Metropolis,' in Rodwin (ed.) *The Future Metropolis.* Constable, London.

Dickinson, R. (1964). *City and Region.* Routledge and Kegan Paul, London.

Dyckman, J. (1962). 'The Changing Uses of the City,' in Rodwin (ed.) *The Future Metropolis.* Constable, London.

Economist Intelligence Unit (1964). 'A survey of factors concerning the location of offices in London.'

EVANS, A. W. (1967). 'Myths about Employment in Central London.' *Journal of Transport and Economic Policy.*

FLEISHER, A. (1962). 'The Influence of Technology on Urban Forms,' in Rodwin (ed.) *The Future Metropolis.* Constable, London.

FLETCHER, B. (1946). *A History of Architecture on the Comparative Method.* Batsford, London.

FOLEY, D. (1963). *Controlling London's Growth.* Cambridge and University of California Press.

GITTUS, E. (1964). 'An Experiment in the Definition of Urban Sub-Areas.' *Transactions of the Bartlett Society,* Vol. 2.

GODDARD, J. (1966). 'Internal Structure of London's Central Area.' Paper read at Conference on Urban Core and Inner City, Amsterdam, Sept. 1966.

GOODMAN (1961). 'Statistical Methods for the Mover-Stayer Model.' *Journal of the American Statistical Society,* 56, pp. 841–868.

GOODWIN (1965). 'The Management Centre in the U.S.' *Geographical Review,* January 1965.

GOTTMAN (1966). 'Why the Skyscraper?' *Geographical Review,* April 1966.

GRAUNT, J. (1962). *Natural and Political Observations upon the Bill of Mortality,* edited with an introduction by C. F. Willcox. John Hopkins, Baltimore and London, 1939.

GREATER LONDON PLAN (1944).

GREIG-SMITH, P. (1964). 'Quantitative Plant Ecology.'

HADLEY, G., and WITHIN, T. (1963). *Analysis of Inventory Systems.* Prentice Hall, New York.

HAGERSTRAND, T. (forthcoming). 'On Monte-Carlo Simulation of Diffusion,' in W. L. Garrisson (ed.) *Quantitative Geography.* Atherton, New York.

HAIRE, M. (1959). 'Biological Models and Empirical Histories of the Growth of Organisations,' in Haire (ed.) *Modern Organisation Theory.* Wiley, New York.

HALL, P. (1963). *London 2000.* Faber, London.

HALL, P. (1966). *The World Cities,* Wiedenfield and Nicolson, London.

HARVEY, D. W. (1965). 'Geographical Process and the Analysis of Point Patterns.' University of Bristol. (Mimeograph.)

HOLDEN, C. H., and HOLFORD, W. G. (1951). 'The City of London—a record of Destruction and Survival.'

INSTITUTE D'AMÉNAGEMENT ET D'URBANISME DE LA REGION PARISIENNE (1966). (Cahiers de l'institution d'aménagement et d'urbanisme de la region Parisienne—9 vols. Paris, 1966–67.)

KAISER, E. J. (1966). 'Towards a Model of Residential Developer Behaviour.' Doctoral thesis in the Department of City and Regional Planning, University of North Carolina at Chapel Hill, N.C. (Mimeograph.)

KENDALL, M. G. (1961). *A Course in Multivariate Analysis.* Griffin, London.

KENDALL, M. G., and STUART, A. (1961). *The Advanced Theory of Statistics.* (3 Vols.) Griffin, London.

LAND COMMISSION BILL 1967.

LEAN, W., and GOODALL, B. (1966). 'Aspects of Land Economics.' *Estates Gazette.*

L.C.C. (1957). 'A Plan to combat congestion in Central London.'

Lichtenberg, R. M. (1960). *One Tenth of a Nation*. Harvard, Cambridge, Mass.

Llewelyn-Davies (1966). 'The Rebuilding of London—Achievements and Failures.' *The Property Developer*, April 1966.

L.O.B. (1967) 'White Collar Commuters—A Second Survey.'

Loewenstien, L. K. (1966). 'On the Nature of Analytical Models.' *Urban Studies*, Vol. 3, No. 2, pp. 117–119.

London Traffic Survey (1964). (2 Vols.)

Lowry, I. S. (1964). 'A Model of the Metropolis.' *The Rand Corporation*, R.N.–4035–RC. Santa Monica, California.

McLuhan, M. (1964). *Understanding Media*. McGraw-Hill, New York.

Marriott, O. (1967). *The Property Boom*. Hamish Hamilton, London.

Mead, M. (1966). *Transactions of the Bartlett Society*, Vol. 4.

Meyer, H. A. (ed.) (1956). *Symposium on Monte Carlo Methods*. Wiley, New York.

Mills, C. W. (1956) *White Collar*, O.U.P., Oxford.

Ministry of Housing (1964). South-East Study.

Ministry of Labour (1965). 'Computers in offices.' Report by the Manpower Research Unit.

Morgan, W. T. W. (1960). 'The Growth and Functions of the General Office District in the West End of London.' Unpublished Doctoral thesis, North Western University, Ill., U.S.A.

Morrill, R. L. (1965). *Migration and the Spread and Growth of Urban Settlements*. Lund, Sweden.

Mumford, L. (1938). *The Culture of Cities*. Routledge, London.

Norris, W. C. (1964). 'Better Offices.' Institute of Directors.

Parker, H. R. (1959). 'Paying for Urban Development.' Fabian Society Pamphlet, No. 207.

Purdom, C. B. (1945). 'How should we rebuild London?'

Prais, S. J. (1955). 'Measuring Social Mobility.' *Journal of the Royal Statistical Society*, Series A 118, pp. 56–66.

Raiffa, H., and Schlaiffer, R. (1961). *Applied Statistical Decision Theory*. Division of Research, Harvard Business School, Cambs., Mass.

Report of the Expert Committee on Compensation and Betterment (Uthwatt Report) (1942). H.M.S.O., London, Cmd. 6386.

Robbins and Terlecky (1960). *Money Metropolis*. Harvard, Cambridge, Mass.

Rogers, A. (1965). 'A Stochastic Analysis of the Spatial Clustering of Retail Establishments.' *Journal of the American Statistical Association*, No. 60.

Royal Commission on the Distribution of the Industrial Population (Barlow Report) (1940). H.M.S.O., London, Cmd. 6153.

Royal Commission on Local Government in Greater London (1957–60). H.M.S.O., London, Cmd. 1164.

Siegel, S. (1956). *Non-Parametric Statistics of the Behavioural Sciences*. McGraw-Hill, New York.

SOUTH EAST ECONOMIC PLANNING COUNCIL: First Report (1967). 'A Strategy for the South-East.'

SPECIAL AREAS (Development and Improvement) ACT (1934). H.M.S.O., London. 'South East England' (1964). H.M.S.O., London, Cmd. 2308.

STANDING CONFERENCE ON LONDON AND SOUTH-EAST REGIONAL PLANNING Report (1967).

STEINDL, R. (1965). 'Random Processes and The Growth of Firms.'

STEVENS, B. H. (1961). 'Linear programming and location rent.' *Journal of Regional Science*, Vol. 3, No. 2, pp. 15–26.

STEWART, H. Q. (1963). 'Empirical Rules Concerning Distribution and Equilibrium of Populations' in *Demographic Analysis* by J. J. Spengler and O. D. Duncan (sds.). Free Press, Glencoe, Ill.

TOCHER, K. D. (1963). *The Art of Simulation.* English Universities Press.

TOWN AND COUNTRY PLANNING ASSOCIATION (1962). *The Paper Metropolis.* T.C.P.A., London.

TOWN AND COUNTRY PLANNING ACT (1932). 'The Land Commission' (1965) (White Paper). H.M.S.O., London, Cmd. 2771.

VERNON, R. (1959). *The Changing Economic Functions of the Central City.* Committee for Economic Dsvelopment.

VERNON, R. (1960). *Metropolis 1985.* Harvard, Cambridge, Mass.

WABE, J. S. (1965). *Office Decentralisation.* D.E.A., London.

WESTERGAARD, J. H. (1964). 'Land Use Planning Since 1951.' *Town Planning Review*, XXXV, Oct. 1964.

WILLIAMS, K. (1965). *Factual Basis of Office Policy in South-East England.* D.E.A., London.

Index